Aby Warburg and Anti-Semitism

Aby Warburg and Anti-Semitism

Political Perspectives on Images and Culture

CHARLOTTE SCHOELL-GLASS

Translated by
Samuel Pakucs Willcocks

WAYNE STATE UNIVERSITY PRESS
DETROIT

KRITIK

German Literary Theory and Cultural Studies
Liliane Weissberg, Editor

A complete listing of the books in this series can be found online at wsupress.wayne.edu

12 11 10 09 08 5 4 3 2 1

Library of Congress Cataloging-in-Publication Data

Schoell-Glass, Charlotte, 1951–
[Aby Warburg und der Antisemitismus. English]
Aby Warburg and anti-semitism : political perspectives on images and culture /
Charlotte Schoell-Glass ; translated by Samuel Pakucs Willcocks. — English ed.
p. cm. — (Kritik, German literary theory and cultural studies)
Includes bibliographical references and index.
ISBN-13: 978-0-8143-3255-9 (hardcover : alk. paper)
ISBN-10: 0-8143-3255-2 (hardcover : alk. paper)
1. Warburg, Aby, 1866–1929. 2. Jews—Identity.
3. Antisemitism—Germany—History—20th century. I. Title.
N7483.W36S3713 2008
709.2—dc22
2007036534

Originally published in German as *Aby Warburg und der Antisemitismus. Kulturwissenschaft als Geitespolitik* © 1998 Fischer Taschenbuch Verlag GmbH, Frankfurt am Main.

The publication of this work was supported by a grant from the Goethe-Institut that is funded by the Ministry of Foreign Affairs.

∞ The paper used in this publication meets the minimum requirements of the American National Standard for Information Sciences—Permanence of Paper for Printed Library Materials, ANSI Z39.48-1984.

Contents

Preface to the English-Language Edition

> I NEED HARDLY SAY that this lecture has not been about solving a pictorial riddle for its own sake—especially since it cannot here be illuminated at leisure, but only caught in a cinematographic spotlight. [. . .] In attempting to elucidate the frescoes in the Palazzo Schifanoia in Ferrara, I hope to have shown how an iconological analysis that can range freely, with no fear of boarder guards, and can treat the ancient, medieval, and modern worlds as coherent historical unity—an analysis that can scrutinize the purest and the most utilitarian of arts as equivalent documents of expression—how such a method, by taking pains to illuminate one single obscurity, can cast light on great and universal evolutionary processes in all their interconnectedness. I have not tried to find a neat solution so much as to present a new problem, which I would formulate as follows: "To what extent can the stylistic shift in the presentation of human beings in Italian art be regarded as part of an international process of dialectical engagement with the surviving imagery of Eastern Mediterranean pagan culture?"[1]

Since 1999 these concluding sentences of Aby Warburg's lecture "Italian Art and International Astrology in the Palazzo Schifanoia, Ferrara," held at the Tenth International Congress of Art History in Rome in 1912, have been available in English as part of Warburg's collected published works, *The Renewal of Pagan Antiquity.* Until then, Warburg had been known to the English reading public almost exclusively through Ernst Gombrich's *Aby Warburg: An Intellectual Biography* of 1970, and, ironically, a lecture on the snake dance of the Hopi, written and delivered in 1923 during his institutionalization in Kreuzlingen on Lake Constance.[2]

In this statement, read closely, much of what accounts for the ambivalent reception of Warburg's scholarship is presented squarely: Addressing questions within the discipline of art history was never, for him, the solving of riddles for its own sake (this separates him from much of the later iconographic riddle-solving that has been under attack for some time now), but always a means to get to questions reaching further toward "great and universal evolutionary processes in all their interconnectedness." However, such hopes for elucidating the very process of culture, in Warburg's intellectual environment, had always to be checked by "taking pains to illuminate one single obscurity," that is, by careful philological accuracy, as put in place in nineteenth-century scholarship. Hence Warburg's favorite motto was "God is in the details." Hence the obvious fragmentary character of his work, published in a coherent way only in 1932, by his collaborators and intellectual heirs, Fritz Saxl and Gertrud Bing, on the brink of the abyss, and, of course, in German, the language that soon was rendered useless for reaching an audience. Disowned by his former friends and colleagues in Germany, only a small community of émigrés would still care about what Warburg himself had seen as his legacy. He offers no neat solutions, but a considered progress to newly formulated problems: this is one of the qualities that make Warburg's scholarship still attractive today. This, and his deep involvement with the power of images as images, rather than a desire to proceed from or arrive at texts surrounding works of art or artifacts. Warburg's methods also, conversely, made for difficulties, arising from claims of universality and the underlying enlightenment paradigms informing his quest of understanding culture and the role of the visual in it.

Warburg's published work rests on the monumental foundations of his extensive archives and correspondence, preserved at the Warburg Institute in London, and, of course, on his famed library. Metaphorically speaking, his published articles could be seen as the surface of a three-dimensional body consisting of the library holdings, the notes and fragments of the theory of culture that inform them, and the correspondence of tens of thousands of letters; to include these unpublished materials brings about, I believe, a more fully resonant meaning of those often pared-down and always provisional texts that Warburg allowed to see the light of publication.[3] His perception of the disciplinary formation of art history as induced in part by "fear of boarder guards," his plea for understanding "the ancient, medieval, and modern worlds as coherent historical unity" and emphasis on the study of the "international process of dialectical engagement with the surviving imagery of Eastern Mediterranean pagan culture" take on an added urgency when his concerns with anti-Semitism are made visible.

For Warburg before and after 1900, it was challenging, and at times troubling, to be German and Jewish, and to belong to a Jewish family whose members were part of the highly influential aristocracy of finance of the time and who later worked most closely with the doomed German Empire during the years of the First World War. To dare aim at an academic career in art history, a field predominantly concerned with the refinement of classifications along the lines of national paradigms and stylistic developments, was, for him, always an exercise in equilibrium, at times causing him anxieties that exacerbated his predisposition for instable perceptions of the Self and others.[4] The mechanisms of inclusion and exclusion of minorities or women, today studied as a matter of course by most disciplines within the humanities and beyond, were a given for Warburg and many of his contemporaries. Understanding them and working against them within the edifice of the German academy was kept under the carpet more often than not. For Warburg the answer was in part a keen interest in the politics of institutions, both with regard to his subject matter, as for instance concerning the role of art and patronage in fifteenth-century Florence, and with regard to his own status within German academic art history. He was a cofounder of the University of Hamburg and the Kunsthistorisches Institut in Florence, a coorganizer of the international congress in Rome (where he lectured on his specific way of "iconologically" understanding European culture[5]) and, most importantly, he founded his own institution, the Kulturwissenschaftliche Bibliothek Warburg. But there is also a many-faceted connection between Warburg's research itself, his questions about Renaissance art and the way he introduced them, and his perception of his own role as a nonobservant Jew both in Imperial Germany and during the Weimar Republic.

It is this connection that I have tried to elucidate and make visible here.

New source material and important new research on Warburg have been published in German, French, Italian, and in English translations since I wrote and researched this book between 1994 and 1996, accepted as a Habilitationsschrift at the University of Hamburg in 1996 and published in 1998. A comprehensive bibliography of publications by and on Warburg was published in 1998 by Dieter Wuttke.[6] For research prior to 1995, this bibliography is an indispensable tool. Two recent publications in English by Richard Woodfield and Philippe-Alain Michaud are noteworthy. The first is a contribution to the history of the discipline, bringing together several generations of Warburg scholarship.[7] The second shows how Warburg's work of the previous turn of the century is embedded in its own time and the early history of photography, moving pictures, and dance.[8] Michaud connects with Warburg's published and unpublished work in an exemplary way in that he takes his clues from Warburg's publications for a study of the history of the media. Both possibilities, one that develops Warburg's approach for today's questions and needs, and one that studies Warburg's position in the history of art history have surely further potential for Anglophone art history and theory.[9]

This study focuses on the traces in Warburg's work and correspondence of anti-Semitism in Germany from the 1870s through the 1920s. Describing the transfer of biographic details into a narrative, particularly if an oeuvre remains as fragmentary as Warburg's, is a task fraught with difficulties. I do not suggest that from the instances collected here all of his achievements could or should be explained. I have come to the conclusion, however, that recording this part of Warburg's legacy touches upon problems still relevant today.

Acknowledgments

EVEN WHEN DEVOTED TO a single clearly defined question, studies in the history of a discipline always challenge our system of subjects and disciplines. Although they can only ever be written from the inside, in this case from within the discipline of art history, they must also justify their claim to be works of history and of sociology. As a rule this claim is hard to defend, even when properly staked, but the problem we set ourselves with such projects necessitates their transdisciplinary nature, which also brings benefits. This study has demanded that I talk with colleagues from my own discipline and from others, asking them for their advice and their opinions, and has thus caused me many debts of gratitude. First of all to Joist Grolle, who has been a generous, patient, and encouraging reader of the work as it took shape; then to Hermann Hipp, who showed his interest in many ways; to Stefan Breuer, who answered and discussed all my questions about sociology and its history, as well as the history of the German Right; to Hedwig Röckelein, who shared with me her wisdom, and particularly her knowledge of psychohistory; to Stefan Rohrbacher, who examined the work carefully in his capacity as an expert on anti-Semitism. Discussions with Carl E. Schorske, with Catherine Sousloff, and time and again with Karen Michels were of great importance to me at various stages of the work. I did not however always follow the advice that was offered, and it is not my intention to pass any responsibility for what I finally wrote to those whom I thank here. Last but absolutely not least I must thank

Sabine Blumenröder, without whose organizational talent and unflappability this work could not have been completed.

My particular thanks go to two institutions. First, to the Warburg Institute in London, whose director Nicholas Mann, with the greatest possible generosity, allowed me to use the archive there in every way I could wish. Also in London, the late Anne Marie Meyer, greatly knowledgeable about the history of the institute, urged me at every turn to honor "God [who] is in the details." Dorothea McEwan, likewise at the Warburg Institute, generously helped me to profit from the ongoing computerization of the correspondence archive. I thank the Warburg Institute for permission to use texts and photographs from their archive. The translator's gratitude goes to Dorothea McEwan as well for her help in understanding the changes that the Warburg archive has undergone since the present work's original appearance in German.

I also owe thanks to the Institute for Advanced Study in Princeton, New Jersey, and above all to Irving Lavin, for a wonderful year (1996–97) in which to catch my breath, talk, write, revise, and reflect. I thank him for his spontaneous and kindly support, and lastly all my friends of that year for offering me a perspective "from the outside."

It is my pleasure also to thank all those who helped to bring about the translated version of this book. I know it was not easy to translate, and it was a long process to get it through the stages of approval and production. I can only hope that so much effort will prove to have been worthwhile.

The following text is a revised version of my postdoctoral thesis, which was completed in the autumn of 1995. Literature that has appeared since that date has been taken into account in particular instances.

Introduction

The Unknown Guest

"Every idea enters our consciousness as an unknown guest, and as it begins to realize itself, it can hardly be told apart from fancy or fantasy."[1] In July 1929 the art historian and scholar of cultural studies Aby Warburg (1866–1929) wrote this citation from Goethe's *Maxims and Reflections* onto the back of a postcard, the front of which showed the facade of the Warburg Cultural Studies Library (Kulturwissenschaftliche Bibliothek Warburg [K.B.W.]), which he had founded.[2] Goethe's observation speaks of the borders of cognition, borders on which Warburg dwelt for the whole of his scholarly life and which lie like a shifting ring around the fields of established, ordered knowledge—no matter where the fields we know happen themselves to lie. Above all, Warburg was thinking of how the his library was itself the result of just such an idea that had come into the world.[3] Between the facade of the library, a realist, strategic manifesto for the institutionalization of knowledge, and the "idea" and its doubtful origins in "fantasy," lies the key to understanding Warburg's life's work and the undeniable difficulties he encountered within the discipline of art history as well as in the broader interdisciplinary field of the humanities.

By 1933, only four years later, the Warburg library and its staff had forever left the building on the Heilwigstraße in Hamburg: neither human beings nor books were safe from their compatriots any longer in their "bookcase-castle."[4] The research institute emigrated to England early, and not a moment too soon. For more than half a century now, one fact has been of central importance for the reception of Warburg's cultural studies in widely varying fields: that Aby Warburg and many of the scholars of his circle were Jewish. This fact did not merely determine the record of continuity and gaps in the history of the Warburg Institute, formed as it obviously was by emigration and by adaptation to a new intellectual climate. It also accounts, at least in part, for the chronicle of postponements, misinterpretations, and omissions that have marked the reception of Warburg's works published in his lifetime and since.

The material presented here documents Aby Warburg's reaction to the anti-Semitism that was ubiquitous ever since the reestablishment of the German Empire in 1871; it also reveals that even the origins of Warburg's work must be seen as conditioned by his Jewish background, to a degree not previously recognized. The historical fracture—the expulsion, persecution, and murder of the Jews—has not yet healed today; here as elsewhere, this fracture marks even more emphatically a preexisting taboo in the human sciences. This taboo dissuades us from seeking motives for the human sciences and decrees that they cannot be spoken of.

This study starts from a different premise. Using the example of Aby Warburg, I wish to show that the question of a scholar's motives for his research and the social action that goes with it need not be seen as a question exclusively for psychologists, or one that concerns only subjective and incommunicable matters. Thus formulated, my study dissociates itself from Ernst Gombrich's remarks on how Warburg had identified himself with his themes, remarks with which he closes the "Mnemosyne" chapter of *Aby Warburg: An Intellectual Biography.*[5] Rather I work from the assumption that the motive for such an activity and its results stand in a relationship that, when recognized, can lend new color and a new tone to the facts in the history of ideas thus examined. This metaphor means to say that the new view offered here of Warburg's research, his methodical aims, and his scholarly-political engagement is a critical view, not in the sense that it denies previous evaluations, but rather that it helps us understand them by situating them in a historical movement that has also given rise to this latest assessment, my own. This explanation recognizes that silence and speech, emphasis and elision, demonstration and concealment in the discourse of cultural history and the history of ideas are revealed (once enough time has passed and new motives have come to the fore) as part of the historical movement, necessary and inevitable. At the same time I wish to show that an unpolitical notion of culture is unthinkable in the cultural sciences, particularly at the beginning of the twentieth century. Only when we see Warburg's achievements within the factual circumstances of their becoming, are they seen also to have been part of that great ideological battle fought over the term *Kultur* in the years before the First World War.[6]

In his published works Warburg took care that anti-Semitism was not seen to be an active force in his life as author—as it was in the life of every Jew: in these works its effects only appear in disguise or at one remove. All the more informative therefore is the trail that his documentation of anti-Semitism left in the archived works, in the library and in his letters. This trail leads to the heart of the Warburg Library's project. As Warburg conceived it, cultural studies was to be a network of questions properly formulated that tacitly seek the answer to a question not formulated overtly: what is the cause of Jew-hating? To answer this question would have been the condition for any possibility to neutralize the threat of anti-Semitism, a threat which Warburg saw and documented with relentless clarity. In 1988 this question—what is anti-Semitism?—was still called "one of the most difficult and most cruelly troubling questions that twentieth-century people can ask themselves,"[7] and was treated as an anthropological question.

The "unknown guest" of Goethe's musing on the question of cognition took many forms in Warburg's life's work. It is the ethnologist's survey of what is closest to him,[8] it works away at language until language as an analytical tool has recovered its relationship to the image,[9] it is the capacity to correlate scattered facts and make them speak—but it is also the ability to order anew the already known, which seems to be firmly ordered into its own classifications. Since then, these efforts have shown a new place for art history in the disciplinary system, and set for it a greater task than can be tackled by questions and answers formulated along stylistic lines. The stylistic paradigm set the questions during Warburg's lifetime and for a long time afterward: whether art history can address the new task is irrelevant to his achievement.[10]

The "unknown guest," however, is also none other than Warburg, who as a student in Strasbourg became ironically aware, and at the same time disturbed to realize, that in the mirror of Jew-hating he was himself an "Oriental" phenomenon. He experienced what Walther Rathenau described in these words: "In the early years of every German Jew comes a painful moment which he will remember for the rest of his life: when for the first time he realizes that he came into the world as a second-class citizen, and that no virtue or service can free him from this position."[11] Warburg noticed and documented the hatred that expressed itself in anti-Semitism, from the smallest everyday taunts to the waves of pogroms in Eastern Europe at the end of the First World War, from the most gruesome excesses to the blowhard pamphlet. This documentation is not neatly separated from that concerned with art history, history, social history, anthropology, and politics: it is built into the broad and branching network of keywords by which Warburg developed his concept of cultural studies, and through which he made his library into a snare for knowledge. In this context we need to reassess the conundrum set by Anne Marie Meyer in 1988: "Exactly what was the relation between Warburg's research on paganism in the Renaissance and his meditations and fears about Judaism (and Jews) remains of course the problem."[12]

One might also describe Warburg's research on the role of "heathen" antiquity in the Renaissance in the much-quoted words of Jakob Burckhardt, from the opening paragraphs of his *Reflections on History:* "We, however, shall start out from the one point accessible to us, the one eternal center of all things—man, suffering, striving, doing, as he is and was and ever shall be. Hence our study will, in a certain sense, be pathological in kind."[13] These words already hint at what Warburg was able to pin down in pictures as the *Pathosformel.* The contradictory tension between hurly-burly life and the human condition, postulated as timeless, is also captured here on the historiographer's desk, as it would be in Warburg's work. The context in which Burckhardt's comment on the "center" of his historical writing appears is a rather brusque dismissal of every available historical method or philosophy of history: "For that matter, every method is open to criticism, and none is universally valid. Every individual approaches this huge theme of contemplation in his own way, which may be his spiritual way through life: he may then shape his method as that way leads him."[14] Warburg never offered any comparable rebuttal, but then he only on occasion spoke about "method" in cultural studies.[15] He held that his method, the "Warburg method," was dictated by the subject at hand: "taking our orders from the problem."[16]

Ernst Gombrich has shown that there is a turning point in Warburg's thought, from the conception of history as proceeding onward to ever higher and more sublime forms of ritual/cultural production, to the realization that there is no such absolute progress. The choice of the term "cultural studies" (Kulturwissenschaft) itself makes a systematic claim that can only be fully understood when we assume that "the problem at hand" remains both constant and *present* beyond its historicity. In 1918 Warburg coined the phrase, "Athens has constantly to be won back again from Alexandria," and thereby brought into this tension of historicity and presence the dynamic of a war that cannot be won, an eternal struggle.[17] Warburg's bellicose metaphor can be interpreted in many ways and has most often been seen in terms of his psychological state, as a man already marked by mental illness desperately proclaiming his allegiance to Reason.[18] It can however also be seen as a metaphor formed by the experience of the First World War, as can the essay "Pagan Prophecy" as a whole. The reconquest of Athens from Alexandria, so appealing that every educated person can effortlessly recast it into his or her own preferred parallel set of oppositions (such as Apollonian-Dionysian)[19]—this metaphor above all encapsulates the conflict between East and West, between an uncanny and unchanging "Sphinx" and all the victorious powers standing under the sign of "Europe." The collapse of the German Empire at the end of the war draws this division between East and West directly through Germany's understanding of itself. At exactly this time, in Warburg's card-index files the uncanny, the unchanging, and the barbaric become dozens of reports on those murderous excesses against Jews that, from Finland through Russia and Romania to Tunisia, remorselessly rolled from east to west.[20] The fate of the threatened and murdered Jews in the East was the blast that jolted the patient observer in Hamburg out of his role as a passive recorder. He had regarded himself and his institute as a seismograph; now, it was impossible to distinguish between "East" and "West" because these were suddenly inseparable in the existence of the threatened Jews.

This reception and transmission of presence and historicity fundamentally distinguishes Warburg's cultural studies (*Kulturwissenschaft*) from cultural history (*Kulturgeschichte*) as practiced by Karl Lamprecht or Georg Steinhausen around the same time. Steinhausen's richly documented and far-reaching studies portrayed a history that was many-faceted yet peculiarly static;[21] Lamprecht could not convince his peers with his concepts of universal history,[22] despite his broad activism in cultural policy "beyond the borders" and his success in founding an institute in Leipzig. Meanwhile, Warburg and the scholars closest to him emphasized the study of symptoms and of formal analogies. Whether in Reformation broadsheets or Florentine portraits of the Quattrocento, in Flemish tapestry or in Dürer's graphic works, the intersection of presence and historicity can be perceived and can be conceived because the pictures themselves are present to us, are doubly active in both history and in the present, in a way unique to images.

This transmission was captured in the term "afterlife," that "afterlife [*Nachleben*] of antiquity" which in the 1920s was formulated as the Warburg library's central research project.[23] The subject of this research was to be the phenomenon of pictorial formulas reused in new historical circumstances, the changing ways in which they were deployed and the ebbing and flowing energies that they stored, releasing or restraining the emotions and affects. Felix Gilbert saw a strange discrepancy, though, in assigning to antiquity this role of a yardstick for the development of European civilization, since Warburg supposedly rejected any concept of historical progress.[24] Gilbert's sociobiographical explanation for this contradiction can be expanded in view of the role of anti-Semitism in Warburg's life. If the European tradition of antiquity is sometimes latent, sometimes active, yet always an effective force in preestablished imagery, then this is paralleled in an equally ancient and similarly accessible tradition of Christian anti-Semitism, a yardstick of that barbarism within civilization that can be activated at any historical moment and can equally easily be transferred to other minorities. One core principle of Warburg's conception of art history as a form of cultural studies is that these traditions are differently brought to life in different historical circumstances, and that within these historical contexts they come to life concretely in the media, in texts and in images.[25] The contradiction between a normative antiquity and an anthropological constant experienced as tragedy is resolved when we break the silence that has so far surrounded the fact of Jew-hating as a historical and human constant in Warburg's historical anthropology.

Warburg provided a corpus of academic work with a silence at its center; my thesis is that this silence may be relevant to the existential question that would explain Warburg's determination and ability to be an academic trespasser, a scholar of the margins—and would explain what makes his achievement so significant. At this point the available instruments of historical examination seem insufficient; at this point, we are tempted to make however dilettantish a use of the tools of psychological analysis, since a comparison of Warburg's life and work with those of Sigmund Freud also seems appropriate here.[26] Although my thesis may indeed profit from looking at Freud's scholarly life, which is so much more deeply researched than Warburg's and so much more self-articulate within its own work, I wish to avoid a reduction of the biographical traces inscribed in Warburg's work. This study will not contribute to the myth of Warburg's mental illness. As a doctor and colleague, Freud had occasion to ask after Aby Warburg's health when the latter was Ludwig Binswanger's psychiatric patient.[27] Yet when we see the importance of anti-Semitism for the two men, there are surprising parallels and structural similarities between Freud and Warburg—however different they were in life and work. Both lives reflect what Hans Liebeschütz called the "dialectic of assimilation," sometimes even in complementary ways.

Warburg did not make much of his political convictions either as a scholar or as a private person, although these beliefs are strongly present in the diverse materials in the archive. Nor did he seek public political engagement for Jewish interests or against anti-Semitic activity. Rather, his activism was a policy of scholarship that always sought new fields, directed at presenting his results to the public alongside the fundamental research in the field of *Kultur*. Different commentators have remarked over and over on the strange dichotomy of this project: Warburg worked on minute problems of historical detail, and then he presented the solutions to those problems as contributions to the understanding of basic questions of European civilization. With one hand he refused any synthetic, systematic conception, and with the other he created a library system that could make sense of the world in an entirely new way. On one side, the concentration on esoteric, recondite questions of pictorial and textual history, and on the other the stubborn instinct and belief that it was exactly such problems that, properly grasped and answered, would solve the vexing questions of his own day. His inability to climb the career ladder in an academic institution was balanced by the determination and self-confidence to found his own research institute.

These inherent contradictions in Warburg's course of action become comprehensible, logical, and determined by a luminous symmetry when we see that the central axis between the work and its public impact was the question of atavism and its role within culture—the problem of how to approach atavism, that historical constant in ever new guises. Again and again Warburg addressed this question in articles on the iconography of astrological images, the role of tapestry in Burgundy, or the message of Florentine pictures and texts of the Quattrocento. At the same time, the inhabitants of Warburg's "bookcase-castle" were reckoning with the atavisms of their present day, which they believed must be fought with reason and investigation. In this context, visitors to the Warburg library were at times called "patients."

This symmetrical axis of research and praxis also bears the aspect of a displacement strategy, at least according to the historian of ideas Hans Liebeschütz, in whose eyes Warburg denied his Jewish identity and never acknowledged this evasion. Liebeschütz is right here. My contention however is that to claim an identity may also hinder any clear view of the basic conflicts of civilization—and Warburg fought for just such a clear view. In other words, his conception of cultural studies can be understood as an attempt at a second Enlightenment, comparable to Freud's project, and this attempt seemed necessary to Warburg because of his own early experience of anti-Semitism, which resists all Enlightenment and reason.

Thus Warburg's scholarly method is revealed as a deeply complex answer to the question of how and under what conditions scholarship was possible in the first third of the twentieth century. His method was fragmentary and oriented to details, because "grand narrative" seemed impossible and easily corrupted by ideology; it did not trust in one man's powers only but was instead interdisciplinary and team-based; it was directed toward fundamental questions that were born of personal experience; it was also pragmatic, striving for institutionalization and public pedagogy, not just because such a precariously modern choice needed a counterweight to be embodied, but also in the hope that *Kulturwissenschaft* could prescribe remedies as well as diagnose symptoms. Born of necessity, this hope distinguished Warburg, the scholar of Hamburg, from Burckhardt, the sage of Basel. These dichotomies in Warburg's cultural studies are precisely what gave his work staying power and account for its continuing challenge as a method of scholarship that embraces its broader responsibilities.

Archaeology in the Archive and Library

My research was prompted by the discovery of a published letter from Aby Warburg in an unexpected place, the notorious anti-Semitic bi-monthly propaganda periodical *Der Hammer*.[28] My method was to take selected samples from various areas and collections in Warburg's published works; in the library of the Warburg Institute in London; in Warburg's working archive there; and in his letters. The examination of these materials was to answer a double question. To what extent did Aby Warburg engage with anti-Semitism? and how, if at all, did this engagement inform his lifetime work of research in cultural studies? The risks of examining the material in such a focused way are obvious: one has to be careful not just to take into account what one is looking for, and then overrate these finds because they cannot be qualitatively or quantitatively related to the rest of the material. Such a relational assessment would require a complete survey, and anybody familiar with the Warburg Institute's archive and library will know that such a survey is inconceivable. Every page Warburg published during his lifetime—about six hundred in all—represents about one hundred manuscript pages found in his unpublished scholarly papers after his death, one hundred books in his library, at least the same number of letters, and at least two hundred postcard-sized note cards in the index boxes (of which there are around a hundred).

If we were to take the visual arts to have been the center of Warburg's research, we could justifiably also refer to other areas in which he was interested, related to this center in the same indirect manner as is anti-Semitism. Air transport perhaps, or to a lesser extent newspapers and philately, on which there are extensive holdings in the Warburg Institute. For this reason the holdings of various sections of the library are examined here with particular emphasis on the early stages of their collecting. Some time ago, a study based on the publications of the K.B.W. and on the library itself showed that in the years between the First World War and the collection's emigration to London, religious studies were most heavily represented in research at the Warburg library.[29] We can safely say, however, that there is much more documentation than we might expect on questions of racism, political science, and sociology, and that these areas form significant holdings in the library. In this context it seemed important to ask how (and when) literature on contemporary themes was purposefully included in the library, which had been collected predominantly along historical and systematic lines.

Despite the difficulty of such a starting point, I have tried to present here all the documentation on anti-Semitism and the "Jewish question" that Warburg collected and that I have been able to find, together with his own letters and other treatments of the theme, and fundamentally there were only two tools I could use to order this material. The first was to read every text closely or even microscopically—however fragmentary or insignificant it may have seemed, from the library catalogue to the keywords in the index boxes and the ways in which they were arranged. I also treated newspaper cuttings I sometimes found pasted into the manuscripts as texts to be read in their context of Warburg's research.[30]

On 10 July 1963 Gertrud Bing wrote a letter to Hans Harder Biermann-Ratjen, the Hamburg senator and president of the city's cultural committee,[31] describing the archive material that must form the basis for a biography of Warburg; she had made a start in systematically ordering this material ("Letters. Diaries. Scholarly notes and records of his public or social activity").[32] Gertrud Bing describes the material with observations that attest to an intimate knowledge of his papers, and she has a keen sense of its material state, just as she interprets it analytically:

> He obviously felt that he had a mission and hoped to entrust it to the future because he felt that his present time had little understanding for him. He hung on to the whole inchoate and untrammeled mess of everyday life, which other people try to dispose of—circulars, invitations, receipts, account books, requests for favors, complaints, all mixed up together with no regard for relevance or otherwise, along with scholarly notes, drafts of his works in print or in the planning stage, and autobiographical writings. [. . .] Nobody has as yet quite agreed with me on the importance of the form (or formlessness) of his *Nachlass.* [. . .] It is not enough to sort the wheat from the chaff in this mass of handwritten, typed, and printed paper. There were no categories in Warburg's life, and whatever happened to come his way was subject to the same standards as his scholarly affairs. Again and again I found that the most trivial-seeming material gave rise to unexpected revelations about connected thoughts or concrete

> situations, so that one has to ask oneself what each item might have meant to him, even where this is not conclusive enough for the report.[33]

This brief outline points out the path deliberately not taken by Ernst Gombrich and takes account of the textuality and materiality of the *Nachlass* in a way that was well ahead of its time, or rather for which there was not yet a method or a set of instruments.[34] Gombrich's biography "sorts the wheat from the chaff" but Bing could only have written her biography by applying an "archaeology of knowledge," a different understanding of what constitutes evidence. This understanding was only just becoming visible at the time; to use Gertrud Bing's own words, in this, her present time held no place for her.

The second way in which have I tried to order the material is to align and compare it with the hinterland of my question, the mountains of historical facts about anti-Semitism and the *Kultur* debate around 1900 produced by other disciplines (such as history of scholarship). These discoveries have so far hardly been used by Warburg scholars, just as the historical sociology of knowledge has likewise barely recognized Warburg; works on a topic such as "Culture and Cultural Studies around 1900" can still be published without any reference to Warburg or to the Warburg library.[35]

The chapters that follow are essentially organized chronologically, so that the continuity can be seen in Warburg's engagement with anti-Semitism. Even as a student he had made thorough and detailed statements on the "Jewish question," and he was still collecting newspaper reports of anti-Semitic attacks for his index-card boxes in 1929, the year of his death. A report on the state of research as regards this question is included in order to allow the reader to assess the relative importance of archival materials here presented—not only within the tradition of previous research on Warburg but also informed by new ways of seeing and reading which we have at our disposal today.

1

Jewishness and Anti-Semitism in Warburg Studies

In 1958 a bust of Aby Warburg was placed in the Hamburg Kunsthalle, and in her speech on the occasion Gertrud Bing made the first public mention that Warburg had "never entirely freed himself from the fear of anti-Semitism."[1] Bing went on, however, to emphasize Warburg's ties to Imperial Germany and his unshakeable patriotism, for "he never forgot that the German Empire treated the Jews well."[2] Ernst Gombrich does not dwell on this aspect of Warburg's life in his own 1966 speech in Hamburg, which celebrated the hundredth anniversary of Warburg's birth. On this occasion he formulated what was for him a tenet of all scholarly work. He said about Aby Warburg: "He was neither the first nor, let us hope, the last student of human nature to be prompted by personal motivations to dare the descent into the darkest shafts of the past. The finds which he brought to surface remain valid whatever had tempted him into the depths."[3] Gombrich the art historian here insists on the objectivity of the process of research and turns his back on what might legitimately interest a biographer. Among the achievements of his intellectual biography of Warburg is its scrupulous separation of facts and their preconditions. The "personal motivations" to which Gombrich refers are psychological or even psychopathological in nature, as referred to in numerous other tributes, biographical sketches, and studies.

There is and always has been a strange fascination among scholars with Warburg's mental instability, and in particular about his period of acute, recurring psychotic illness between 1918 and 1924 that he himself described as a "Passion."[4] Not only those who write about these topics, but also quite a few of those who keep silent about them have felt this fascination. This may in part be because knowledge about the nature of Warburg's illness was until recently only fragmentary and supplemented by fantasies. Above all, however, this fascination reflects widespread and individual attitudes to mental aberration and illness in general, which vary from outright denial to mythologizing idealism.[5]

Scholarly biographical interest in Warburg's state of mind can however legitimately argue that he himself drew a connection between his work and his mental state, even if not publicly: "Sometimes it seems to me as if, in my role as psycho-historian, I tried to diagnose the schizophrenia of Western civilization from its images in an autobiographical reflex. The ecstatic 'Nympha' (manic) on the one side and the mourning river-god (depressive) on the other."[6] We must ask here whether we are really to follow the writer of these words; that his most important biographer so far had decided not to should command our respect. A comparable reading of the life and the work that takes Warburg's Jewish origins as a point of departure can only make use of less startling comments, and no use at all of his public pronouncements—although there may yet be unnoticed documents in the archive. Nevertheless scholars attempted such readings and sought relationships, albeit cautiously and tentatively. "*Ebreo di sangue, Amburghese di cuore, d'anima Fiorentino*" ("Jewish by blood, Hamburger at heart, of Florentine soul")[7]—Warburg's oft-cited, epigrammatically concise self-description indicates that he himself saw his Jewish origins as the foundation of his identity.

If we disregard the obituaries and tributes from the time closely following Warburg's death,[8] Carl Georg Heise's *Persönliche Erinnerungen an Aby Warburg* ("Personal Memoir of Aby Warburg") is the first major biographical portrait. Like Gertrud Bing later, Heise reports Warburg's personal choice of a "low-profile" policy when it came to Jewish matters. As a young man Heise went to Rome with Warburg in 1912 to meet the great minds in the field—for the last time, as Warburg is supposed to have said at the time. Among these was "Henry Thode, son-in-law of Richard Wagner, who persuaded and inspired the Italians, and whose engagement Warburg thus welcomed for cultural-political reasons."[9] Heise goes on to report: "[Warburg's] sense of things to come was in every respect extraordinary. He had been asked to preside at the congress [the International Congress of Art Historians] but had declined. He said that a Jew may not be president of a worldwide organization since that could only discredit the cause. He would gladly have undertaken the task but sadly could not accept the honor."[10] Instead Warburg suggested Rudolph Kautzsch as president. Heise was writing after having experienced the war and the Nazi era,[11] and he reads with hindsight and therefore only partly correctly: Warburg's circumspect reaction was of course not based on things to come, but on his own experience.

Another episode that Heise recollects concerns Warburg's keen sense for intellectual and scholarly integrity:

> I remember the inordinate hail of imprecations against Gobineau's *Renaissance,* which I had been talked into admiring; I had to name the man who had recommended the book to me, and I was forbidden to have anything more to do with him. For Warburg, the pseudopoetical violation of history was always cause to let rip. He showed me the place in his library where the book stood, next to Mereschkowski's *Leonardo*—he called the whole section his cabinet of poisons. My question as to why he would make room for such poison in the first place occasioned another stormy outburst. He almost shouted as he said that one must have the devil at hand, always be able to cite him, in order to fight him with his own weapons. Were we supposed then only to acquire books that we happened personally to like? I fell silent: [. . .] any inclination of mine to the purely aesthetic had to be fought with every means.[12]

This glance into the "cabinet of poisons" that Heise here allows us is more informative than the young student (or the reminiscing eyewitness) could have known. One look at the Gobineau section of the Warburg library reveals that this collection of writings by and about Gobineau was unrivaled, at least until the end of the 1920s.[13] The collection furthermore documents the Gobineau who wrote the *Essai sur l'origine de l'inégalité des races humaines,* an obvious subject for Warburg's dictum that one must have the devil at hand in order always to be able to fight him with his own weapons.[14]

Heise held that Warburg's years of sickness, once researched, would be the key to understanding his work, and this opinion contributed to the further mythologization of Warburg the "figure of legend."[15] He recalls two episodes in which he himself observed Warburg's "descent into the deep shafts of ancient wisdom," "the journey to the Mothers."[16] Heise visited Warburg in Hamburg in the early stages of his illness, and the scholar took him to one side:

> He told me that he had a dreadful confession to make to me, and that I could judge for myself how far he had forfeited any claim to be considered a decent human being. In conversation with a university professor he had apparently said, "In the depths of my soul I am a Christian!" Now he accused himself of the indignity, the utter surrender of such an impulse in his heart, which moreover he had expressed in words that could be totally misunderstood. He said that a Jew who confesses himself to be a secret apostate is a coward who suffers no consequences, or a man who does not know what he owes to his people and to his family.[17]

Writing of a visit to the sanatorium in Kreuzlingen where Warburg was being treated by Ludwig Binswanger,[18] Heise describes his "delusion that in Hamburg his wife was in deadly danger."[19] Heise observed that despite his symptoms "his logic was by no means confused, albeit that it was very abrupt and he often interrupted his thoughts; rather it was the precision and thoroughness of his reasoning that made it meaningless in our nebulous everyday world. [. . .] He saw danger and destruction everywhere, and blamed himself with fearful imprecations."[20]

Heise's memoirs form a marked contrast to Ernst Gombrich's *Intellectual Biography,* which appeared in English in 1970 (and in German translation in 1981). Although Gombrich tried to exclude from his work everything that was solely biographical, in particular any psychological analysis, he nevertheless included some details concerning Warburg's attitude to his own Jewish origin.[21]

Thus Gombrich emphasizes that Warburg's preoccupation with Renaissance art and culture must be seen as part of a tradition stretching back to the eighteenth century, in which this period is understood to have given birth to modern man. This trope in historiography is useful and significant because it cut the cloth with which Europe costumed its self-image throughout the nineteenth century and into the twentieth.[22] Gombrich does not explicitly address the question of how this trope of writing cultural history had become so politically loaded. One measure of this, though, is his analysis of how Warburg differs from Burckhardt and others in his view of the Renaissance. According to Gombrich, Warburg gives a new bearing to the cult of the Renaissance that was his own received tradition. While previously the Golden Age of the Florentine Quattrocento was thought to have been a carefree awakening from the nightmare of medieval vassalage, Warburg began to see it as a period of painful emancipation. In Gombrich's view, Warburg's own experience of life influenced this new perspective: "His own emancipation from Jewish orthodoxy, and the conflicts this engendered with the family, was one of the experiences which pointed in this direction."[23]

Yet Gombrich points out that this stripping away of ideals from the Renaissance had in its turn a model and a parallel in the new view of classical antiquity developed by nineteenth-century historiography. Nevertheless he finds Warburg's early estrangement from the Jewish religion so important that, following Warburg's own example, he quotes extensively from Warburg's recollections.

Warburg reports the early trauma of his mother's serious illness in Ischl in 1874. He remembers a visit to the Calvary there, in which his mother, carried in a litter, took part: "It was on this occasion that I saw for the first time and dimly experienced in the Stations of the Cross, executed in a debased peasant style, the stark and tragic power of the Passion of Christ."[24] For Warburg the memory of this summer was connected to his estrangement from Judaism:

> A single visit to the bedside of my poor and distracted-looking mother, the company of an inferior Jewish-Austrian student who had to function as my tutor, made for an atmosphere of inner despair which came to a climax when my grandfather arrived and said: "Pray for your mother," whereupon we sat down on the suitcases with Hebrew prayer-books and rattled out something. Two things served as counterpoise to these deeply disturbing events: a grocery

> shop downstairs where, for the first time, we could contravene the dietary laws and eat sausages, and a lending library which was full of stories about Red Indians.[25]

Gombrich further shows how Warburg freed himself bit by bit from religious life and defended his choice of career against his family's disapproval: he not only rejected his grandmother's suggestion that he become a Bible scholar or a rabbi, he also insisted on studying art history. Gombrich reports strong resistance most of all from his mother's relatives in Frankfurt, who would have found a career in any other branch of scholarship more acceptable. Warburg though was not the only art historian around that time to choose this path despite such a family and social background: Adolph Goldschmidt and Max J. Friedländer also came from Jewish banking families.[26] Gombrich briefly notes the dispute about keeping kosher,[27] and in connection with Warburg's reading of Vignoli points to the model of religious evolution found in the young student's notes in 1888, which set out a steady development from "personal gods" through Jewish to Christian religion and onward to a form of secularized Protestant work ethic.[28]

Gombrich's biography contains no hint that alongside Warburg's rejection of Jewish religion, anti-Semitism might also have held some significance for him or even for the genesis of his work, any more than it recognizes a religious or cultural influence from Judaism. The act of cutting himself loose from the religion into which he had been born is shown as a central event in Warburg's life and work. Gombrich considers this event to have been definitive and important to any understanding of Warburg's views on religious history and on the process of Enlightenment in its broadest sense.

It seems that with his 1971 essay "Aby Warburg (1866–1929) as Interpreter of Civilization," Hans Liebeschütz wished to fill a gap that was quite evident in Gombrich's biography, characterized by Liebeschütz as "distanced" and "respectful."[29] In an early passage Liebeschütz stresses the great importance that Warburg's birth into an influential family of bankers in the comparatively liberal Hanseatic city of Hamburg was to have for his life: their place among the city's ruling class defined the family just as much as did their adherence to strict Judaic orthodoxy. Religious identity as part of the Jewish community formed the basis for their relations with Christian society on equal terms of respect.[30] Liebeschütz too stresses Warburg's concern to find a new position for himself within the Jewish-Christian cultures; he reports especially the difficulties Warburg encountered when he wished to marry Mary Hertz, a Protestant. After their engagement each had to confront their families, who sought to obstruct the match. It was obvious that the difference in religions was the real obstacle. Here the fact that the Protestant, senatorial Hertz family itself had Jewish ancestry played no role.[31] The difficulties of a denominationally mixed marriage in those days, especially the problem of the religious education of the children, allow Liebeschütz in a second passage to compare Warburg's attitude to his Jewishness with that of Fritz Saxl, whose career was closely connected to the Warburg library.[32] Saxl and Warburg are presented as representative of two generations of Jewish scholars, whose behavior as Jewish contemporaries differs significantly even though they start from similar premises, since "Saxl's own experience in the Austrian world had made him see both Synagogue and Church as outdated antagonists of free thought."[33] Saxl included the study of the thought and art of the Christian Middle Ages in his work, and he put medieval studies on an equal footing with the study of antiquity and its transformations; nor did he exclude themes from Jewish tradition. Warburg meanwhile firmly staked out the boundaries of his areas of research; for him secular culture was distinct from the culture of this or that faith. Interpreting the fragmentary description of his position as a psychologically and de facto "modern" Jew that he jotted down at the time of the Konitz Affair (see chapter 3), Liebeschütz states that "knowledge about his own past and the attitude of his ancestors remained a *silent but powerful force* in his intellectual development" (my italics).[34] Although he remained constantly aware of them, Warburg's "Jewish roots" were not a source of positive identification, but rather the source of a never-ending disquiet.

According to Liebeschütz, Warburg's areas of interest, his questions, and his scholarly conceptions were formed by the force of that unrealized identity. He sees this drive ("perhaps unconsciously"[35]) at work in Warburg's understanding of Luther as a quasi-Enlightenment figure, a view shared in some ways by other Jewish scholars such as Hermann Cohen and Ernst Cassirer. Liebeschütz recognizes in this common approach and interpretation an attempt to anchor the tradition of the Enlightenment into German intellectual history. The sociology of scholarship sees this as an outsider's position, which Liebeschütz invokes to explain the points of affinity he finds between

Warburg and scholars as diverse as Franz Rosenzweig, Moritz Lazarus, and Karl Lamprecht.[36] There are clear traces here of what Peter Gay had just a few years before Liebeschütz described as constitutive for the culture of the Weimar Republic as a Republic of "Outsiders as Insiders": that "Weimar style had developed before the Weimar Republic."[37]

Warburg's concept of cultural studies is presented by Liebeschütz biographically and through the history of scholarship, and unlike in Gombrich's *Intellectual Biography* it is shown in its context. Where Gombrich proceeds genetically, Liebeschütz seeks parallels. Where the former had drawn an almost completely isolated portrait, the latter presents us with a scholar anchored in his historical situation, whose achievements and contradictions can be if not wholly then at least partially explained by this very same situation. At the center of Liebeschütz's explanation stands Warburg's ambivalent relation to Judaism, an ambivalence that never really gave rise to a new identity. Liebeschütz, comparing Warburg with the next generation of Jewish scholars to which he himself belonged, writes as though the inner conflict were resolvable if only he had been able to achieve a serene attitude toward Judaism: "Warburg did not forget his roots, but he did not allow himself to be proud of them."[38]

In 1972, the following year, Felix Gilbert made a similar assessment in a review of Gombrich's *Intellectual Biography*. His essay "From Art History to the History of Civilization: Gombrich's Biography of Aby Warburg" starts in a sharply critical manner by establishing that Gombrich's thorough biography "does not place [Warburg] adequately in the framework of intellectual history" and that Anglophone readers are thus being set on the wrong path and their image of Warburg distorted.[39]

Gilbert attempts to supply and elucidate what Gombrich's biography had not shown clearly enough. He emphasizes the importance and the unprecedented nature of Warburg's insight that it is only by studying the whole range of a period's cultural history that we can attain productive insights into the role, function, and even specific form of artworks. He points to parallels that place Warburg's work in the context of a "general trend toward broadening the framework of history which would make [. . .] the entire civilization the subject of investigation."[40] In particular, Gilbert sees a connection between Warburg's concept of cultural studies and Wilhelm Dilthey's work in cognitive theory and psychology, a deeper study of which he pronounces necessary. He also holds that Gombrich's biography had not taken sufficient account of the shift in German intellectual history after the First World War, which saw results from the impulses of Max Weber's historical sociology and would also have been ready to receive the impulses set in motion by Warburg. Finally, Gilbert characterizes Warburg's original contributions and most important innovation (taken up by the next generation of scholars) as the method of precise empirical study based in thorough examination of the documents. Every work of art is situated in a complex context: Gilbert maintains that Warburg's insight into this complexity rendered inconceivable any received ideas about the direction in which a historical process might be moving, and that this complexity even excluded the idea of an historical process itself. In this attitude, which set Warburg apart from Dilthey and Lamprecht, Gilbert sees a precondition for the picture-atlas project *Mnemosyne,* which occupied Warburg from 1924 until his death. The atlas was intended to develop a typology of the expression of fundamental emotions, and this entirely rejects, according to Gilbert, the thought of a teleological process on the one hand, while on the other hand it assigns a normative character to the forms established in antiquity.[41] Gilbert explains this contradiction by means of Warburg's background: "Clearly, he was inclined to identify with the social upper group of the empire,"[42] since he came from the only family of great financiers that had kept faith with the Jewish religion while he himself had turned away from that religion. The difficult balance of irreconcilable contrasts that Warburg described in his essay on Francesco Sassetti's last will and testament can be seen paradigmatically as the condition and first cause for any kind of cultural progress—and according to Gilbert, Warburg indeed saw it as such.[43] Like Liebeschütz, Gilbert locates Warburg's research in the historical context in which he worked, biographically and within the history of scholarship. Gilbert makes much of the fact that Warburg was born into high society and thereby shared a certain value system with the upper classes, and he finds hints that allow him to postulate Warburg's relative conservatism, without however addressing the problem of Jewish assimilation.

Georg Syamken takes a different tack in his article "Warburgs Umwege als Hermeneutik 'More Majorum'" ("Warburg's Digressions as Hermeneutics in the Tradition of the Elders") in order to establish a connection between Warburg's method in cultural studies (for which

Syamken uses the terms "dialectics" and "hermeneutics") and the "rabbinical practice of Torah exegesis." Since there are no works on dialectics or hermeneutics to be found in Warburg's library, and he used each term only once in his published work, this was supposedly an "acquired behavior," the origin of which might be sought in "Warburg's life before scholarship." Although there is no documentary evidence available, Syamken presupposes for Warburg's work an early familiarity with Torah exegetical practice.[44]

The significance of Georg Syamken's article is that (apart from R. B. Kitaj's artistic appropriation of the theme[45]) he is the first to connect the roots of Warburg's work and his methodical innovations explicitly to his Jewish background. It is however not easy to defend the tacit adoption of the quotation "*Hermeneutik More Majorum*" from its original context, which had referred to Franz Boll's impressive application of philology to the reconstruction of astrological texts.[46] One might also consider how Warburg gently suggests an ironic distancing from his own working practice as well as from Boll's ("assuming a great deal of patience, we only need a faithful philological art of exegesis in the good old style—*Hermeneutik More Majorum*—in order to achieve a longer view").[47] It is hardly convincing to point to early religious schooling as the source of Warburg's art historical approach, supposedly informed by Jewish orthodoxy.[48]

In the afterword to his 1988 edition of Warburg's lecture "Schlangenritual: Ein Reisebericht" (The Snake Ritual: A Travel Report)[49] Ulrich Rauff touches on this and a whole series of other problems variously connected with Warburg's biography and work. Warburg had traveled in the lands of the Pueblo Indians in 1895–96, and he delivered this lecture on their cultic practices in April 1923 in the Bellevue Sanatorium in Kreuzlingen, where he had at this point been a patient for exactly two years. The lecture was intended to demonstrate to himself and to the doctor treating him, Ludwig Binswanger, that he was on the road to recovery, could carry out scholarly work, and could therefore be released to live with his family. Raulff remarks on the onset and course of Warburg's illness[50] that "We can only speculate whether it was in fact nothing more than a mind that had been fragile all his life and that now gave way, or whether it was not rather an outright complex and fragile political-ethnic-religious identity that could no longer withstand the pressure of circumstances: an identity, to be sure, having been formed in congruence with the political system of Wilhelmine

Germany and, at the same time, in opposition to it, by the identification with Judaism and the abandonment of religious practice."[51] Raulff offers this as a "speculation," but it deserves to be called an informed intuition that approaches the facts very closely, and he introduces into the discussion of Warburg's biography two terms of central importance for the role of anti-Semitism in connection with the biography as we examine it here: "identity" and "identification." The *identity* is complex and fragile because it must unite within itself contrasts that ultimately do not allow for reconciliation—at least not in the long term, and not during the First World War and afterward. At the very least the part of this identity that Raulff calls "ethnic" was threatened by racial ideology.[52] The *identification* on the other hand involves the Hamburg high-society background that Gilbert had indicated and that—to borrow a formulation from Peter Gay—allowed the outsider to be an insider even before the liberalization of the Weimar Republic had made such a paradoxical role conceivable, and (albeit for a short time only) livable.

Apropos of Warburg's American journey, Raulff offers further conjectures about Warburg's experience of his own Jewishness:

> The self-confident and engaged Jewishness of the New York and Washington circles in which Warburg then moved (and into which his brothers were so soon to integrate) is remarkable. Cyrus Adler's biography reports that J. H. Schiff's "active engagement against anti-Semitism was notorious, and since the early 1890s he was the driving force behind the diverse American protests (some of them diplomatic) against the Russian pogroms." [. . .] Warburg cannot have remained unaware of at least those cases where pro-Jewish engagement and anthropological interests came together, as they did with Adler. He was after all himself intensely interested in the "Jewish Question" and five years later in 1900 was to work on a (never completed) "Psychological Survey of German Jews." The question remains as to how far the concern for Jewry and the interest in anthropology spoke to Warburg.[53]

Answering the question he has posed here, Raulff goes on to say not merely that Warburg was "abreast of current anthropology"[54] but that his articles on the meaning of myth, the formation of symbols, and their function in the human psyche stood in a European tradition of thought that had been grounded theoretically in the eighteenth century and reached back to Greek antiquity. This tradition is based on the postulate that there is a general, prescriptive development or history of human capacity to explain and exploit the world, and that this history allows us to identify the different stages of development at which various human populations stand. This perception of the exotic "Other" as an earlier (more primitive) stage of one's own development is the basis for the idea that "savages" are phylogenetically at the childhood stage.[55] Raulff's section on Aby Warburg as anthropologist ends with the suggestion that the "problem of survival" of elements of earlier cultures into later ones was somewhat inspired by lessons and reading in ethnology.[56] This suggestion might be further accentuated: "survival" (or after-life, *Nachleben*) is a phenomenon related not only to the memory of such coping strategems but above all to their causes. Warburg's ethnological readings and experiences could be seen as part of a scholarly strategy to cope with problems posed by contemporary life.

Also in 1988 appeared Anne Marie Meyer's essay "Aby Warburg in His Early Correspondence," a biographical study which ends in the year 1910, on Warburg's forty-fourth birthday. The study concentrates on Warburg's relationship to his Jewish parental household and his family background, but it also allows a glimpse of the contacts he made on his journey to America. In this context a plethora of facts is presented from Warburg's correspondence with his parents and his brother, some of which are of decisive importance for knowing how Warburg reacted to anti-Semitism.[57]

Meyer's article was the first to examine Warburg's family background in connection with his biography and his scholarly career: for instance, the strongly matriarchal element in the family exemplified by the dominant role of Warburg's grandmother Sara Warburg and his mother, Charlotte Warburg, née Oppenheim.[58] Both women raised their children with a stern sense of duty and a patrician outlook. One hitherto overlooked fact in Warburg's student years is of importance: in his first semester in Bonn (1886–89) Warburg shared rooms with Paul Ruben, who was later to become a renowned scholar in the field of Old Testament studies. Meyer holds that Warburg learned more from him than from anybody about Judaism and its history, even if he had to wait until he was in his early twenties.[59] The years in Bonn also saw Warburg's decision no longer to observe Jewish dietary laws.[60] Having renounced his religion, Warburg remained steadfast from then on. In 1908 he called himself a "dissident"[61] with regard to Hamburg's Jewish community; he declined to take part in his father's funeral. Meyer maintains that ever since his student days in Strasbourg, Warburg had had a lifelong interest in questions of Jewry and the place of the Jews in German society, and that he closely observed all symptoms of anti-Semitism.[62]

Lastly, Michael Steinberg has written extensively on Warburg's relation to Judaism. He appended to his new English edition of Warburg's 1923 lecture on the Hopi snake ritual an essay that also takes a critical stance against a tendency toward omission and suppression[63] in English-language scholarship on Warburg—particularly Gombrich's excision of the years following Warburg's breakdown in 1918. Steinberg established that "[a] source of (great) inner conflict for Warburg was his intransigent insistence that Judaism retained a primitive, pagan presence in the modern world."[64] Pagan antiquity and its survival, and even the Hopi (equating "heathen" Indians with pagan antiquity)—these objects of Warburg's studies were thus connected to him personally. Warburg never bound up the contradictions of rationality and irrationality into a theory that would have allowed equilibrium between paganism and reason. Steinberg believes that Warburg had drawn "a connection between Hopi and Hebrew culture," and asks, "what is the nature of the recurring irrationality of culture which precludes a victory of modernizing rationality?" In this context Steinberg quotes a passage from the notes Warburg had jotted down in the sanatorium for his lecture, in which he wrote a few lines about "anti-Semitism in its creeping form," calling it a fundamental danger for Germany.[65]

Steinberg's analysis touches partly upon questions that are also examined here, and at the same time achieves some of what Felix Gilbert had stipulated: it anchors Warburg's work into the social and intellectual history of his times. He concludes that Warburg's rejection of "aestheticizing art history" must be seen alongside the "recognition of cultural violence": "In this respect, the aesthetic analysis of Warburg is anti-aestheticist; it stands militantly on the critical side of European intellectual life, next to Benjamin, and opposite, ultimately, the fascist energies that proceed according to the aestheticization of politics."[66]

2

"This of Course Does Not Make Life Much Happier"

Two Letters (1887, 1889)

Two letters that Warburg wrote to his mother, one from Bonn in 1887 and the other from Strasbourg in 1889, show him as a student at twenty-two and twenty-four years old, self-confident yet loyal to his family and his background; troubled by the role of the outsider that he must internalize; outraged by anti-Semitic episodes; reflecting on his own situation and on that of German Jews in general. These few pages contain key words and themes, and they set a tone in which the political and social dimensions of these questions can be (and are) discussed even today. The identity of individuals and groups; nationalism as a pervasive quotidian attitude; the ever-present hostility and stigmatization that knows no class boundaries; the role of the "Eastern Jew" for assimilated Jews, but also the assimilated Jew's own participation in Orientalist constructs; and lastly, in a final sentence, reference to a silence broken here exceptionally. Both letters are also documents of the age in which they were written, and their terms and conclusions can be read with regard to the political tendencies and social developments of Wilhelmine Germany. The second letter in particular defines areas that, modern scholarship confirms, lead to larger themes of central importance for the situation of the Jewish minority in Germany and for the renewal of a rejection of, and a contempt for, Jews which had never really fallen silent.

The first letter refers to Warburg's decision no longer to follow Jewish dietary laws, which he and his parents saw as extremely significant.[1] He would thus no longer eat kosher, since the "Rothschilds," the only kosher lunch table in Bonn, did not suit him. His letter also answers the remonstrations from his father, Moritz M. Warburg, that even hinted at the possibility of Aby's changing universities: he was not prepared to organize his studies according to the availability and quality of kosher food, but could only choose a place to study according to the quality of teaching.[2] For his mother he phrased this cool declaration somewhat more considerately. The decision seemed so drastic that Warburg or his parents found an intermediary, Dr. Unger, who should explain (in Hamburg) the situation of the student in Bonn. No matter what, Warburg had made up his mind; but even if he could not have their acceptance, the son needed his parents' acquiescence to a decision he had reached on his own, for reasons of his own. These letters, and other letters from the time, show that his parents never considered that he had left the family by breaking with matters of faith. Yet his mother must have referred in her letter to the symbolic importance of the dietary laws, since for all its assurances his reply shows that this was precisely his concern.

We know from Warburg himself that his estrangement from the Jewish religion had its roots early in his childhood.[3] Elsewhere he wrote that he had been "raised entirely in this orthodoxy and until my fifteenth year was a pious observer thereof."[4] In her memoirs Ingrid Warburg Spinelli describes this "orthodoxy" and how it was lived in her own family, that of Aby Warburg's youngest brother, Fritz: "My grandparents Moritz and Charlotte Warburg were still orthodox or, as my father used to say, 'orthoprax.' The observation of all laws and commandments of the Jewish religion was as it were a self-evident habit, a lifelong rhythm to which [Fritz and Anna Maria Warburg] conformed out of respect for their parents."[5] If we follow Ron Chernow's conclusions,[6] gradual relaxation of strict observance by Aby Warburg's generation went together with growing optimism and the belief in a secure future in a prosperous Imperial Germany; it also found expression in an affectionate disrespect for the old-fashioned, devout father. Or, as Warburg Spinelli reports of the period after the turn of the century: "In those years our family pride could be clearly felt; we had felt German for decades and had above all felt 'at home' in Hamburg, and finally felt that we could take part in Germany's social, economic, and political life on a more or less equal footing."[7] All of Moritz Warburg's sons "gave up Jewish dogmas sooner or later, and their Judaism survived as a cultural tradition but also as an awareness that they were at once Jews *and* Germans. [. . .] My father Fritz's and my uncle Max's brief but intense engagement with German politics can only be explained as a Jewish sense of community responsibility. They felt this responsibility for Germany not so much as a state but rather as a human community in which they could take an active part for the sake of social progress."[8]

These words relate to the Warburgs specifically, and can be complemented by broadly consistent descriptions of Hamburg Jews and their social position from the mid-nineteenth-century onward: "Long since politically emancipated, on equal terms with their Christian neighbors as businessmen, lawyers, judges, scholars and the like, and often occupying prominent positions, the [. . .] Hamburg Jews were all in all an uncommonly industrious and productive element of the population."[9] Julius von Eckardt notes that of the years after 1870 the Hamburg Jews were well treated by "old Hamburg" and that "those who had been strangers" thus became "good Hamburgers, devoted to the civic interest."[10] Nevertheless, Eckardt reports, old Hamburg closed itself off from "the Jewish element" socially: "With a very few exceptions even the rich Jews stood outside of 'society.' Whether baptized or not they formed a world of their own, which—as everywhere—was characterized by intellectual ebullience and a lively sensitivity for the common good, and appeared just about as Hamburg as it possibly could be."[11]

From all of this one can conclude that because of the favorable conditions under which he had grown up in his home city and the especially privileged position of his family, Aby Warburg was not quite prepared to cope with the daily hostility and insults he encountered in his student years. He had already experienced how difficult it was to break with the conventions of his background (even in choosing a subject of study, which his family at first vehemently rejected[12]), but the second front of this "war on two fronts"[13] (as Warburg later described this aspect of his student life) always stupefied him: "How such things can happen at all!"[14] The stark contrast between Warburg's privileged individual and family situation in liberal Hamburg and the atmosphere at the universities was surely among the reasons for Warburg's particular sensitivity, his analytical and perceptive acuity, and the extraordinarily long-lasting impression that anti-Semitic insults made on him; this contrast could only have arisen at precisely this point in time. It was only the security of his situation, combined with the confidence that emancipation was an irreversible process, that allowed Warburg to dare oppose his own family: the second "front" of social exclusion therefore must have found him particularly vulnerable.

Warburg's university years coincided with a wide-ranging change of climate in German student society that had been making headway since the mid-1860s.[15] German liberal nationalist students had frequently been politically disappointed: after the founding of the Reich in 1871 they turned ever further toward corporatism, and to forms of student fraternities that wished to be exclusive and followed military codes in their outlook and their exaggerated concepts of honor. In 1891 Wilhelm II pronounced that the spirit prevailing in the student corps should set the young men who belonged to them onto the right path for their later lives. As they competed with the corps, liberal-national vestiges within the fraternities changed, and their "liberal impulses increasingly atrophied into pure nationalism."[16] They were intended to turn out "citizens of a unified German fatherland, domestically strong, powerful abroad, free and self-confident in their thoughts and actions."[17] More and more fraternities followed the example of the corps and became dueling societies whose central features were an outward formalism, a pronounced ritualism (with dueling at its core), and a clear hierarchy which promised entry into the elite.[18] Although they were supposedly apolitical organizations, in truth their "old boys" were heavily over-represented in all high political offices and leading positions in finance.[19] When for whatever reason a student group rejected fencing and duels, the group seems in return to have been almost of necessity second-rate: Catholics had been explicitly forbidden to fight student duels by a papal letter of 1891,[20] and Jews were socially discriminated against, as were of course women. For such groups and their forms of organization "a decisive role was played by defending themselves in a male, Protestant world of old boys' clubs."[21]

We can distinguish three ranks in the hierarchy of student organization and inclusion: the corps, which above all served to secure social status; the fraternities, whose members were more ambitious to improve themselves socially; and groupings of those who were relatively excluded from "respectable society,"[22] such as Catholics and Jews.[23] In the universities of larger cities about one-quarter of all students belonged to such organizations, while in smaller towns two-fifths (in Bonn) to over half (in Marburg) of university students joined.[24]

During his first semester in Bonn Warburg also belonged to a group of students who regularly met in a wine cellar and about whom he wrote to his friend Paul Ruben during vacations. Although members adopted the jargon of established student clubs the group seems to have been informal, albeit one that was of personal importance to its members at this time.[25] There are no comparable letters or documents from his time in Strasbourg.

In Warburg's letter from Strasbourg the problem of exclusion is only hinted at, and the wish to belong is merely touched upon and then immediately called a weakness: "I am still governed by the rather lamentable wish to enjoy the tacit respect of everybody with whom I have to do, as I go about my business (which I know to be quite respectable)." It seems unlikely that Warburg joined any of the societies that would have taken him at this time. Since he belonged to the upper class, joining a Jewish student fraternity would have been tantamount to publicly acknowledging his social exclusion. Aby Warburg and his brother Fritz, a jurist, were the only ones in the family to face this, while the other brothers, Max, Paul, and Felix, were not educated at universities but were trained in banks. His "self-chosen place" had to be won "as an individual": first of all in conflict with his family and then in his milieu, which for Warburg was the university and academia.

Development of Culture and the State

The dispute about dietary laws was not an argument merely about good or bad food in more or less pleasant company, but rather about the meaning of emancipation as a Jew and as a person.

> When you write, dearest Mama, about the things that will go by the board through eating differently, I must tell you that you are doing me an injustice. I am not at all ashamed to be a Jew; on the contrary, I am trying to show others that representatives of my kind are well suited, in accordance with their talents, to insert themselves as useful links in the chain of present-day developments of culture and the state. But precisely because I want to do that I must strive to shake off whatever will not fit organically into my activity. I want to act as I am; I want to be regarded by people as I am.[26]

Although understandably he does not lay out the actual reasons for his decision in the letter to his mother, it did indeed represent exactly what the family had feared: a renunciation of Jewish religion and of Jewish ritual that only grew more uncompromising as the years went by.[27]

What Warburg represented as "contrary" to denying his origin shows, in his choice of words and metaphors, a complex and almost overly precise definition of this difficult process; whatever he set out to do, he would always be a "representative of his kind" and not simply himself. He feels the need to show that he is a useful citizen; the role in which he sees himself is that of a link in a chain. This image evokes a sense of undifferentiated conformity, of tradition and community, perhaps also of functionality and necessity. The idea of complete assimilation implied here is conditional upon the concept of a fully secularized Jewry. The young intellectual seeks a way of life that can reconcile historical and theoretical insights with life as it is lived.

The basis for such a way of life is the belief in basically positive and progressive "present-day developments of culture and the state." This conjunction deserves closer examination. It implies that here we have a concept of culture that is fundamentally politically determined, or at the least has political connotations, and this can hardly surprise us when we remember how the concept and phenomenon of culture attracted intense, politically motivated attention in the second half of the nineteenth century. It was not merely in the recently founded sociological sciences of, for instance, Max Weber and Georg Simmel that this concept has political connotations, but also in history (with Karl Lamprecht), in philosophy (Heinrich Rickert), in national economy and the theory of the state and in "those schools of cultural philosophy which set themselves the task of interpretation."[28] It is however significant that Warburg speaks here of "development of the state" (*Staatsentwicklung*) and does not use the term "nation" already prevalent in the general and the specialist discourse on "culture." At that time and long after, the concept of culture,[29] with its broad meanings in many different disciplines, could not be thought of except in conjunction with the nation, the German nation, the *Kulturnation*. As George L. Mosse said, "while it was the state, then in formation, which emancipated [the Jews], it was the nation they faced once they were emancipated."[30] The young Hamburg citizen writes to his family from just such a situation, which is to some extent clear and comprehensible with hindsight and from the outside, but which as the letters make clear, when lived from the inside was paradoxically hemmed in by a frustrated new beginning.

Identity: The Representative of His Kind

Developmental psychologists would understand the wish to "shake off whatever will not fit organically" as a search for identity, along with the passionate desire to reach a unity in essence, activity, and reputation.[31] As a young man Warburg insisted on being himself, on taking his "self-chosen place" in life even at the risk of causing pain to those closest to him.[32] The insistence on the right to an "ego-identity" independent of tradition and background, freely chosen by a free individual, seems to point decisively to a modern self-image—and to this extent it is prefigured in the German tradition of *Bildung*,[33] the tradition of the *Bildungsbürger* as Goethe formulated it in *Wilhelm Meister's Years of Apprenticeship*, when Wilhelm confesses to his brother Werner in a letter: "To put it to you in a few words, it was my wish and intention in a vague way from childhood onward to develop and educate myself, entirely as I am. I still cherish these very views, it is only that the means which will make this possible for me are rather clearer to me."[34] Warburg's "organic" was Goethe's "harmonic" ("that harmonious formation of my nature"), and Goethe does not hold back either from sociopolitical conjectures that of necessity define the limits for free development of the free individual.[35] Warburg's claim to an "ego-identity," however, is bound up inseparably with the problem of Jewish group identity and the question of what defines it.

The amalgamation of an adolescent's search for identity with the problem of belonging to a minority group seems almost paradigmatically suited to an explanation through Erikson's and Goffman's theories of identity as developed in the 1950s and 1960s. Erikson showed how (and under what circumstances) identity can be developed and realized by stages in each individual's life cycle; Goffman used the term "stigma" to show how identity can be attained under the circumstances of "being other."[36] In both cases the underlying models of successful identity formation presuppose coherence and continuity, the unity of the person—the organic and harmonic unity that we have already discussed.

Regarding the problems of the young Jewish intellectual from a family of the *grande bourgeoisie* searching for a "self-chosen" place in society in the nineteenth century's last quarter, Erikson's model of identity appears in a particular light. This model, conceived of by Erikson to explain certain phenomena, can be taken as a *parallel* of what is to be explained; as a postulate developed in a biographical context comparable to Warburg's.[37] His model of identity as a universal human concern that must be worked out is really a concept pushed to the fore by social conflict. Goethe had formulated it as a conflict between the aristocracy and the bourgeoisie, Warburg perceived it as the search for a place in society in Imperial Germany at a time when that society was defining itself as anti-Jewish, and Erikson understood it as a healing factor in a fragmenting society of immigrants and disenfranchised "natives." The identity that Warburg evokes, an identity of what one is and does, is a confrontation with those who are stronger, with the majority. The subject of individuality, selfhood in its division or integration, can be called one of the great European themes,[38] and ever since Kant we have talked of "subjectivity"; but it is only since the middle of the twentieth century that "identity" has been a term in this context.[39] It is a term borrowed from logic, where one can apply it to the formula $a = a$, but it proved too strict for the field of social psychology.[40] That this inflexible term would be introduced in political debate is explicable through the documents used here. Especially today, "identity" has become a slogan in cultural politics, and the notion of group identities has become so fixed that the historical genesis of the term, and what it postulates, is no longer questioned.

It seems that the problem of identity, like the concept of culture with which it intersects, first appears as a term in political discourse and contexts at the time when Warburg was a young man and a student.[41] Identity means to be something, and not to be some other thing. Every Jew found that he had to "answer the question at pistol-point"[42] (Warburg's phrase, which he used often, sometimes in the context of discussing style): either a German or a Jew, either a Frenchman or a Jew, either nationally committed or a traitor.[43] Against this background we see played out the drama that is manifest in Warburg's two letters. It is not merely that to be "true to himself" meant, for Warburg, giving up his religion; it also meant that as a scholar and art historian he entered a world whose unwritten rules had long ago decreed that Jews were unwelcome, especially at the rank of professor in the German universities;[44] lastly, it meant that he already saw, but long refused to recognize, that he could not access German national identity even if he wished to find his place in society—a place that would allow him to make his contribution.

The "Jewish Question" and Praxis

The second letter to his mother, written from Strasbourg in the winter semester of 1889/90, is a progress report on his attempt to orient himself within a reality riven by contradictions. Here we no longer see simple strategems and clear decisions intended to make possible an "organically" unified personality in deed, thought, and feeling. Instead young Warburg regards the dovetailing of Jewish identity and "ego-identity" as a problem so difficult that he takes its "practical solution" as, perhaps, a lifelong task; he seems to see a process that might need several generations to work out: "My great-grandchildren or rather my great-grandnephews may perhaps become full professors." Upon the first page of this letter Max Adolph Warburg had written "Important: the whole letter";[45] this was Max Adolph's reaction to a text that does not pretend to be anything more than a student's letter home but that is also a sharply observing document and a merciless piece of youthful self-examination. Its analytical remarks are socially critical and its conclusions political.

The letter opens with a report on a paper Warburg successfully presented in Theobald Ziegler's philosophy seminar,[46] on Kant's *Prolegomena to the Critique of Pure Reason.*[47] He writes that although he finds it hard to understand Kant he earned his professor's respect, which had pleased him and given him a fillip. He regards it as a weakness to be so dependent on favorable reactions that he hopes to have them from everybody whose path he crosses—and indeed he experiences the opposite "at every turn." "The German people, whom we so deservedly love" choose to "see every Jew as above all a foreign interloper with dubious manners." It "depresses" him that such discrimination is unavoidable. Yet the letter immediately contrasts to this experience of group stigma a second and more positive experience: "Everybody whom I have come to know a little better shows me good faith and good will." On the one hand, the individual in his relation with others, and on the other hand the "German people" who treat "every Jew as a foreign interloper": these two contrasted levels of experience introduce the two motifs that will be repeated and varied in what follows. Thus the next paragraph addresses the political feasibility of "integration" (*gesellschaftliches Durchdringen*). Again Warburg sees any chance to combat anti-Semitism at the level of the individual man of good will, and is thoroughly skeptical about parliamentary committees debating the place of Jews in the military: "Neither are the debates in the Reichstag committee encouraging: even if there is no official regulation that Jews should not be made reserve officers, the will to recognize an individual's worth is still lacking." At this point, too, Warburg mentions as if in passing a problem that was symptomatic of the policy of exclusion, a problem that affected the Jewish bourgeoisie in particular: the conflict over the rank of reserve officer, "which in many circles was seen as proof that the holder was socially acceptable and politically reliable, which offered him better chances for advancement in many civil careers."[48]

As he experiences and recognizes his status as an outsider his response is a retreat into the self and into scholarly work as a place of safety. From this standpoint he writes that he intends to "seek a practical solution to the Jewish question later," which he now sees is a task that life has set him. It may disconcert the modern reader to hear Warburg declare that he will devote his life to the "solution to the Jewish question."[49] Warburg used this phrase at a historical moment when the "Jewish question" (which had its analogues in the "women's question" and the "social question") was changing. These "questions" had been formulated in reaction to the emancipatory and progressive movements of the eighteenth and nineteenth centuries. Only later did the "Jewish question" become an anti-Jewish and anti-Semitic slogan: Warburg still understood it as referring to emancipation at all levels of politics and society, "integration," but at the same time the same words were used elsewhere to question this process, to stop it, and where possible to reverse it.[50]

We must however ask just what weight this declaration of intent should be given, and how far we can dimly see here a serious plan to undertake a lifetime task: should we not rather assume that while these were indeed intensely felt experiences, they were not concrete plans? After all, he writes as a determined future bachelor, at the most uncle to great-grandnephews, whereas whatever his resolutions he became a husband and father not much later. All the same we should take his phrase, "the solution to the Jewish question," seriously insofar as it uses the same term by which the future role of the Jewish minority would be focused on in the German nation-state. This is especially obvious if we compare it with another phrase he uses, "social mingling," which is in contrast a "soft" description of the social process described. We might in any case take this resolution to mean that because he had experienced discrimination, Warburg as a young man thought practical political engagement viable, and we may thus remain all the more alert for later signs of politically motivated engagement.

Nothing to Do with Us: *Mauscheln*

The "revolting mob" on the street never grew tired of picking out a passerby as a Jew; in their Alsatian dialect, "*Desch ischt a Jud!*" Much like this mob are the "Christian gentlemen" who murmur while playing cards in the Germania building[51]—and here Warburg uses the Yiddish word *mauscheln,* "murmuring." The word *Volk* can mean the German nation, or the mob on the street—and the mob and the Christian "gentlemen" are in agreement when it comes to the Jews. Warburg counters the inconsiderate and insulting way strangers invade his privacy with distancing language, sarcastic ("The German people, whom we so deservedly love") or dismissive ("Nothing to do with us"). Neither sarcasm nor distancing, though, can save him from feeling injury and indignation; rather, they reinforce his status as a stranger and his exclusion: "How such things can happen at all!" The briefly sketched episode in the Germania throws a sharply contrasting light on young Warburg's particular situation and on wider, general developments which affected him or in which he took part. In this respect the parodistic Yiddish *mauscheln* of the men playing cards is significant, as is Warburg's reaction.

The episode described here happened at a time when Eastern European Jews fleeing the pogroms in Russia, Poland, and Galicia were becoming more numerous, more visible, and more audible in the big cities of Berlin and Hamburg; many of them were emigrants on the way to America.[52] The refugees were particularly noticeable because of their unusual, archaic dress and appearance, because they spoke Yiddish, and because they were greatly impoverished: "When assimilated German Jews were confronted with a Jewish nation in Eastern Europe, with all the attributes thereof, they mostly reacted negatively by shutting out; they wanted to have nothing to do with the 'Eastern Jew' [*Ostjude*]. It seemed one more proof that German Jews belonged to the German nation and not to this other *Volk,* which was foreign to them and sometimes repulsive."[53] Parallel with this exclusion, however, there was a positive reaction from some Jewish groups who for the first time saw in their midst "Jewish masses with their own way of doing things and folk customs."[54] This led to the "invention of the Eastern Jew,"[55] which is to say to the attempts by a small yet important group of the Jewish minority to set themselves apart from prejudice by accepting and studying this particular wellspring of Jewish identity, which they felt was an enrichment to themselves.[56] The central importance of *Kultur* as a bond and a generator of ideology in the new nation-state can be said to have resulted in "the invention of a culture."[57] Warburg did not see this option for himself. With Heinrich von Treitschke's insult of the "Jewish trouser-selling youth" in mind,[58] it is obvious that the pressure on the majority of the Jewish population in Germany to assimilate was so great that for their part, they felt the need to exclude in turn: "It's nothing to do with us." However, the Eastern Jews were not enough for anti-Semitic stereotyping and this scarecrow was soon replaced by another: "The negative image of the Eastern Jew was displaced by the image of the nonassimilated Western Jew (or at least the Jew in the West), by *Mauschel*."[59] The accusation that Jews were corrupting the language,[60] and the conjecture that there may exist a "hidden language of the Jews," were together to become one of the most effective and at the same time one of the most hurtful and spiteful anti-Semitic tactics. Sander L. Gilman holds that it particularly contributed to the development of a negative and divided self-image, which in an early twentieth-century debate has been labeled "Jewish self-hatred."[61] There is no question then that the cardplayers who pretended to speak Yiddish as a parody were aiming at a central point of Warburg's identity. It is however not possible to assess his description of the episode or to read his commentary, at once distanced and indignant, without going deeper. The reference at the end of the letter to the effect of his own "Oriental appearance"[62] lends more weight to what he had already reported to his mother. Those sections of the letter speaking of the experience of everyday anti-Semitism and its effects also talk of the self, reflected in a wickedly distorting mirror. Warburg perceives how others perceive him and is shocked: this shock releases his thoughts about himself, the situation of the Jews, and ways to possible remedies.

To examine *mauscheln* in its meaning of bad, corrupted language means to think also of a larger theme that is central to Warburg's later work: his own use of language. Ever since Gertrud Bing planned a study on this topic[63] it has been a commonplace in Warburg studies that

Warburg's language, or the wrestling with the German language that yielded his texts, was a fundamental prerequisite for his methodological innovations. His virtuoso use of metaphor is one way in which Warburg opens the reader's eyes and brings us to insight, as is his almost inexhaustible gift for neologisms that can say what had never yet been said (for example, *Schlagbild*, "pictorial slogan"; *Bildervehikel*, "pictorial vehicle"; *Pathosformel*, "expressive formula"; and countless others that of course depend on the fact that such constructions are possible in German). He himself recognized the danger this gift represented, and he sometimes spoke of his *Aalsuppenstyl*, his "eel broth style."[64] His biographer (and the translator of long sections of his texts) Ernst Gombrich realized this as well.[65] One would not choose to call Warburg's intensity of language masterful, since it always shows how hard he had worked at the texts: but the innovative power of his works depends in large part on their linguistic creativity, as in the text "Pagan-Antique Prophecy at the Time of Luther." This "civilized" way with words, using mastery of language as a means of self-expression, plays a central role for modern Jewish self-awareness.[66] It has sometimes been said that for Warburg the tradition of the Talmud and Haggada is of eminent importance for an art history that wishes to be a cultural study of word as well as image. It has not been acknowledged, however, that working against the myth of a hidden language of the Jews may have played a more important role in this respect.

Parvenus of National Sentiment

Young Warburg is clear-sighted in his analysis and observation of the background to anti-Semitism in Imperial Germany: one is dealing with "parvenus of national sentiment." We can only conjecture from what vantage point Warburg spoke of "parvenus." Certainly he spoke as a historian in an only recently founded German empire; perhaps he spoke also as the scion of a highly regarded Jewish family that had been in Hamburg for three hundred years. Since then it has become a basic historical tenet in speaking of recent German history that the Germans were to be seen as "parvenus of national sentiment, not yet certain of themselves"—much later, during the First World War, Max Weber saw them as such and said so publicly,[67] and in 1974 Helmuth Plessner coined the term "belated nation," which became the definitive formulation.[68] It is however uncertain just how much one can ascribe to this "belatedness" and to the peculiarly strong drive for modernization that it occasioned. To look at the Third Republic in France is to learn how at the end of the nineteenth century, the least politically "belated" nation in Europe could undergo a phase of anti-Semitic propaganda just as intense as that in Germany, culminating in the "Dreyfus affair." Most convincing, it would seem, is a historical concept that identifies the formation of nation-states throughout Europe as the central reason for calling into question the emancipation and equal rights that Jewish minorities had enjoyed in modernizing states since the eighteenth century. Perhaps this view of history can also best explain the different forms this process took in different nations. In other words: since the "Jews" of the anti-Semites can only be understood as a construct, it is to be expected that the European nations would each imagine their own Jews to suit their own particular problems. It seems undisputed, however, that after the founding of the Second Empire in 1871 there was a concerted attempt to forge a "German identity" not least with respect to its rapidly built military strength, while also at that time full equality in civil rights for German Jews was achieved between 1869 and 1871[69] (and in Hamburg in 1868[70]). There is a bitter irony (and perhaps a measure of logic) in the circumstance that the full emancipation of the Jewish minority should be almost immediately followed by their renewed stigmatization as "foreign interlopers with dubious manners," to use Warburg's words. The process of national self-assertion badly needed outsiders, who were thus duly constructed.

A relaxed and even optimistic commentary by Warburg's father on these "national parvenus" is preserved in the Warburg Institute archive of family correspondence, dated 29 November 1889:

> It is with regret that I learn from your last letter that the Strasbourgers are still very coarse in some ways, yet one can only regard such people with contempt and be glad that one does not oneself have such debased views. You are right that the national sentiment of the Germans as it is currently expressed is often reminiscent of parvenus. Such people need time to become decent human beings. A few days ago an anti-Semitic scandal sheet was being handed out on the street here, *for free* of course. At the same time Herr von Liebermann-Sonntag[71] held [gap in text] a lecture that was very sparsely attended. H. D. Levy alerted the Lord Mayor to the scandal sheet, and Mayor Petersen then wrote a very

> fine letter that I read, in which *inter alia* he wrote that "we in the Senate are all agreed that this publication broadly conforms with the Anti-Semite Union [*Antisemitenverein*]." Petersen writes "we are lucky that there is no place for such vulgarity here in Hamburg. The whole Union consists of 17 members although the men are making every effort, thus we confidently expect that the [gap in text] will very quickly right itself." . . . May we not be *happy* that we are Hamburgers? Your loving father.[72]

Yet the times in which Hamburg had been a world apart, where one had long been accustomed to wait calmly for "parvenus" to become decent human beings, were coming to an end. The son could no longer attain the security his father had enjoyed.

Breaking the Silence

Warburg ends his letter to his mother parodically, with an allusion to Nietzsche; he signs off "Greetings to you all from your 'blond.'" He apologizes to his mother for having even touched upon the theme of anti-Semitism and for having written about it so extensively—"but I do not see why we should not speak out on this point just once." "Pardon me for singing the ballad of the good Jew."[73] he writes. This could be near-naïveté excusing itself to worldly wisdom and experience; it is also however the consciousness of having transgressed the rules. Between Aby Warburg's generation and that of his parents there was for a while the possibility for each individual to decide what stand he wished to take toward Jew-hating, which in itself seemed unchangeable.

Silent acceptance of insults and humiliations such as Warburg reports has a long and sad history. Jews of Warburg's generation began to take their stand against this silence and consciously to reject their elders' experience and the careful restraint that they had observed in their own families. Ever since legal equality for Jews was introduced, the modern state had become a court of appeal that was supposed to function as a guarantor of civil rights for all. The Enlightenment project of Jewish emancipation was to be completed now. Prudence in dealing with the non-Jewish majorities had for centuries been practiced as a wise necessity but now had become questionable: "integration" seemed a realizable Utopia, as did activist engagement to achieve it.

Freud's family background could hardly have been in starker contrast to Warburg's, yet an episode from his life captures the traumatic quality of this historic change—although Freud reports the episode in his *Interpretation of Dreams* precisely because he saw in it a particular significance for himself. His father, Jakob, told Sigmund "to show me how I had been born into better times than he had. . . . 'When I was a young man I went for a walk on a Saturday in the town you were born in, wearing my best clothes and with a new fur cap on my head. Then a Christian comes along, knocks my cap in the mud with a single blow, and shouts: "Jew, get off the pavement!"'—'And what did you do?'—'I stepped into the road and picked up my cap,' came the impassive reply. That did not seem to me very heroic of the big, strong man who was leading me by the hand."[74] According to Yosef Yerushalmi, as an adult Sigmund Freud mostly reacted to everyday anti-Semitic incidents forthrightly and without backing down: "better times" were times when to defend oneself was not to endanger one's life.[75] As Carl Schorske has shown, he also spent a great deal of intellectual and mental energy in successfully avoiding manifestly political threats by showing their "actual" apolitical nature.[76]

In his essay on "the nervous years" of 1887–91 Jakob Toury sets the scene for this situation, between a new beginning and a new threat to what had been guaranteed rights:

> The years since Germany's unification and the constitutional foundation of equal rights for all citizens seemed to the Jews to be the high tide of integrative tendencies in the economy, in culture, even in day-to-day dealings with others: yet ever since the so-called *Gründerkrach*, the economic crisis, and countless bankruptcies of 1873, shrill tones of hatred had broken the incipient harmony of coexistence in state and society. The tactics of silence that Jews usually adopted toward all such attacks could no longer be deployed once the pastor at the Berlin royal household, Adolf Stoecker, and the Hamburg journalist Wilhelm Marr had made "anti-Semitism" into an ideology acceptable even at court.[77]

The "tactics of silence" were, however, the age-old tradition: when silence over the attacks and insults was broken, so was another, larger silence that went beyond what is normally understood as tactical, and beyond even the respectful silence toward the parents' generation. Warburg could not achieve a "solution to the Jewish question" any more than could many others,[78] since it was so closely bound up with other "solutions." Instead he began to search for an *answer* to this question.

The letter from Strasbourg especially shows that Warburg was not merely turning his daily experience into keen political analysis, and not merely summarizing and examining essential themes and aspects of the "Jewish question" on a few pages of stationery. His letter also shows that these themes were not among those that could be naturally and freely discussed in the Warburg family. The reasons for this are not named, but their outlines can be recognized: personal dignity, integrity, and not least social status forbade one to descend to the level of these crude everyday insults by confronting them. This attitude is quintessentially aristocratic, or better yet it is that of a "cosmopolitan,"[79] and it allowed Warburg as the intellectual of the family to approach the phenomenon of anti-Semitism through a useful paradox. The dramatist Nestroy is supposed to have coined the phrase for this paradox—"hardly worth ignoring"—and this shrewd oxymoron allows the option of doing something, without doing anything.[80]

The two youthful letters record the beginning of Warburg's difficult and lifelong confrontation with the experiences he describes in them for the first time, and with the problems and questions to which they gave rise; the letters also document the limits of such confrontations. There is a great difference in tone between the two letters, and this points to several conclusions: Warburg believed that a scholar and modern citizen could not combine such a career with Jewish orthodoxy, and he originally saw his confrontation with his parents on this point as only one step toward inner independence and to the clear understanding of the necessities of his own existence. The first letter lays the groundwork for distancing himself from Jewish religious observance, "orthopraxis," and thereby from his parental home, and was clearly written in the hope of setting things straight. The second letter reports on slights and insults and the necessary engagement with "identity" to which they gave rise: his own identity, Jewish and German. Turning away from the religion of his fathers did not alleviate the problem, and a rational decision on one's own behalf did not at all influence the reactions of those around one. German nationalism was belated and therefore all the more self-important, and in such times the broad education of an individual to be a useful link in civic society, his

Ausbildung, was not enough to show that he belonged. Thus at the center of this second letter stands the relationship of the individual subject to the demands and expectations of the group, and whether by accident or design this is set between Kant and Nietzsche ("your blond"), held in high tension; the group is the *Volk,* in its oscillating meanings as a political or a sociological category.

3

Modernity and the Eternal Recurrence of the Beast

In the years from 1900 to about 1908 Warburg's lectures, publications, and unpublished writings concentrated on the fact that opposing styles nonetheless coexisted alongside one another, as a problem in historical psychology.[1] Florence under the Medici and Valois Burgundy were the realms that gave him problems, characters, and objects as ever-evolving aspects of these questions. The common denominator for Warburg were kaleidoscopic sightings from many different perspectives on the iconology of form, on form as a vehicle of meaning.[2] In his dissertation he had identified "accessories in motion" as the traces of a confrontation with antique forms occasioned by reasons of historical psychology, and he refined his results with further material. Warburg read and deciphered these signs above all as traces of a liberation—the freedom to show lively feeling through unimpeded motion. As we see in the Dürer lecture in particular, he also perceived ever more acutely the "dangers" of classical pathos when it manifested itself as a superlative expression of emotion in rhetorical formulas and formulas of violence. These studies gave rise to Warburg's coining the widely accepted term *Pathosformel* (emotive formula).[3] We can now show that this change of emphasis, from liberation to threat, is closely connected to Warburg's perception and assessment of anti-Semitism.

CHAPTER 3

Dürer and Italian Antiquity

Warburg spent the years 1897 to 1902 in Florence, the second time he had lived and studied there for a longer period. The first result of his study of the artworks and archives was a lecture on Leonardo given in Hamburg in 1899.[4] An unfinished project on the Nympha dates from shortly thereafter, in 1900; together with André Jolles, Warburg had planned an exchange of fictitious letters on which he began work.[5] The Nympha was a female figure that appeared under many different guises in the works of the Florentine Renaissance (Salome, Judith, an angel, a fleeing mother), and Warburg believed that it was nothing other than the embodiment of a principle: "It was always she who brought life and movement into an otherwise calm scene. Indeed, she appeared to be the embodiment of movement."[6] In the Nympha, both scholars ultimately saw the personification of passion. Here as in other areas of Warburg's research, Gombrich points out how modern parallels, in this case the women's liberation movement of the time, may have determined and reinforced this identification of the figure as a pictorial metaphor for liberation and emancipation in general. For Warburg, its appearance in the sober civic context of Florentine art signaled that aspect of the Renaissance which showed the epoch to be a positive departure for modernity.

The lectures and studies of the following years, however, show that Warburg became ever more aware of the dangers of unrestrained passion,[7] and in particular he observed these perils in Florentine bridal chests (cassoni) decorated with mythological scenes. At the same time he was turning to the "commerce between North and South," the interest shown by Florentine patrons in art and tapestries from the Low Countries, and the study of Italian art undertaken by artists from Northern Europe. Compared to his dissertation on Botticelli, this was an expanded historical horizon, and for Warburg it encompassed alongside Franco-Flemish art an exceptional case in Italian art studies, Albrecht Dürer's interpretation of "Italian antiquity." Warburg was interested in the question of what the Northern milieu took from Italian art and why, as well as how Burgundian court art was received in Florence and to what end. Warburg refined his conception of "impulsive and inhibitory forces"[8] over the years. He had once written that "we must see the culture of Graeco-Roman antiquity also in the symbol of a 'dual herm of Apollo-Dionysus'";[9] this assessment was then refined through an evaluation of the mental energy contained, transported, and received through the exaggerated, "Dionysiac" form in violent motion. It is astonishing to see Warburg pose questions here that can be found a decade later in new configurations and with a specialized technical meaning; Heinrich Wölfflin was to raise these questions in addressing "questions of national psychology of forms."[10]

In a passage of his *Intellectual Biography,* Ernst Gombrich develops modern parallels to these historical enquiries as he addresses this decade of Warburg's work.[11] Gombrich demonstrates how Warburg's work as an art historian was bound up with his own times, and conversely how his scholarly work gained impetus from an identification of Hamburg in the 1890s with Quattrocento mercantile Florence. The "modern" parallels are mostly found in the areas of artistic and cultural policy, such as Warburg's opinions on Hugo Lederer's Bismarck memorial in Hamburg or on Hugo Vogel's frescoes for the town hall.[12] For Warburg this always involves a political ethics of art, just as ultimately he assesses Florentine painting of the Quattrocento in ethical terms. For instance, when he considers Ghirlandaio's fresco of the Massacre of the Innocents,[13] these ultimately normative criteria assign to the picture an effective force that is otherwise only attributed to actions.[14] A representation, or the deed that it implies; an act itself (murder, orgiastic dance, battle) and its translation into an image fraught with affect and the energy represented as movement: from Warburg's point of view, pictured actions, in terms of the energy they impart to a society, cannot be distinguished from the actions themselves.

Against this backdrop we can see a second "modern parallel" that Warburg kept to himself; he included it in the manuscript of his lecture "Dürer and Italian Antiquity" (1905).[15] Warburg gave the lecture to the forty-eighth congress of German philologists and educators in Hamburg, and it was published as an abstract of only a few pages.[16] When we compare the abstract to the manuscript preserved in the archive, which covers fifty-eight pages,[17] the publication is an extreme of concision and summary, and it documents only the basic structure of the argument. Warburg takes as his point of departure two prints owned by the Hamburg Kunsthalle, both of which show the Death of Orpheus. One is an engraving from 1465 now identified as Ferrarese, and one a drawing by Albrecht Dürer from 1494.[18] Both show a group of three figures identical in all details, consisting of Orpheus kneeling on the ground and two Thracian Maenads on either side of him, swinging their clubs with exaggerated bodily movement. Warburg shows that Dürer's drawing, the anonymous engraving, and a woodcut that he also included from a 1497 Venetian edition of Ovid, all vary an antique original formula that he sets alongside the fifteenth-century images by showing Greek vase-paintings. Warburg shows that "this archaeologically authentic emotive formula [for the Death of Orpheus] . . . had taken root in Renaissance artistic circles."[19] Poliziano's 1471 stage adaptation of the material, *Orfeo,* showed that for humanists as well as for artists it was well understood that drama, and later painting, was giving contemporary form to "the dark mystery play of Dionysiac legend, passionately and knowingly experienced in the spirit and through the words of the ancients."[20] Warburg goes on to show that there were different modes in which antique *pathos* could find concrete form in variously corresponding media: he points to Antonio Pollaiuolo's "exuberant rhetoric of muscle," Poliziano's "graceful flutterings" (as painted on the cassone by Jacopo de Sellaio using motifs from his *Orfeo*), and the "heroic, theatrical, emotive intensity of the antique figures of Mantegna."[21] He also posits

Ferrarese, *The Death of Orpheus,* engraving, ca. 1460.
Hamburg, Hamburger Kunsthalle. Photo by Elke Walford.
Bildarchiv Preussischer Kulturbesitz/Art Resource, New York.

Albrecht Durer, *The Death of Orpheus,* drawing, ca. 1494.
Hamburg, Hamburger Kunsthalle. Photo by Elke Walford.
Foto Marburg/Art Resource, New York.

that although Dürer was willing to learn from the Italians in his studies of antiquity, "Nuremberger as he was, he instinctively countered the pagan vigor of southern art with a native coolness." Though his figures are faithful copies from the Mantegna prints they have "an overtone, as it were, of robust composure." Warburg sees Dürer as an artist who clearly studied the antique emotive gestures of Italian painting yet "assumed his rightful place among the opponents of the Baroque language of gesture, toward which Italian art had been moving since the mid-fifteenth century."[22] The danger of "Baroque aberration" (the quote marks are in Warburg's text) had its "climax" in the discovery of the Laocoön in Rome in 1506, and is bound up with the chance of liberation from "medieval expressive constraints": the two had to be balanced against each other.

In the manuscript for the lecture these remarks are placed in a frame that sets them in almost palpable tension—as though further tension were necessary. On the back of the first sheet Warburg noted down the following list of quotations, which he dated 11 and 12 July 1906.

> Cf. Jessen, *Heinses Stellung zur bildenden Kunst* [Heinse's View of the Visual Arts, 1901], p. 71.[23] Winckelmann, *History of Art* . . . 1776, p. 53: "Dürer would have been greater than any, had he known and understood antiquity."
> on which Heinse . . . *Heft* 55: "Here again the antiquarian pedant"
> Wackenroder: *Herzensergießungen*[24] 1797, p. 24
> on Winckelmann's opinion "I find nothing to regret here and am rather glad that fate had granted Germany a *truly* patriotic painter in this man"
> Jessen p. 72 "This is how we too feel"
> Even down to today the historical phenomenology of stylistic development has been shoved aside in favor of the antithesis of "Greek stillness and grandeur" or "Teuton simplicity"; Greek culture [*Griechentum*] however does not exclude the liveliest forms of expression, any more than German culture [*Deutschtum*] excludes the purposeful adoption of traditional forms: thus:
> [here a hand pointing overleaf to the next, unnumbered, page] A. Warburg, Dürer and Italian Antiquity, 12. VII. 1906.

What Warburg presents here as a collage of quotations and what he concludes from them can be read on two levels. The German Romantic tradition is briefly touched upon and characterized, with its departure from what was seen as Winckelmann's normative Classicism and its discovery of an inherent value in each artistic culture. The quotation from Jessen's study of 1901, in which he succinctly affirms the Romantic tradition, shows that this departure from normative antiquity will not as elsewhere result in a neutral, value-free "phenomenological" art history—it still takes Albrecht Dürer as its leading and therefore normative figure. Warburg emphasizes the ironic distance he takes to such terms as "*truly* patriotic" and "Teuton" (*ächt* and *teutsch*) by underlining and ironically using archaic terms. At this point, Warburg's conception of an art history that must be true to the historical facts intersects with his alertness as a man who closely watched for particular definitions of "Germanness" (*Deutschtum*). Warburg emphasizes "purposeful adoption" and fruitful exchange to counter those constructed oppositions that depend on the exclusion of the un-German. In the lecture he emphasizes with particular weight that "the castle we see on the left, the mountainous landscape to the right, and the group of trees in the background are the meager remains of Dürer's own creation, thus the unpleasing fact for the 'aesthetic of circus artists' is that Dürer, the pride and pinnacle of German native art, had enriched himself by using foreign work!"[25] Warburg's response to Jessen goes on: "This irrefutable documentary proof of the artistic process thus shows the utter inadequacy of the usual 'aesthetic of the artists.' Clearly if we were to treat this process as would a judge, examining the artist's personal effects to establish whether he has ever stolen, or to approach the artist as would a rude exciseman searching luggage for contraband imports, then Dürer is in our modern sense not an individual."[26]

The Death of Orpheus

The abstract of the Dürer lecture as it appeared in print is not least remarkable because the main theme of the pictures examined, the Death of Orpheus, which was also the title of a picture portfolio printed for the occasion, disappears almost completely in the lecture as a pictorial subject or a topic.[27] In the printed version of the lecture Warburg emphasizes insights into the meanings of the *Pathosformeln* as expressed in Italian art and in Dürer's work; the motif of jealous amorous revenge on a loved one and orgiastic murder merely seems to be the occasion for Warburg's specific contribution to this question of the "psychology of styles." The last paragraph presents the two essential insights developed in the lecture: that the "antique superlatives of gesture" came to Nuremberg via several staging posts, and that "Dürer's response to this migrant rhetoric varied at different times." Radicalizing the problem posed in the collage of quotes that preceded the manuscript version, Warburg states that "the psychology of style is not the kind of issue that can be forcibly brought to a head by imposing the categories of military and political history, 'winners' and 'losers.'" Rather a problem that is "far wider, though hitherto barely formulated: the interchange of artistic culture, in the fifteenth century, between past and present, North and South" can yield "a clearer understanding of the early Renaissance as a universal category of European civilization," one in which "great individuals" are seen in the greater context.[28]

The shocking story of Orpheus is visible only in the illustrations, and Warburg does not refer in so many words to these actual representations nor to the texts; yet to a certain extent his choice of language is markedly bellicose and thus (re)presents the violence in the "categories of military and political history" in which there are only winners and losers, in "hero-worshiping dilettantism" that is satisfied with "rough conclusions," in "Baroque aberration." The print version, cleansed of all direct or graphic representation of the theme, only prepares us with its turn of phrase for what remained hidden in the archive: the modern parallel, the description of an orgiastically violent murder published in the *Frankfurter Zeitung* under the title "Russian Revolution. Cossack Atrocity" on 6 December 1905, two months after the philologists' congress in Hamburg.

> A Russian student living in Nice, Nikolev, has told a reporter from the *Temps* of a barbarous act by Cossacks that he witnessed in Stavropol (Caucasus). In Stavropol there are few revolutionaries and the "intelligentsia" is represented only by schoolteachers. When the Tsar's decree was published the clergy was very much enraged and the Orthodox priest marched to the school at the head of a mob and attacked the teacher Praskovja Dugentzova. Nikolev protested the actions of the priest, who threatened him in turn. When Cossacks arrived under the command of the hetman, Bratkov, the teacher believed that they would protect her. Nikolev re-

ports what followed in the following terms: the hetman grabbed the teacher roughly by the hands and forced her to kneel. "First answer me this," he said while keeping her in this humble posture. "What religion do you belong to?"—Since the teacher kept silent, he struck her a fearful blow with his knout.—"Let me go!" the unhappy girl cried. "You know that I am an Orthodox Christian. The priest can tell you so." "Yes, yes, we know that you go to church," said the hetman, "but you are against the Tsar, like the Jews are." "That's not true," cried Miss Dugentzova, "I am not against the Tsar, but I want freedom for my country." "Ah, you want freedom!" yelled the Cossack, letting the knout lash down on her shoulder again. "I thought so from the start. And that's why you were so happy to read the false decree that the Jews dreamed up and ascribed to the Tsar."—"You are mistaken," protested the teacher. "The Tsar himself has finally given freedom to his unhappy people."—"Ah, you want to spread revolutionary propaganda," screamed the hetman. "Here, my brothers."—Then a dreadful scene followed. The Cossacks and fanatics flung themselves upon the girl, threw her to the ground, and trampled her. Covered in blood, the miserable woman succeeded in standing again and in a pitiful voice called out, "I shall die then; my Creator, make it so that my blood will serve the welfare of my people." The hetman, probably fearing that these words might move one of his hoodlums to pity, threw the girl to the ground once more. The bloodthirsty mob engulfed her and these beasts beat her to death with hammers. Their rage was not yet satisfied however. With animal howls the bandits lifted the body and threw it in the air, playing a game of catch. Shreds of the unhappy martyr's clothing flew in all directions. Soon only the body was left and blood ran down from it onto the murderers' heads. They continued their dreadful game however and shouted in animal frenzy "Death to the students and the Jews!" The notables of the city have petitioned the government to punish the hetman as harshly as possible, but there have so far been no reports of his punishment.

Warburg incorporated this report from the *Frankfurter Zeitung* into the lecture manuscript as collage, and wrote alongside it: "Death of Orpheus. Recurrence of the eternal beast, called: homo sapiens." A short article from the *Hamburger Correspondent* briefly reporting the lecture is pasted in on the next page with no commentary.[29] The handwritten fair copy of the lecture manuscript, in the bound ledger along with the two newspaper cuttings, shows the same problem that Gertrud Bing describes when talking of the biography she wished to write: "Again and again I found that the most trivial-seeming material gave rise to unexpected revelations about connected thoughts or concrete situations, so that one has to ask oneself what each item might have meant to him, even where this is not conclusive enough for the report."[30]

The newspaper articles filed with the manuscript represent Warburg's habit of documenting exactly every detail that had to do with his publications or other public utterances.[31] However, the article on the teacher's murder is essentially different from these records of public appearance, such as in the *Correspondent*'s brief article on the lecture. The report from the Caucasus is constructed dramatically and has all the qualities of a literary text. After a brief introduction establishing the authenticity of the eyewitness along with the location and further details, there follows a long passage characterized by direct speech, rapid changes of perspective, and the escalation to a frenzied ending. The depiction of the bloodthirsty murder culminates in the cry "Death to the students and the Jews!" and then breaks off with a laconic phrase such as might end a story by Heinrich von Kleist—"there have so far been no reports of his punishment."[32]

Beasts and "Primal Dances"[33]

Warburg's comment about "man, the beast" is prefigured several times in the newspaper text pasted in alongside, where "beasts," "animal howls," and "animal frenzy" are evoked. Contained in this discourse of primitive, pre-human wildness is a shared assumption that fits the article seamlessly into the void of the scholarly text, cleansed of all emotion, and fills its vacuum.[34] Read through the newspaper report of a counter-revolutionary atrocity in the East, the myth of Orpheus in which violence has found a meaningful place is once again enacted and remythologized.[35] Questions of *historical* psychology that Warburg had addressed as an art historian are at the same time shockingly contemporary: death by dismemberment threatens Jews and students, and thus potentially the Jewish academic in every aspect of his self. The complex of texts and images surrounding the theme of the death of Orpheus as it appears in the archive represents various reactions to the threat of violence that confronted him. And this is not simply a function of the very different sorts of media in which the theme appears. There are pictures from different periods, and texts from widely separated areas of life, and the scholar allowed or denied himself measured amounts of public engagement with each: it is precisely here that we see fresh spoor, a clue "entrusted to the future."[36] Warburg's unpublished commentary on the "Cossack atrocity" resembles a stenographic abbreviation, standing for a whole field of background thought against which the "historical psychology" of style must be considered. The notion that civilization is a thin veneer that simply obscures our view of the wildness lying hidden beneath, the "dark continent," the bestial that is always present and poised to leap: this fantasy of the beast in Modern Man is one Warburg shares with Nietzsche and Freud, with the anthropologists and ethnographers of his age, and with a broad current of nineteenth-century thought.[37] The dichotomy "wild" versus "civilized"[38] is so deeply anchored in thought about culture as such and about individual—contemporary and historical—cultures, that it was thought of not as a polarity but rather as a necessary vector of development, which again and again dashes itself against the intransigence of the "wild." It appears almost to be a secular form of salvific history, whose universal validity throughout time and space could not be questioned. Such thinking informs Warburg's perception of the past when he contrasts Dürer's "Nuremberger . . . native coolness" with the "pagan vigor of Southern art," or when he invokes the double head of Apollo and Dionysus as a figure of Antiquity; it informs his self-image when he speaks later (1923) of the "eternally unchanging Red Indian in the helpless human soul,"[39] and finally offers a possibility of understanding the age-old hatred of Jews in its modern manifestations.

A pattern becomes visible into which the most varied findings can be placed; at the same time, different grades of *distancing* become apparent in the variations on the theme. In the lecture itself the pictures are present, as is the theme itself, both preserved in a portfolio on the Death of Orpheus. In the abstract written for publication, the theme is objectified to a question of modes and styles and historical psychology; as deposited in the archive copy, the explosive political implications and relevance for the present day are both concealed and preserved. But the archive material attests equally clearly to a continuing *identification* with the role of one potentially threatened, with the victim; an identification underlined by the prominent place given in the newspaper article to "Jews and students" as victims of further collective murders.

In his analysis of the Freudian construction of the "primitive," Raymond Corbey concludes: "The wildness of the other, according to psychoanalysis, is an imaginary construct, a projection of a real wildness deep in ourselves on others. I put it that this wildness deep in ourselves is itself an imaginary construct, too, that an archaic, animal other within is hypostatized from the bourgeois self precisely to constitute that self by the repudiation and exclusion of 'low' and 'other' anti-values."[40] This examination draws a critical conclusion that is a subtle variant of Karl Kraus's satirical criticism of psychoanalysis.[41] According to Corbey "[a]lterity is a discursive structure, and has slipped into psychoanalysis from hegemonic, disciplining cultural discourse: on culture and nature, man and animal, the civilized and the primitive, male and female, the ascent from wildness to civilization."[42] It may be that this deconstruction goes a little too far, as its goal is simply to make visible the gradual dislocations of the topos "wild-civilized" as a historical process. Yet the parallel examples of Freud's and Warburg's research teach us that these related questions, concentrating on the "eternal beast" and the role of civilization, stem from the real and deeply felt experience of being threatened by hatred of Jews. To understand how it was possible that this hatred (in its mutation as anti-Semitism) could withstand all enlightenment, both scholars examined the received body of knowledge for traces of just such resistance to reason. Themselves trapped in a construction that made them into "others," they searched out the necessary preconditions of these constructions, one studying his patients, the other the history of images. From this perspective the search for and discovery of the "other" at the heart of one's own tradition and one's own person seems a heroic exertion rather than a conjuring trick of bourgeois consciousness.[43] Such a search, and such a discovery, can be found in Freud's "Moses and Monotheistic Religion"[44] and in Warburg's lecture on the snake ritual.

In the collective fantasy of "the primitive" that threatens from within as well as from without lies one central crux of Warburg's work: between art history as the study of culture as it is performed in the Dürer lecture, the role of the image in the history of civilization understood as a struggle for equilibrium, and the biography of a Jewish scholar as a life latently and manifestly threatened by Jew-hating.

The Fragment on Characterology of the Jews and the Konitz "Ritual Murder"

The Stavropol pogrom was not the only manifestation of modern Jew-hating that Warburg documented and that we may conjecture to have influenced his conception of what emotive formulas (*Pathosformeln*) convey. Folders with newspaper clippings, the *Zettelkästen,* and the library itself all attest to Warburg's awareness of pogroms, and of the blood libel in particular, as an anti-Semitic strategy and cultural phenomenon. The earliest document is dated 1892 and can be found under the keyword "anti-Semitism" in box 27, which in turn is labeled "Oriental Region" (*Sfera Orient*). It is a copy of the Hamburg anti-Semitic newspaper *Die Abwehr,* and the editorial (called "Talmud and Shulchan Aruch") is underlined and annotated by Warburg and by another hand.[45] It purports to give Judaic laws prescribing ritual murder, and these are marked with the word "fabrication" (*Fälschung*) and other remarks. In a box-file marked "Jewish questions I, 1901–1914" (*Judenfragen I, 1901–1914*) are two dossiers concerned with the so-called Konitz Affair and with a ritual murder trial which took place in Kiev in 1913.[46] A further dossier assembles cuttings that report on pogroms, particularly in Russia.[47] There is a single historical source about alleged desecrations of the Host in Nuremberg and Passau in 1491, indicating that Warburg was not deeply concerned with the medieval prehistory of nineteenth-century trials.[48] Library acquisitions on such topics do not seem to have been made systematically,[49] although they include one of the most important publications on blood libel, by Hermann Strack.[50]

The documents attesting to Warburg's engagement with anti-Semitism and "German Jewry" are preserved in the archives of the Warburg Institute; among them is a rough draft of an unfinished text whose purpose can no longer be established, a fragment with the title "Konitz" added later. The fragmentary character of this document is all too evident, as there is almost more text crossed out than had been left as satisfactory; after a barely formulated introduction and a few further sentences about Jews and anti-Semites it breaks off. Nevertheless this incomplete text has its own archaeological value precisely because it fails in what it wants to articulate. The author dated the fragment himself, "1900," and added the two comments "put aside" and "Konitz."

In his essay "Aby Warburg as Interpreter of Civilization" Hans Liebeschütz summarized this draft and saw it as recording the one moment in Warburg's life when he felt called to "a public declaration of his personal commitment" as a Jew.[51] It did not come to this, and the document was "put aside" to await its readership:

> If in these days, when anti-Semitic journals are blossoming and bearing such imposing flowers [*fruit*], the Jewish press has unfairly suspected that the government
>
> With the [*slogan/motto*] war cry "be slightly more modest" the national [*solemn and serious*] [*anti-Semites began their battle against Jewry at the end of the 70s*] Prussian Protestants began [*had begun*] their battle against Jews at the end of the 70s. The disciples of this [*Berlin*] movement [*growing up (educated) in the German tradition*] in the mood of the resurgent [*nascent*] German Empire
>
> Generation which [*made a great impression*] had a great influence and in the name of these men now around 35 years old [*I feel*] I—one of these Jews—[*compelled*] in these days of the Konitz murder [*compelled*] to say directly what [*thousands*] hundreds of modern Jews feel dimly as I do. [*Perhaps not so sharply as I, for only a very few modern Jews yet know what*] [*under favorable circumstances independent*]
>
> [*Perhaps*] do not see so [*keenly*] clearly, [*because they*] and no longer feel entitled to speak in the name of all able to speak, because their [*repr*] they about [*are*] [*own*]. Of the religious life of their own lineage no longer know anything; I however was raised in such Orthodoxy and until my fifteenth year was a pious adherent, and then broke free through hard struggles within and without, in order to devote myself [*my life*] to [*modern*] study as a private scholar
>
> [*Since I do not*] The time now seems to have come to share my own experiences, because I see [*no better*] nobody else who might be prepared (psychological survey of German Jews) to draft such a portrait of typical character.
>
> The anti-Semitic movement's flaunted (and in many of its leaders quite sincere) idealism initially

> —
>
> The most difficult thing for a Christian-minded German is perhaps not to follow his first instincts; not to let the irksome and distasteful behavior of the propertied parvenu sour [. . .] He should however not simply imagine that there is a just greasy populism is particularly noticeable when the [*A Jewish*] state very much less dangerous than the apparently feigned restraint of the anti-Semitic . . . and the indifference of the R.
>
> —
>
> more moral to let the Teutonic wrath run its course
>
> —
>
> This is exactly the moment at which real poise and genuine calm should be evident, [*not that of the however*] but at such times inner calm is lost completely, while outward calm seldom is, for it is an outward mask rather than the product of an inner development.[52]

The text might be read more or less as follows: a charge of ritual murder in Konitz in West Prussia was the spur for this attempt at writing. Warburg believed that, compared with other assimilated Jews, he had a better knowledge of Orthodox Jews. Inner conflict, and conflicts with those around him, had marked his own breaking free from the tradition into which he had been born, in order to devote his life to study as a private scholar: "Warburg did not wish to claim any general interest for his personal experience, but he saw such development as a presupposition of his project to define the 'typical character' of an enlightened and assimilated Jew."[53] The planned title for this treatise was to have been "A psychological survey of German Jews" (*Psychologischer Querschnitt der deutschen Juden*): "Some fragmentary sentences reveal the conflict in the writer's mind. He cannot get over his antagonism to the ostentatiousness shown by wealthy Jews, an attitude which gave the anti-Semitic reaction an appearance of idealism. But further experience had shown Warburg that the very conspicuous complacence on the Jewish side was less dangerous than the 'teutonic wrath' hidden behind a pretension of restraint. In this situation Warburg found it difficult to preserve in his mind the genuine composure corresponding to human dignity without which the gesture of self-control remains a mere mask."[54] Such is Liebeschütz's summary, which gives the content of the fragmentary draft at least in its broad outlines but spends little time on the details: the spur of "Konitz," the assessment of political developments, and the contradictions with which Warburg visibly struggles here.

The "days of the Konitz murder," or the "Konitz Affair" as it is listed in the relevant handbooks,[55] refers to a dreadful and never fully solved murder in the small West Prussian (now Polish) town of Konitz (Chojnice) not far from Danzig (Gdansk). On 15 March 1900 the torso of nineteen-year-old high school student Ernst Winter was discovered; his body had been expertly butchered, and the head and other parts of the body were later found elsewhere. It appeared that the murderer had some basic knowledge of anatomy and for that reason the (Christian) town butcher was the first suspect, but could not be convicted; nor could several Jewish suspects. Nevertheless the anti-Semitic Berlin *Staatsbürgerzeitung* took up the cause and raised the suspicion that it had been a ritual murder; the newspaper accused the judiciary of protecting Jewish suspects. The forensic doctor at the scene had established that the body had been bled completely dry (although a medical commission later found that this was false) and various Jewish suspects were arrested. By April and May 1900 there were attacks on the synagogue in Konitz and on houses of Jewish families; the military was called out to prevent pogroms. Subsequently there were attacks on the Jewish population of other West Prussian cities as well, attacks that were repeated in the following year on the basis of false accusations.[56]

The Konitz Affair aroused widespread public interest, and also led to the trial and conviction of breach of the peace of the publisher of the *Staatsbürgerzeitung* along with one of his reporters, both of whom nevertheless became members of parliament in the Reichstag in 1903. The shocking aspect of the case was that since the 1880s there had been ever more blood libels and accusations of ritual murder, mostly in Eastern Europe: these now began to come closer to home. "In these days of the Konitz murder": we can no longer exactly reconstruct what this meant to Warburg. It spurred on his impulse to introspection, but also marks the beginning of an interest in the themes of ritual murder and Host desecration that lasted many years, and is documented in both library and archive.

The "Blood Libel Legend" and accusations of ritual murder are an essential component of European Jew-hating, and one which has been adapted again and again to new circumstances over the centuries since the high Middle Ages.[57] The accusations are patched together from rumor, from confessions extracted under torture, and from projection, and they broadly claim that Jews require human blood for secret ritual purposes, among them baking unleavened bread for Passover. Above all, Jews were said to abduct and murder Christian children in order to obtain this blood. A crime that never took place, an action that never was performed and that therefore never could be proven, led over the centuries to countless trials and persecutions all over Europe. Such "historical rumors of murder"[58] now seem more atavistic than ever, but their study has only recently moved on from the litany of accusation and refutation.

Georg R. Schroubek has written on the "transmission and diffusion" of the blood libel and about the character of this "delusion": "Even at its first appearance in late antiquity it already shows the complex formation, with the essential characteristics, the like of which we still can observe in late occurrences in the twentieth century. For the cultural historian it therefore poses questions about this phenomenon's roots, evidently very strong, and about the efficient means of transmission which can allow continuity over eight-and-a-half centuries and dispersal through almost all of Europe, as well as Asia and the trans-Atlantic world."[59] These roots are to be sought in anthropology, since they touch upon the complex of "sacrifice, human sacrifice, child sacrifice [and] sacrificial blood"; in the twelfth century above all they are to be sought in theology, since the blood libel becomes "domesticated among the elite,"[60] and especially among the clergy to a much greater extent than one would expect for a phenomenon of "superstition": "Only a knowledge of the theological content of the liturgies of the Passion and Easter, and contact with the pious mystical view of the Passion that was then developing, can explain the details of the charges leveled against the Jews."[61] The first charge of ritual murder was documented in England.[62] Geographically speaking, the notion of ritual murder seems to have spread from the West, and went ever further East until it reached Orthodox Christendom. In the nineteenth century there was then a reversed diffusion from East to West, in which historians, Orientalists, Church historians, and the Romantic heralds of ethnography played a transmitting role—some of them opposing the belief in ritual murder, but some as pseudo-scientific collaborators in anti-Semitic propaganda. In the Middle Ages it was the clergy, and above all the mendicant orders, who played the most important role in transmitting the idea of ritual murder, but also lawyers and doctors, particularly in early modern trials.

There is a great deal still undiscovered or disputed in this context concerning individual cases as well as the motives of the (Christian) perpetrators. Even very basic questions, about for instance the way in which the isolated cases are connected anthropologically, psychologically, and sociologically are answered differently. Regarded as symptoms, blood libel and the charge of ritual murder call into question any belief in the progress of civilization or enlightened humanity: they force us to ask fundamental questions about the societies and cultures that can give rise to them, and which transmit them for centuries. Recent research and opinion holds that at least from the nineteenth century onward, nobody really believed in ritual murder, although there is some evidence that this belief could easily be rekindled. Implausible charges were coldly and calculatingly brought to bear by those with an interest in doing so—we must therefore assume that a conspiracy of silence existed about the fact that everybody knew better.[63] Warburg's documentation indicates that he too had reached the same conclusion. He was interested in the use to which anti-Semites put this easily roused fear of ritual murder, and he began to look for the anthropological roots of a fear summoned so easily from the "social memory," and set to work at the spur of a moment.[64]

Learning to See the Dionysiac

The metaphor of "anthropological roots" calls to mind a living plant, and thus a nourishing soil in which these roots are sunk: the substrate of time and of the past. Historical memory does not reach back to this past, which must therefore be reconstructed by looking at the sediments and residues of myth and ritual.[65] Warburg collected such material in a *Zettelkasten* labeled "Primal dances" (*Ur-Tänze*). Here we find material on "eating, cultic eating, persecution, Christian feast, Communion, transubstantiation, dance, sword-dance, concepts of sacrifice, human sacrifice, plaint," and other related themes. Several newspaper cuttings reporting blood libel trials from Europe and Asiatic Russia in the years 1907–11 are collected under the keyword "concepts of blood and human sacrifice," under "non-European sacrificial cult" and "cannibalism."

The necessity of reaching back to the "primal causes" of human behavior in order to be at all able to write a "characterology of the modern Jew" finally prevented this text entirely. Unlike Nietzsche, Warburg balked at creating the myths to fill in the "missing links" of such a story. He revisited, however, his early reading of Nietzsche for the lecture on Dürer, as his notes in the Warburg Institute's copy of *The Birth of Tragedy* attest.[66] We can only confirm Gombrich's pithy assessment that Warburg was no Nietzschean, and that his criticism of Nietzsche's working method that such reading occasioned expresses a basic reservation: "If Nietzsche had only been familiar with the data of anthropology and folklore! Even in his case their specific gravity would have served as a regulating force for his dream-bird flight."[67] However Warburg himself concedes that Nietzsche's polarity of "Dionysiac" and "Apolline," and some of the insights and constructions set forth in *The Birth of Tragedy,* had taught him to see one particular aspect of the Classical tradition: in connection with his lecture "The Gods of Antiquity and the Early Renaissance in Southern and Northern Europe" he remarked, "Every age can see only those Olympic symbols that it can recognise and bear through the development of its own inner visual organs. We, for instance, were taught by Nietzsche a vision of Dionysos."[68] As with the "primitive," so with the "Dionysiac": we find what we look for and what is useful to us. This is what Warburg's comment seems at least partly to imply. In *The Birth of Tragedy,* Nietzsche had constructed the Dionysiac-Apolline opposition that supposedly had been brought to fruition in the Greek tragedy. The Dionysiac-Apolline, in a further opposition, was seen in contrast to "aesthetic Socratism."[69] Logic and conscious thought are denounced and their opposite, Dionysiac "life-force," is lauded even though in breaking the shackles of the *principium individuationis,*[70] it always also implies death, or rather, killing.

It appears that as a young man, Warburg had patiently read through his copy as far as page 58—which is where the annotations cease. We might suspect that had he read on, he would also have continued his skeptical—even ironic—pencil markings. Faint underlinings mark the almost innumerable instances where Nietzsche uses the German prefix *Ur-* (primal, original): from *Origin* to *primal unity,* via *primal desire* into the *primal process,* and thence to *primal suffering* with its *primal resonance* and into the *primal image* and the dramatic *primal phenomenon.* Also underlined is the passage on "Apolline phenomena in which Dionysus is objectified" in which now "Dionysus no longer speaks through powers, but as an epic hero, almost with the language of Homer."[71] Warburg comments: "hexameter." Two passages in particular are heavily marked up: that discussing metaphor as a "vicarious image," and the phrase "enchantment of individuation."[72] Rereading Nietzsche in 1905 was a process of rediscovery for Warburg, as with the passage on page 108: "Because he has no notion of the Dionysiac depths of music, he transforms musical enjoyment into a rationalistic words-and-music rhetoric of passion in the *stilo rappresentativo,* and into a voluptuous sensuality of vocal music;"[73] Warburg comments: "On the formation of *stilo rappresentativo* cf. my work on *costumi teatrali* etc. (noticed Sept. 1905). I did not have Nietzsche with me in Florence at that time and the problem of the 'Dionysiac' was still a long way off."[74]

The *problem* of the Dionysiac, which drove Warburg in his analysis of the Orpheus prints, is entirely different from that in *The Birth of Tragedy.* In studying textual and pictorial sources Warburg had gained a clear view of the subject at hand: unlike Nietzsche, he relied on "documented cases" in the history of orgiastic release. A marginal note in his essay "Francesco Sassetti's Last Injunctions to His Sons" makes this clear. In a footnote, Warburg addresses the portraits of Francesco Sassetti and his contemporaries, including the Medici partisan Antonio Pucci, which he believed he had found "on the cassone of scenes from the legend of Nastagio degli Onesti that was painted in Botticelli's workshop for the Pucci-Bini wedding in 1483."[75] In the addenda, Warburg's further note on one of the four *spalliere* that Botticelli and his workshop had decorated with a motif of sexual revenge from the *Decameron*[76] abruptly drops the theme of the portraits and digresses: "A wild chase, with scenes of orgiastic cannibalism, here storms in upon a sedate family celebration: daemonic undercurrents burst through the thin veneer of Christianity, Catholicism and courtly culture[. . . .] Something rather similar took place in real life: at the Colonna-Baglioni 'Blood Wedding' of 1500, Filippo di Braccio tore Astorre Baglioni's heart from his breast and ripped it apart with his teeth."[77]

Warburg never lost sight (perhaps, since the shock of Konitz at the latest, could not lose sight) of what the Dionysiac unleashed and the "breakdown of the *principium individuationis*" could mean: frenzied bloodlust. That some could propose an aestheticizing, Dionysiac ersatz religion that remained blithely unaware of its own dangers, was therefore a way of thinking Warburg found absolutely unacceptable.[78] Warburg gives a factual grounding, in the historic period that he researched and in his own time, for the dread that Schopenhauer describes and Nietzsche invokes, horror in the face of the inexplicable.[79] Gombrich's assertion that Warburg *would have* distanced himself from the cult of the irrational that was gaining ground in Germany in the 1920s[80] must be modified: Warburg was well aware of this cult and had responded to it with good reason and keen insight, not just in the 1920s but ever since the turn of the century.

Francesco Sassetti: The "Modern Man"

A further aspect of this investigation can be seen in the 1907 essay "Francesco Sassetti's Last Injunctions to His Sons." First, however, it is important to understand that in the lectures he held after the turn of the century and that in part were published later, Warburg was, among other things, concerned to show the advantages of the cultural studies method as he employed it. As also in the Dürer lecture, Warburg's art historical enquiries and his political insights are inseparable.

He constantly reformulated what it was that set him apart from connoisseurs and dilettantes, as well as from art historians working in style criticism: "Nothing could be further from my mind than to elucidate these things, because it was I who discovered them: that is an irrelevant personal detail. Nor do I wish to set choice mouthfuls in front of those gourmets who appreciate art: I am only concerned that the broader public might help art history equally to avoid both a barren style-critical tendency that clings to detail only, and (more than that) the irreverent dilettantism which breaks in with its self-satisfied chatter at points where the past itself could speak to us in its own voice. I want us finally to have an artistic history of culture."[81] In the same lecture Warburg calls this patient attentiveness to the voice of the past "the indispensable condition for experiencing the 'beautiful' and the 'sublime' and for comprehending it as the product of serious and inmost cultural labor."[82] This third lecture contains the germinal thoughts for the 1907 Sassetti article ("Francesco Sassetti's Last Injunctions to His Sons"), which bears the subtitle "An Essay in Character, as Related to the Stylistic History of the Florentine Early Renaissance."[83]

The first lecture in this series does not have a title as preserved in the archive,[84] but it gave rise to the article "The Art of Portraiture and the Florentine Bourgeosie."[85] Here Warburg stresses that the religiously motivated use of wax votive figures was a constitutive factor for Ghirlandaio's portraits, as was above all the central role played by the cooperation of patron and artist in his art. He explained his contextualization in these words: "I need bravery if I am to exhort you to hike over difficult detours and uneven ground, and I gain this courage from the conviction that a thoroughly detailed knowledge of men's civic and social background is absolutely necessary in order to understand the artistic language of forms in its peculiarities, and to grasp its style in comparison alongside lifestyle. I also pluck up my nerve because the study of art has thus far neglected to establish systematically this necessary cultural-historical basis."[86] Here as elsewhere, Warburg urges the most complete possible search for documents that might have any bearing on a work of art—today, of course, a self-evident basis for art historical interpretation.

> Florence, the birthplace of modern self-awareness and of civic mercantile culture, yields to us not merely in unrivaled fullness and striking vivacity the portraits of those long dead: the voices of these departed also live on in the archives, in hundreds of recorded documents and thousands that have not yet been read, and historical regard may yet lend these unheard voices a living tone, if we do not shirk the task of establishing afresh the natural coherence of word and image. Florence answers all cultural-historical questions if only one never grows tired of asking, and if one is sure to restrict oneself to a narrower scope of questions.[87]

In Ghirlandaio's frescoes Warburg sees the embodiment of the Florentine citizen of the Quattrocento, and he believes he can hear their voices in the archives: he calls the method of his *Kulturwissenschaft* an "attempt at resuscitation" that allows the "lifestyle" and "artistic style" to reflect on one another, so that a vanished reality is brought to light in the present day. In the manuscript of the lecture, two exuberantly handwritten words "Dark" and "Light!" mark the beginning and end of the conjuring trick, the flourish that prominently sets out this methodical premise. The "contrast" between medieval and Renaissance, the ambiguity between loyalty to tradition and setting out into a new age, is shown to be not just the fundamental condition of Francesco Sassetti's life but also the leitmotif of his testament and of his program for the family chapel and tomb in Santa Trinita. Around this contradictory biography Warburg constructs the program of the Sassetti chapel and every circumstance of the life of this worthy, pious merchant, who was so proud of his lineage, who was a friend of humanist scholars, a patron of the arts and a collector of rare books.

The archive holds a dossier of fragments, notes, and attempted formulations ordered by the author, and through it runs with overwhelming insistence the idea of the epochal contrast between "medieval considerations" and "modern progression,"[88] between "subjective energy" or "historically fixed *Weltanschauung*,"[89] the "enemy armies whose routes cross in uncanny fashion, between the dark medieval and bright modernity."[90] Five years later the author was critical of, almost disgusted by, his first formulation of the problem: his comments (with date) show that he found in his own earlier text exactly that tone of the lecture circuit he so despised in others, "a physiologist's convoluted way of speaking."[91] Apparently, the sharp juxtaposition of two epochs and ways of life needed no further justification. Warburg shared this idea with Burckhardt and with the historians and cultural historians of the nineteenth century, and a view that today has largely been eroded in favor of a far less spectacular divide, foregrounding continuity, imperceptible joins, and contingency. For Warburg, the model of history that held the Renaissance to have been the birth of "modern" man was still an unassailable myth, in the sense, perhaps, of a founding legend of the bourgeois age.[92]

It hardly needs pointing out that the more recent comprehensive studies of the Sassetti chapel have shown a new emphasis, after the collapse of this constructed dichotomy between piety and the study of antiquity, between adherence to tradition and risk-taking in a mercantile career, between medieval and Renaissance.[93] We are shown a coherent and homogenous program, backed up by a survey of all the material and archival documents, which harmoniously unites the patronages of Saint Francis and the Nativity, the variously prioritized themes of peace and reconciliation with the pope, and finally the idea of Florence as a New Rome.[94]

The "Spirit" of Capitalism

In his lecture, his working notes and eventually the published article on Francesco Sassetti, his last will and testament, and the decoration of the chapel and tomb, Warburg undermines a myth and raises an objection to underlying assumptions of very recent date; he calls into question Jacob Burckhardt (and his followers) but also Max Weber. The working notes name neither of these scholars but contain unmistakable references to core concepts in the work of both. In neither case is there a radical rejection, but rather a divergent interpretation of the historical material. The central question is what distinguishes "Renaissance man," the "modern individual": what sets him apart, where it was that his new characteristics were formed, or as Warburg formulated in his notes, where we should seek "the headwaters of the Nordic ethic, that view of life which bends nature to its will."[95]

For Warburg, Burckhardt's portrait of Renaissance man showed egocentrism, impetuosity, and the "primitive" naïveté of the man of action as characteristic traits,[96] and this he opposes with the portrait of Francesco Sassetti, who lives his contradictions and thus brings them to a new synthesis, "the organic compatibility of opposites."[97] As in his essay on Dürer, Warburg counters the "either-or" with a "both-and" that he had developed from his observations in the archives. Thus the "heightened self-awareness along the lines of antique precedent" is made from "conscious self-cultivation with the help of antiquity consciously received." In order to show clearly the high degree of self-confidence in this "gradual change from medieval to modernity" Warburg tries out imaginative turns of phrase: "Attempts to reconcile the old and the new through a steadfast, thoughtful reasoning that reinvents itself as it goes."[98] The old way of thinking, the "contrast field" (*Contrastgebiet*) is not simply a matter of piety and adherence to faith; Warburg sees it above all as represented by the phrases in the last will that appeal to the binding loyalty of the family lineage, to the mutual loyalty of the heirs and to family honor. The medieval is represented by descent, family, and honor, with regard to the last of which Warburg remarks "realism ceases here." He confronts Burckhardt and his epigonal populist successors; above all he confronts Gobineau. Warburg shows us a complex man, who knew that he was living in a time of transition and who sought out antiquity (or let others seek it for him) in order to amplify and thus command the vital energies therein; this amplification can be explained in economic terms. Antique art serves to "stylize energy," it is a necessary medium and it partakes of the "genesis of modern (observing) energy."[99] Thus at a time when the sharp divide between old and new, medieval and modern, "modernity" and what came before, was invoked all around, Warburg constructed the possibility of gradual transition, dichotomies to be lived through, even as mutually exclusive world views.

Warburg's notes indicate that the article might have been subtitled "An Essay in Character, as Related to the Stylistic History of the Florentine Early Renaissance" in reaction to yet another concept of history,[100] a different sort of founding legend, to Max Weber's first essay in the sociology of religion, "The Protestant Ethic and the Spirit of Capitalism."[101] The two-part publication of Weber's essay in the *Archiv für Sozialwissenschaft und Sozialpolitik* of 1904 and 1905 is bound together in the library of the Warburg Institute as one volume with the accession number 07/153.[102] This copy is heavily corrected for printers' errors, but Warburg has underlined only sparsely and written few marginalia. There is a reference to his reading while he worked on the Sassetti article, in a letter which he sent to his wife from Berlin: "Now I am reading Max Weber's essay on the spirit of capitalism; most interesting, and just as I would have written it, even with the same phrases used; we are thus (both of us) mouthpieces for the unknown, as the times demand."[103]

Weber's work sought to explain the conditions whereby "Occidental" capitalism arose as a force that would compel and control modern society; on publication it caused great interest, but it was at first merely a legend in the making.[104] In a broader sense Weber's essay contributes to explaining the process of rationalization that early sociologists had established to be a constituent part of contemporary, "modern" society and had analyzed as such. At the same time Weber insists, "If this essay makes any contribution at all, may it be to bring out the complexity of the only superficially simple concept of the rational."[105] Weber explicitly states that he uses the term "spirit of capitalism" only provisionally;[106] his main theses on the concept are as follows: although capitalist economic behavior (that is, an economy aimed at the accumulation of wealth) has existed all over the world and even in the earliest times, the particular economic rationalism characteristic of modern capitalism only won through in the West, particularly in New England, and since the seventeenth century. This economic rationalism arose alongside the Reformation through a new conception of work and of a "calling" (*Beruf*) as an end in itself, inasmuch as the Puritans, and the Calvinists in particular, declared that the sacralization of everyday life was pleasing to God. While "the normal Catholic layman lived ethically, so to speak, from hand to mouth," Calvinist and Puritan strains in Protestantism made "systematic self-control" over one's own life into a method that also denied any sacrament to the Christian, whose spiritual life was to be led in absolute isolation with God. This enormous weight of responsibility could not be relieved by confession or penance. Christian asceticism that had developed in the monastic orders of the West entered into the world and gave rise to a "reining back of consumption" and to an ascetic thriftiness necessarily leading to the accumulation of capital. Thus the Puritan concept of economics "stood at the cradle of modern economic man."[107] Weber emphasizes that irrational and religiously motivated element in the modern concept of a calling. He then transfers his analysis to the whole of Western capitalist culture and concludes: "One of the fundamental elements of the spirit of modern capitalism, and not only of that but of all modern culture: rational conduct on the basis of the idea of the calling, was born—that is what this discussion has sought to demonstrate—from the spirit of Christian asceticism."[108]

Iron Cages

There can be no question here of sketching even the rudiments of the reception history of *The Protestant Ethic*.[109] Weber's text itself passes on some of that painful pressure, originating from the "iron cage" (*stahlhartes Gehäuse*) that,[110] like the shell left behind by a dead creature (in this case, the Calvinist with his anxiety about salvation), now without any religious rationale holds captive a whole society that believes itself to be universalist.[111] The method of enquiry is determinedly antimaterialist and this, perhaps along with the painful pressure and Weber's clear-sighted conviction, was enough for Warburg to feel that although the answers reached were not his own, their ways of asking questions were related. At least, once his article was complete and had been set in type for the *Festschrift* for August Schmarsow, Warburg sent an offprint to Max Weber with a covering letter in which he uses a telling metaphor for the relationship in their methods: "please accept this essay as the sign of a colleague's thanks for your treatise on 'the spirit of capitalism and the Protestant ethic.' All the while when writing, I had had the feeling that my unconventional method was setting me to work on the borders of the disciplines, where I could not hope for much comprehension of the inmost core of my problem: yet shortly before I finished, your thoughts gave me the cheering proof that there was indeed somebody digging away at the tunnel from the other end. Certainly we are working with very different tools and I well know that yours are the better; nevertheless I hope that you can make use of this study as material on some occasion."[112] Weber's reply can no longer be found in the Warburg Institute's correspondence archive.[113]

For Warburg, the question as to the genesis of modernity appeared in a different light. From Weber's work he took the concept that "the modern idealism for labor was not in fact formed rationally," and under the keyword "headwaters of the Nordic ethic" he notes, "Attempts to reconcile the old and the new through a steadfast, thoughtful reasoning that reinvents itself as it goes—lead to the cultured, backward-looking, and historically aware Catholic Italian merchant under the influence of antiquity—the chivalric, medieval *paterfamilias* [. . .] becoming the self-assertive, daring energetic man who is resigned to his work."[114] This staccato formulation was obviously written down as an objection to Weber's thesis—"Catholic, Italian"—but entirely lacks the cultural criticism underpinning Weber's analysis, set out explicitly at the end of its second part. If Warburg felt the pressure of an "iron cage" then it was wholly different in kind. "Reasoning," "idealism for labor," "steadfast"—all the terms and evaluations that Warburg uses here are, in the end, positive. Whereas Weber was analyzing rationalism as a "world of contradictions,"[115] Warburg set out to do exactly the opposite. In his interpretations and his "characterology" everything aimed at "the organic compatibility of opposites," which Gombrich also emphasized as a central concern of the text ("Harmonizing Opposites"[116]).

Warburg's points cannot then be called an adequate "answer" to Max Weber's thesis, since they do not even begin to address his arguments. Warburg's ideas were already formed *in nuce* before Weber's text was published and were evidently written down after he had read Weber, with a new emphasis and under the pressure of a different, serious stress—which seems to have been one reason for the intensity of Warburg's formulations. Against the thesis that the modern "individual" was set free and then immediately imprisoned again by Protestantism in the North, Warburg insists that this individual was born in Catholicism, in the culture of the Mediterranean basin, and from the recollection of recovered antiquity. He also insists that there was a hope of salvation to be found in what he called resigned, daring, and energetic work. Warburg does not take account of Weber's genuinely sociological insight that the true difference between the Quattrocento and the eighteenth century was a specifically individualist attitude, that life was lived according to a system within a collective attitude.[117]

This is a mixture of acceptance of Weber's work and of a counter-thesis; of agreement, understanding, and outright denial of Weber's conclusions. A hint toward the reasons for this can be found in Warburg's working notes on how to turn Weber's postulates on cause-and-effect on their head for the late fifteenth century: "Consequences of the adoption of the idealistic demand—an ethical identification with mercantile worldly realism of the calling—new trust in conditions of life—Fortuna—with the struggle over the real goods of this world and [*breaks off*]."[118] The word "identification" is written on the left of this sheet five times, one above the other. The note serves two purposes: it is an interpretation of the mercantile spirit as a new worldly ethic in the fifteenth century, but it is also a clue left by an author wrestling with his text, and as such shows how he had realized his own proclivity to identify with his topic. Warburg is obviously referring to this problem in the letter to his wife from Berlin, where he was struggling with his difficulties in writing the Sassetti text; he writes, "It's dreadful that my profession sits so ill with little everyday worries. It comes from the way I have to seize onto every part of the past, passionately and feelingly, in order to see a thing, and I carry this over into real life. I have no control over this. What is really incredible is that for me there are no degrees of sympathy, no step-by-step; I can say 'no' to a great deal, but when once I say 'yes' then I am defenseless at least as long as my nerves are still drawn tight."[119]

It is not my concern here to tease out this clue as to how Warburg's studies of Florentine civic culture can be explained by means of a scholar's affinity with the subject of his research—although the letter as cited does show that this is a plausible view.[120] Rather it is exactly the engagement with Weber's work that shows a possible second reading for the Sassetti article: that Warburg stood by a Mediterranean-Catholic rather than a Nordic-Protestant "headwater" for at least parts of the "spirit" of modernity, can also be applied to Warburg's other contemporary interests not shared by Weber. Whereas Weber wished to show that the concept of Europe's entry into modernity as into a prison could be traced back to Protestant theology in its most oppressive rejection of the world, Warburg was concerned that the transition from tradition to modernity be seen as a reasoning act, which was to be attributed not just to Protestantism but to other religions as well. Both texts examine the cultural rather than the material conditions of historical movements: yet while the sociologist emphasizes the qualitative leap from an individual attitude to a social culture, the art historian sees the free individual as the most important point. It is tempting to conjecture that the word "identification" jotted down in the notes can be explained by the hopes and several setbacks bound up with complete "assimilation";[121] it holds firm to the meaning of man alone, to self-examination, to liberation from tradition. Although the "characterology" of the modern Jew was never written, parts of it at least went into the text on the Florentine merchant who "organically" held together the centrifugal elements of the age in which he lived, in the life as he lived it.

Warburg saw just such a balance of tensions in Sassetti's motto "*Con Dio e Buonaventura,*" which yoked together "God" with the pagan "Fortuna," and early in 1907 he noted, "Emancipation of the energy forms of earthly life but not of the whole spiritual man."[122] Here he names the dilemma he could not or would not address for his own life.

4

The "Jewish Question" in Wartime

Documentation and Intervention (1916)

"Anti-Semitism," "The Jewish question," "Splendid Aryans"; "Jews," "Characterology," "Race"; "Superstition," "Sacrifice"; "Schmoller," "Jeering," "Ritual murder": these are some of the keywords in the folders and index-card boxes under which Warburg collected documents, mostly newspaper cuttings and excerpts from articles on anti-Semitic statements, incidents, and campaigns in the press. Above all these folders and boxes contain daily testimony to a conflict that today is much researched and written about as part of the prehistory of National Socialism and of the German genocide against the Jews. However, Warburg's concern with anti-Semitism is not merely attested in the Warburg Institute's archive dossiers and boxes under the headings "Jewry" or "Anti-Semitic politics, government." Items dealing with related incidents can also be found again and again under more general headings, such as "Study of expressions," "Concepts of history," "Sfera Orientalis," "Historical synthesis," and "Politics."[1] The period after 1913 is notably poorer in such material. The collection of newspaper articles deals with cases of anti-Semitic agitation or with the (public) careers of individual anti-Semitic politicians and members of parliament, and largely concerns the time from the turn of the century to the First World War. The immediate reasons for this are external: Warburg lived in Hamburg from about 1900 onward, and from 1914 introduced newspaper indexing, so that the index cards and excerpts gave an overview of the bound volumes of complete newspapers.[2] The material in *Zettelkasten* 36, "Jews," refers to these now lost volumes and thus largely to the time of the First World War.[3] Many cuttings came from a professional newspaper clipping service in Berlin and had thus been collected specifically as touching on these themes.[4]

Anti-Semitism in Imperial Germany

The assaults upon the Jewish minority that began after the founding of Imperial Germany and mounted in intensity have been seen as a last, unsuccessful attempt to limit the development of a civil society: they started only after the decades-long process of civil and juridical emancipation of the Jewish populace had been completed. There is however no longer any doubt that the anti-Jewish attacks that came in wave after wave from 1879, made socially acceptable by Adolf Stoecker, a Protestant pastor and court preacher in Berlin, fostered anti-Semitic attitudes or at the least the acceptance of such attitudes at all levels of society, particularly among the educated classes.[5]

As Thomas Nipperdey and Reinhard Rürup have demonstrated,[6] the history of the term "anti-Semitism," its origin, application, and widespread use (and indeed those of parallel formations), cannot be explained without recourse to nineteenth-century racial theories that in turn rely on analogies formed with reference to historical linguistics. The existence of "Semitic" and "Aryan" language families was used to infer the existence of a Semitic and an Aryan race. Ideas, developed in the eighteenth century, about the origin and nature of the different races were used in the nineteenth century to create evolutionary theories, scaffolded by a little empiricism and a lot of imagination. Neither the existence of language families, nor the idea of the origin of species through natural selection, need in themselves to have led to the idea that the races were intrinsically more or less valid. Ingrained historical constructs such as "the primitive" worked together with barely concealed party interests to modernize European xenophobia and its most typical form, anti-Semitism; this was a complex interplay of the power struggles within society ("rationalization") and European nationalism as an unassailable doctrine, which with other factors gave rise to modern imperialism. The prejudice against Jews, as old as Christianity itself, could now be performed in a modern key, and thus became an instrument to be used in daily political life in the nation-state.[7]

Faced with the abundant literature on anti-Semitism and Jew-hating in Germany and Europe, it would be problematic here to give a short overview that might allow us to evaluate the documents from Warburg's archive in terms of today's research on anti-Semitism, as well as for Aby Warburg himself as an art historian working within *Kulturwissenschaft*. The fundamental problem with research on anti-Semitism, which has as much to do with philosophy of history as it has with methodology, is that of a historical teleology,[8] it is a problem as pressing here as it is nowhere else. In concrete terms, we can only write the history of anti-Semitism with knowledge of its outcome: that it led to the death camps and to the murder of millions of Jews, planned and carried out by Germans. Yet at the same time we must not write this history as though it were inexorably to lead to this end, for to do so would be to afford history a function of exoneration, of cause-and-effect explanation that it cannot bear. This aporia also characterizes the way in which the holdings of the Warburg Institute archive are classified and interpreted here. Yet precisely the fact that these holdings exist in the library that once was the Kulturwissenschaftliche Bibliothek is revelatory: while Warburg's collections do indeed document stages and samples of a prehistory, they also represent a possible counterfactual history taking the correct diagnosis at the time, and thereby aiming to find the means with which to counter this ill.

We come to this realization by understanding the division of the Warburg collection as a dual cognitive strategy. On one side, the collage of articles on individual cases and persons, such as the collection of cuttings on the rise and fall of the Hamburg anti-Semite Wilhelm Schack and of other professed anti-Semites,[9] or the patiently assembled dossier on the question of reserve officer status for Jews and why it was impeded: on the other side, the holdings of books acquired over decades, thematically centered on the ideological foundation of these current events.

The origin and internal organization of the Warburg library has been explored extensively and in detail.[10] The library was arranged into four broad areas in which books were shelved: word, image, orientation, and action. The shelving system changed several times over the years, but in Hamburg (as later in London) the organization corresponded to the four floors in the building. Within these broad areas numerous subdivisions were introduced. "Racism" and "Pan-Germanism," with texts by or about Gobineau, Lagarde, and Chamberlain, form their own sections in the library's fourth broad category, "Action," which is today "Social Patterns and History." "Anti-Semitism" follows on from "Judaism" in the third broad category, "Religion, magic and science, philosophy," which was earlier "Orientation."[11] It is only through their mutual function of explanation that the two areas, archive and library, can achieve the urgent clarity that allowed Warburg to attain the specific results he sought in the politics of scholarship, under the pressure of specific social and perhaps psychosocial circumstances. Everyday incidents gave rise to the need for explanation; isolated cases were understood symptomatically, and this clearsightedness is explained by the knowledge of the origin and spread of racial myths. The cuttings dossiers on anti-Semitism are concerned with a considerable number of different themes and personalities, yet they yield as it were a mosaic picture of Warburg's interests that he saw as a symptomatology, a diagnostically important tool. This is true even (or especially) when we compare his picture of "public" anti-Semitism with the far-reaching and detailed studies now available on the same theme in this period of Imperial and Weimar Germany.[12] Warburg was not primarily interested in collecting material with which to fight in the anti-Semitic battles waged ever more intensely in the press as the years went by. Although there are fifteen cuttings devoted to "Zionism,"[13] Warburg kept himself at a cautious distance from any public political action, whether to counter anti-Semitism or to further a Jewish national politics.

Warburg's case studies well demonstrate the ebb and flow of political-party-related anti-Semitism, which has also become a subject in recent historiography. Anti-Semitic delegates take over constituencies and are themselves overtaken by scandal; the citizenry, even Jewish citizens, lose interest in what becomes known as "squalling anti-Semitism," in the hopes that the problem would blow over. Warburg's dossiers follow the headlines and collect what is most notable. Alongside an interest in documenting anti-Semitism, the archive also reflects his interest in the function of the press as a medium that spreads and reinforces opinions. This explains the dense documentation of any given event—such as the Konitz Affair—over long periods, systematically put together for just this reason.[14]

Recent research has attempted to see the phenomenon of long-lasting Jew-hating in Europe, with its pre-rational pattern, alongside political history;[15] it is surprising how closely Warburg's analytic documents, which are those of a contemporary, agree with the analytical findings of these historians almost a century later. We must remind ourselves that this attempt at fundamental research was undertaken not at an institute for social research but at the Kulturwissenchaftliche Bibliothek. Sociologists only much later approached the anti-Semitic theme empirically—one might well say too late[16]—and their studies concluded that anti-Semitic attitudes frequently appear together with superstition and belief in astrology.[17] Recent publications and research on anti-Semitism are characterized by just such a picture of how long-held attitudes are woven together with ideological justification and are then politically functionalized. The basis for this work is the exacting and detailed research largely sponsored by the Leo Baeck Institute since the fifties, and by the Berlin Zentrum für Antisemitismusforschung since 1978.[18] All aspects of the relationship between Germans and Jews in the period 1890–1932 have been portrayed in the yearbooks of the Leo Baeck Institute, in particular in three compendious collections.[19] It is self-evident that this relationship was not exclusively or even primarily determined by anti-Semitism.

To present and appreciate this situation is difficult precisely because political and social anti-Semitism was reacting to the inexorable political, economic, and social integration of large parts of the Jewish minority.[20] At the turn of the century or even before, this made it possible for Jewish authors and others to call anti-Semitism a thing of the past, God be thanked.[21] This is an explicable assessment, if anti-Semitism is regarded as a political or a political party-related movement, for the history of modern anti-Semitism in Germany does not run in straight lines but is characterized by its greater or lesser political importance, by the success of anti-Semitic factions in elections to the Reichstag, by the rise and fall of supra-regional anti-Semitic and *völkisch* organizations, by the official treatment meted out to Jewish soldiers and officers at the beginning and end of the war.

The Anti-Semitism Debate

The "anti-Semitism debate"—occasioned by Adolf Stoecker, Protestant pastor, court preacher, and tutor to the Imperial princes—in September 1879 is of great importance in every respect, and its effect in the whole of the period under discussion here cannot be overestimated.[22] Stoecker let loose an avalanche with two speeches to the Christlich-soziale Arbeiterpartei intended to win workers away from socialism and for his own party by playing upon anti-Jewish feelings, particularly envy.[23] As we read in a newspaper cutting in Warburg's collection,[24] even twenty-four years later the party founder looked back with great satisfaction; this was at a congress to celebrate the twenty-fifth anniversary of the party on 2 January 1903: "Our party has led a very vigorous struggle against Jewry. [. . .] I am proud that the thought of fighting against Jewry has made its way from two congresses of the Christian-Socialist party to all civilized nations. (Tumultuous applause) With the help of the Conservatives and those who also wished to fight Jewry in their own way, we started the 'Berlin movement.' In the Reichstag elections of 1881, 1884, and 1887 we scored great successes." Stoecker's anti-Semitic speeches were indeed a sensation and packed the halls. That his tactic scored no short-term or middle-term successes with the workers, although it found favor with the petty bourgeoisie, does not change the fact that "Stoecker's public engagement marked a change in the climate."[25]

In November of the same year Heinrich von Treitschke published a polemic in the *Preußische Jahrbücher,* in which he called the mood whipped up by Stoecker a "marvelous and mighty stirring in the depths of our national life"[26] and took it as the occasion to reflect "as do thousands of others [. . .] on the worth of our humanity and reason."[27] Treitschke describes signs of a renewal in the (Protestant) church, hails the "conscience of the *Volk*" in its turning away from "the feeble philanthropy of our age," and sees the tide rushing toward "the implacable stern majesty of justice which must come into its full force, in our laws as in their application." He then attempts to describe the change in attitude, the "impassioned movement against Jewry," as part of an antiliberal, conservative moral revival. As this movement is fundamentally justified, it will excuse any unpleasantness and "coarseness."[28]

At the end of his polemical tract Treitschke uses his authority as a university professor and historian to proclaim his notorious motto "the Jews are our misfortune!" His repeated polemics became emblematic for anti-Semitic stereotypes and accusations, lending them the appearance of respectability; or as Ingrid Belke put it, "Stoecker brought these to the hustings and preached them from the pulpit. Yet in order to become acceptable to the 'educated' bourgeois, they had to be declared *ex cathedra* in the university."[29] It hardly mattered that Treitschke did not think of himself as an anti-Semite, that unlike other anti-Semites he demanded that the Jews assimilate themselves completely (in order to forestall the evil that they would otherwise represent for German society), or that his polemics did not go unchallenged. Among the Gentile authors who opposed Treitschke, Theodor Mommsen in particular put his reputation at stake as a historian and a moderate liberal, and spoke out forcefully against his colleague.[30] Treitschke's political engagement against Jews in his lectures and seminars established the tradition of academic anti-Semitism in Germany, which proved to be stronger than any words of warning about the separation of scholarship and activism such as Max Weber pronounced.[31]

Jewish reaction to Treitschke's provocations was equally vehement and deeply felt,[32] as we know from Warburg's rough draft.[33] That this might result in a "Jewish helplessness" in arguing their case is only too credible; for Jews were German patriots, just as much as were Prussian Protestants. Because of the hopes they had vested in the first German civil state, a division into "Jewish" or "German" was inconceivable.

Such a division was first prized open by Treitschke's outbursts and was a contributing factor to Warburg's tactical silence about his strategy for resolving such cultural tensions; this tactic in turn led to his institute largely being seen as an apolitical or politically neutral establishment even today. Such a view is correct and also mistaken, as shown by the following two letters written in 1926 after the war. They may be cited here despite their late date, because they set out especially clearly the view from within and from outside of the same situation; what is important here is not that these two aspects exist side by side, but rather the way in which the emphasis changes. The letters concern a report on the K.B.W. that Johannes Geffcken[34] had written for the *Süddeutsche Monatshefte.*[35]

> Dear Max, dear Fritz, I enclose a report on the K.B.W.'s contributions to German cultural policy by Johannes Geffcken, who is a professor at the university of Rostock and at the moment, Rector. I believe that you will be pleased by this sympathetic mention, as I was—I have thanked him for it in a letter, of which I enclose a transcript since I also talk therein of diverse fundamental experiences.
>
> There is something ulterior to mention here as well: this article is by a professor of philology at Rostock, a reactionary university, and appears in the *Süddeutsche Monatshefte,* a reactionary journal. If the K.B.W. can find favor in such a place, which is by no means free from internal resistance, it

> is in keeping with the fight for the rights of German Jewry, or the way in which I think we can best lead the struggle for the rights of German Jewry, as I believe it should be fought: to prepare to teach well the Germans of tomorrow, or even of the day after, to make them recognize (whether or not they will say so during our own lifetime) that their elder brother Shem has their best interests at heart, is a more productive expense of spirit than the conceptually empty call to arms against anti-Semitism.

The letter to Geffcken has a different emphasis:

> Even long before the war it had been my goal to help in the work of salvaging Germany's idealism from its entrapment in somatic narcissism: a goal born of enthusiasm, stirred up ever and again by the chatter that passes for cultural commentary, even if this enthusiasm itself had to be coaxed each day from a physically and psychically delicate nature. It now becomes clear (and I never had doubted) that though they were concealed until now, the weapons have long been readied for battle against the "Culte de l'incompétence"; a few more years, and the mollycoddling advocates of "education-free schooling" will see that a pedagogical reformation has taken hold root and branch, whereby Germany in its intellectual life shall at last regain that place, seat, and voice in the intellectual life of Europe that it had perhaps externally forfeited for a little while, but that internally it never had lost.[36]

The problem of anti-Semitism appears in this second letter only encoded, as "entrapment in somatic narcissism": a formulation that a reader unfamiliar with Warburg's nomenclature may not immediately have understood as a reference to Gobineau's and Chamberlain's racial ideology and its reception.[37] A backdrop to all of Warburg's far-reaching "cultural policy" and "pedagogical" measures is the removal of the need to confront explicitly the threat posed by anti-Semitism, for to do so would acknowledge its claim that German Jews were not Germans. This attempt to dissolve the anti-Semitic threat by starting from its roots is also the intellectual and mental construction embodied by the Kulturwissenchaftliche Bibliothek. In Warburg's view the Kulturwissenchaftliche Bibliothek was a deeply German and patriotic endeavor, which indicates that he never gave up those hopes he had expressed in the letter to his mother, hopes that for Jews were bound up with the young German nation.

"The Jewish Question in the Context of Germany's Entire Policy"

Among other items in Warburg's archive from shortly before the outbreak of the war is the parliamentary record of a debate on the army budget;[38] this annual budget debate was regularly used by liberal members, particularly by Georg Gothein of the Freisinnige Partei[39] to ask why Jewish one-year volunteers were still de facto denied the status of reserve officer. That this was not the case as the war began is surely explained by the "truce" proclaimed by Wilhelm II ("I no longer recognize parties, for I know only Germans"[40]), in which Jewish patriots could also feel themselves included in the first two years of war.

Warburg gave particular weight to the place of Jews in the German army, as an indication of how far anti-Semitism actually was politically possible and tolerated by the state. There is already a sign of this in the letter to his mother from Strasbourg in 1889.[41] A little later (1892–93) he did his own voluntary military service in a cavalry regiment in Karlsruhe,[42] and we may suppose that he too felt the refusal of reserve officer status as an insult. An interest in this question is attested by newspaper clippings on the theme, as well as by records of Reichstag debates. Several speeches made in the budgetary debate of 6 May 1914 addressed the question of whether Jewish one-year volunteers had been denied the rank of reserve officer in Prussia ever since 1885—not by law, but de facto—and if so, why this was happening.[43]

Recent historical research has concluded that although the perennial debate on access to the officer ranks may today seem to be an offshoot of Prussia's Wilhelmine militarism,[44] we must remember that in peacetime the army's function was primarily political, and that the Prussian army formed the core of the establishment in Imperial Germany.[45] The exclusion of Jewish one-year volunteers from the ranks of reserve officers crystallized all of the unspoken, stubborn, and dogged resistance to the integration of the Jewish minority on the part of the aristocratic and bourgeois power élite. It could be argued that only this fundamental resistance among the élite allowed explicit and activist anti-Semitism to flourish, even if they themselves took no part in it. Especially in Prussia the rank of reserve officer was the entry for a career in the civil service and the judiciary, just as it was the minimum of integration needed truly to belong in Wilhelmine society. The institution of the reserve officer rank was itself the fruit of just such a social compromise between the aristocratic military caste and the social-climbing bourgeoisie.[46] It is clear that in this respect we can speak of what amounts to consensual anti-Semitic sabotage of the constitution right up to the end of Imperial Germany, which even the "truce" of 1914 changed only for a while.[47] The "free choice of the regiment" whereby the officer class was coopted proved to be a tried and true tactic for conservative politicians who could thus wash their hands of any wrongdoing in public. Such double standards were documented in the Reichstag records, and any strategy was basically helpless against them. These tricks and loopholes for discrimination were notorious, and together with the attempts to counter them, symptomatic of the whole situation; they throw a harsh light onto the trap in which the Jewish minority found itself even when (or especially when) they were particularly successful in many ways—as were the Warburgs. In his dossier on the "Jewish question" in the Prussian army Warburg documented the dangers of this trap.

In the second summer of the war—in 1916—Warburg had the chance to use his documentation for a direct political intervention. His brother Max had written an "opus" that in its first draft was titled "The Demand of the Moment (the Jewish Question)" (*Ein Gebot der Stunde [die Judenfrage]*), although the occasion for writing it remains unstated.[48] Max calls the text an "indictment" in a letter to his brother, and this term (*Anklageschrift*) also occurs in the text itself, although it was later cut. In November 1916 Max M. Warburg gave copies of the text to "leading personalities" in Berlin; he had revised it several times together with his brother and titled it "The Jewish Question in the Context of Germany's Entire Policy." The distribution of the text probably took place under pressure of time due to the "shock" of the Jewish census.[49] On 11 October 1916 the Prussian Minister of War, Wild von Hohenborn, had used an anti-Semitic campaign against Jewish combatants as the occasion for a statistical study of German Jews in the war. This "Jewish census" was supposedly undertaken to refute accusations against the Jews, but in truth was itself underpinned by anti-Semitic notions.[50]

The Warburgs' pamphlet was at first just under ten pages long, and in its final form seven pages, and set out the Jews' situation in the war as Max and Aby Warburg saw it. It argues for the civil rights of Jews in wartime (as secured by the "truce") to be maintained, extended, and guaranteed in the new peacetime order, arguing that the conditions of the "truce" must persist, for reasons of state if nothing else; that a great deal that would be decisive depended on the approach the government took to the question of equal rights for Jewish soldiers—Germany's strength and feasibility as a state, the legitimation for her campaign of conquest in Eastern Europe, the nation's international reputation, and her bargaining power in a future peace settlement. The Warburg Institute archive has a thorough (if not absolutely seamless) record of how the pamphlet was conceived, written, and received. Letters found in the correspondence archive only become comprehensible when read alongside documents that can be found variously shelved in section IV of the archive.

A letter from Max Warburg dated 13 June 1916 briefly sums up the text as it would later be printed.

> I enclose my opus for you. It is by no means complete; e.g., it occurs to me that I really must devote a paragraph to Zionism, and that secondly, I could give the whole matter a different tone were I to assign to Germany the solution to the international Jewish question. Germany has a better right to undertake this than any other state, for just as anti-Semitism has a scientific basis in Germany, the solution to this difficult problem can (paradoxical though this sounds) be addressed here. In the final analysis, philo-Semitism in England is merely a means to an end; the Gallic countries' passion for justice in the Jewish Question is, as we have seen in the Dreyfus affair, on shaky ground. If German science and the German talent for organization were to tackle this question this would also be (as I have hinted) good publicity for Germany all around the world. Add to this that Germany is best placed to satisfy certain Zionist wishes in Turkey. Thus this whole indictment will not simply end in a call to action within Germany-rather it shows the way to a world-changing mission, which may yet lead to the estab-

> lishment of a Department for Jewish Affairs in our own foreign ministry.[51]

It is not clear how far the brothers had agreed on the urgency of the memorandum and on its contents before this letter was written. A letter from Max Warburg to Aby of 23 October 1916 characterizes part of the background against which the pamphlet was conceived: "The situation in Germany is most troubling. The whole Reventlow clique is abhorrent,[52] and the Reichstag has behaved idiotically in the question of Jews in wartime society. I am taking all these things calmly; two years of war can only provoke the worst passions, especially when one is not well fed. This too shall pass."[53] Max's assessment may have been softened to spare his excitable brother: yet however realistic it may sound, the very fact that he had written and distributed a position paper on the "Jewish question" shows that he did not dare hope that the "worst passions" would pass so simply. In any case Aby Warburg added several paragraphs to the first draft; this draft is not preserved in the London archive, but the section Aby added can be found as a text in its own right. It is held in manuscript along with several sheets of notes, and in typescript under the title "Directives concerning the military promotion of religiously non-conformist persons, suggested by a . . ."[54] The first printing contained these paragraphs, as well as the passage on Zionism that Max had promised in his letter: the second version is considerably curtailed, with much removed that was important—foremost a judicious and distanced take on Zionism, and a lengthy passage in which Max Warburg anticipated the likely negative reaction to the intervention. Max made these changes himself. Aby justifies his own suggested changes in a letter of 25 November preserved in the handwriting of Mary Warburg, strongly worded and showing that he saw the essay "as a work common to us both, even if you have done the greater part."[55] There then follow detailed suggestions for changes, each in turn rejected or taken on board in a letter from Max Warburg of 25 November 1916 headed "Not via secretary"; the pamphlet's possible recipients also become recognizable, in outline at least:

> Of course I do not take your changes amiss, that is self-evident[. . . .] It is only that early next week I shall most probably see the leading figures in Berlin and would have much

> liked to be able to put this pamphlet into their hands. I really do not know whether that will now be possible, since I will send it off to the printer's again this afternoon. I have accepted all of your editorial changes. I have also struck out the passage on Zionism and the passage on who may win the war. On the other hand I do not accept your introduction. We have no such thing as new territorial conquests[. . . .] I have now addressed the census of Jews, in one sentence. It is a measure that in this context, we cannot avoid. I have also changed the title[. . . .] I hope that I will have the galley proofs tomorrow morning and I will then send you a copy, so that you have another opportunity to have your say in all points. I have also used your concluding passage only in part. I have dropped the grounds of excuse, about that you are right, but when one speaks to these military types it is best to end with a certain manly pride. There are after all not many who know how to say such things modestly, yet also confidently.[56]

The second printing, with further suggestions by Aby Warburg, is archived together with the first version, as is a third printing showing that these changes were not incorporated.[57]

The pamphlet's effectiveness with the "leading figures" of the foreign ministry goes undocumented in correspondence or in the archive, but is visible in an epilogue that might almost be called satirical. Max Warburg obviously distributed the text more widely and thought it very persuasive. In the dossier on the "Jewish question" pamphlet is a copy of a letter dated 28 May 1917, bearing Aby Warburg's jotted note "Börries von Münchhausen to Max M. Warburg." Baron Börries von Münchhausen (1874–1945) was Germany's last ballad-maker; his work was very popular above all with youth groups, and his 1900 collection *Juda* had been a great success.[58] Older reference works do not mention his career as a *völkisch* writer and later a National Socialist, which has, however, been thoroughly detailed by Werner Mittenzwei.[59] The letter is six and a half pages long and begins as follows:

> I would have written to you some time ago and thanked you for so kindly sending me your pamphlet, had I not been waiting each day for an essay for the *Kunstwart* to arrive,

> which I would have liked to enclose here. [. . .] now I shall no longer delay in answering your kindness with something in exchange, nor in writing down for you my own thoughts on the Jewish question. As you will see from my book *Juda* (which follows in the posts), this problem has occupied me artistically: yet long ago it also caught my attention politically and humanly. [. . .] 1) *The Nature of anti-Semitism:* anti-Semitism, that is the *awareness* that Jewry is in many respects very alien to the Aryan nature, and the conscious refusal of Jewry's essential and characteristic traits, is not a sentiment that can be spread as it were by infection, but rather one which anyone will feel who has taken the time to think more deeply about the world in which he finds himself. [. . .] We must not delude ourselves. Each and every Aryan has and will always have the sense of otherness from each and every Jew.[60]

With this in mind the author (who was also a cavalry captain) lays down the law in setting out rudiments of the *völkisch* racist worldview, always emphasizing that right-thinking people such as Max Warburg cannot help but reach these same conclusions. Among other things he calmly puts discrimination against Jews into its racist context, while the Warburgs had presented it in their pamphlet as religious intolerance: "anti-Semitism is a racial feeling, not a religious one, and furthermore it is in no way a feeling of hatred or contempt." Münchhausen also points out the justifications for anti-Semitism: "I therefore feel that anti-Semitism is justified as a defensive phenomenon wherever I see German nationhood and German culture in danger of being taken over by Jewry. In my opinion this is especially so as regards the way in which our cultural legacy is handled." He dismisses as secondary all the concrete points that the Warburgs had raised in their pamphlet: "for the army has nothing to do with our cultural legacy" since "experience has shown that the Jew is incapable of comprehending the depths of German being and culture, just as the Aryan is incapable of feeling Semitic culture deeply." He closes the letter in the hopes that he has succeeded in convincing Warburg of his good intentions, and that they should get together and talk these things over one day soon.

In a letter of 6 June 1917 to his brother Max, Aby Warburg comments on all five points of Münchhausen's creed, which had also addressed the question of Jewish soldiers.[61] His conclusion: "Pity, such self-satisfied narrow-mindedness behind a tactful façade; all in all it is nothing other than the clipped tones of the noble paleface."[62] There are few phrases among Warburg's pointed political aphorisms that so exactly skewer the fantasies of which Wilhelmine anti-Semitism was the syndrome. When Warburg describes the tone and tenor of Börries von Münchhausen's letter as "the clipped tones of the noble paleface," he points straight to where European delusions of superiority (in their Prussian version) converge—we see them most harmlessly in Karl May's novels.

Max replied on 7 June 1917 and was clearly in no mood to address the issues raised: "As soon as I have finished my present work I shall think through the whole matter again more closely, and then reply to Herr v. M. I will send you the reply before I post it."[63] This reply is not extant in the Warburg Institute archive and may well never have been written; as far as the archive documentation shows, here ends one of Max Warburg's attempts to influence Germany's wartime policy regarding the "Jewish question," with Aby Warburg's counsel.[64]

Although this episode can hardly be rated as very important in the course of events or for dominating trends, it does very tellingly attest to Max and Aby Warburg's particular position as insiders and outsiders. Alongside their acuity in judging certain facts as symptoms of a social reality there is a blindness to how impervious the pamphlet's recipients would be to rational, sober, and moral arguments; this blindness was real but may also have been tactical.[65] In this respect the text is above all a document of helplessness, its thirty paragraphs ringing the changes upon a few themes and offering (again, perhaps tactically) disconnected concepts of nation and state that are in the final analysis mutually exclusive. German and Jewish patriotism and devotion to one's country, the German and the Jewish cultural task in the East, blood-and-thunder chauvinist phrases—these all stand in contrast to a repeatedly invoked *raison d'état* in the idealist tradition, which in turn contradicts a technocratic and utilitarian view of the state presented as the actual basis for argument and the proper perspective. The state is portrayed as a disinterested, nonpartisan arbitrator, and only this view allows the two advocates of the Jewish cause explicitly to write "not as Jews" and to let the frequent "we" of the text mean a majority that tends toward anti-Semitism and must be brought to reason: "For love of our country we must decisively banish to distant regions long-planted disagreements, for otherwise we will never be able to work together in the interests of the state."[66] This first-person plural seems even more precariously constructed when it addresses foreign affairs: "We have no right to make Poland independent, to free the oppressed—which means millions of Jews as well—if we do not show in our own land that we are also just to Jews who have for generations shown themselves to be good Germans, *for he is not suited to care for other children who is an unjust father to his own*" (emphasis in original).[67] Such disavowal of one's own self provoked increasing displeasure among the Warburgs' American relatives, and most recently caused indignation and incomprehension in the Warburg family's biographer.[68] In the name of *raison d'état*, interest of state, and the interests of the German Empire,[69] and with reference to the Jews' particular patriotism and whole-hearted identification with Germany at war,[70] comes a warning that though "natural differences" may be recognized, "disagreements of a religious nature" no longer have a place in a civil society.[71] "In recent times the feeling of solidarity has calmed the battles of Protestant and Catholic despite their intensity, yet the struggle against Jewry has been waged openly and secretly in a hateful manner."[72] Equal treatment for German Jews, particularly in the army, is demanded in the name of justice: "As well as its military importance, the non-promotion of officers has a far-reaching effect on the possibility of partaking in civilian life."[73] Only when reason of state suppresses anti-Semitism can Germany expect true international regard, especially from Jews living elsewhere.[74]

The oppositions constructed here are especially obvious at the end of Aby Warburg's contribution and at the end of the larger text: "A stream of our nation's blood shed in this sacrificial war must wash away this uncouth blot on the German army's pristine shield [i.e., discrimination against Jewish one-year volunteers]."[75] At the end of the text we read: "Without false modesty and without undue pride I must warn of this danger, as a German and as a member of a family that can be traced back in both lines in Germany for more than 300 years, which has honorably contributed to art, to science and to philanthropy, which shed its blood sacrifice in the war of 1870/71 just as in this present war."[76] Self-sacrifice, blood sacrifice, and the "stream of our nation's blood" appear inchoately alongside phrases so coldly calculating that they achieve a certain pathos. "After the war its own people will pitilessly ask, 'How, my state, did you handle your human resources? Did you not besmirch the great will to sacrifice by intruding in personal matters of conscience, and where men were ready to give their all, did you not deny them this joy?'"[77] Taken together, these metaphors, intentionally both chilly and heated, supply the meta-metaphor for the wartime situation, in which the patriotic, nationally minded German Jew Aby Warburg—and perhaps to an even greater extent his brother Max—sought to create an awareness of the danger which anti-Semitism posed not just to Jews but also to Germany. Anti-Semitism had long been endemic in the officer corps, and had long been part of that struggle for survival that Wilhelmine Germany experienced externally and internally; and at least to this extent it had been a part of national "identity."[78] Only this can explain the letter from Münchhausen, who wrote to Warburg with the great self-assurance of just such an identity. Münchhausen's untroubled assumption that Warburg might come to agree with him is also a distorted echo of that impossible construction, a "we" that is only German and not Jewish.

Statistics as a Weapon

The land that "nurtured anti-Semitism scientifically" could also be called "to find a scientific basis for solving this difficult question."[79] Max Warburg called this a "paradoxical" hope and Aby Warburg held it to be a self-evident truth: and there were others who shared it. This can be shown by the statistical survey of the army in 1916 and by works on Jewish demography held in the Warburg Institute library.

The "Jewish census" ordered by the Prussian Ministry of War on 11 October 1916 supposedly took place in order to defuse accusations of Jewish "draft-dodging," but there were in fact anti-Semitic motives behind the survey itself.[80] The results of this statistical enquiry were never published, and this gave currency to yet more rumors about the results, which supposedly would have been damning for the Jews and went unpublished in order to protect them.[81] Two tracts by the anti-Semite Alfred Roth, using the pseudonym Otto Arnim, which used these statistics to defame Jewish soldiers, only appeared after the war.[82] One of these two texts was held in the Kulturwissenchaftliche Bibliothek, along with a publication by Franz Oppenheimer, who sums up the events and refutes the rumors with fact.[83] Statistical survey as a weapon in this dispute had acquired a whole new importance after the turn of the century,[84] and this too is documented in the K.B.W. library.[85] Each side hoped to justify their political beliefs with the hard facts of descriptive demographics, or conversely to refute badly interpreted figures with better, objective statistics on the Jewish population:

> For longer than a lifetime, Jewry has been the focus of searching interest. For decades it has been the object of a more or less unfavorable verdict. Jewry is scrutinized down to the smallest drop of its blood, and always in one-sided fashion, in order to paint smirch after smear upon it and to prove scientifically an inferior status that its opponents have decided a priori. Jewry can only welcome a study of its population trends, of its anthropological structure and pathological features, of the life and activity of its social body. Just as we Jews have always relied upon ourselves, so now have we seized the initiative in this regard in order to solve the questions mentioned above in a way that is free from prejudice, interest, and assumption. To this end Dr. Nossig has established the Bureau for Jewish Statistics, which has a secure basis in the Society for Jewish Statistics.[86]

The reliance on "science" as an ally in the battle against anti-Semitism is among those points of Warburg's pamphlet that sound like a conjuration, included only sketchily. It is not only Warburg, or the statisticians and social scientists of the "Bureau for Jewish Statistics," who parade science in two costumes; as "free from prejudice, interest, and assumption," a rational and quantifiable view of reality, but also as a magical practice. The unconditional belief in the possibilities of science, in the possibility of using knowledge to act upon prejudice, distrust, even hatred and antipathy, lends a tragic dimension to the Warburgs' essay. This attempt at influence was clearly motivated by a proper recognition of how crucially significant was the exclusion of Jews from the officer corps in Wilhelmine society, yet "[i]f ever there was a lost cause, this was one of them, although this fact is more easily perceived in retrospect than it was by those who fought for their rights sixty odd years ago."[87] The Wilhelmine state stood or fell by its ideology of a homogenous officer corps, and the political anti-Semitism fostered by the government stood or fell alongside it: Warburg had recognized this, yet he shut his eyes to the inevitable consequences.[88]

Max and Aby Warburg's efforts remained futile, like earlier arguments that used sober analysis of what had taken root in Imperial German society to appeal to the righteousness of a supposedly reasonable bourgeois class. A comparison with Walther Rathenau's 1911 text "State and Jewry" (*Staat und Judentum*),[89] which was subtitled "A Polemic," shows that Rathenau had already said everything that the Warburgs' pamphlet had in the way of motifs, themes, and arguments, and had said it more clearly. Rathenau's essay is rightly celebrated and much quoted, not least because of its devastating clarity and prophetic conclusion: "I battle the injustice that takes place in Germany, for I see shadows rise wherever I turn. I see them when I catch sight of the insolence of our wealth, which has become madness; when I hear the emptiness of boastful words or hear of pseudo-Germanic exclusivity[. . . .] Not for decades has Germany lived through a more serious period, but the strongest act possible in such times is to destroy injustice."[90]

Giving Names to Threatening Shadows

In his magisterial *Deutsche Geschichte* Thomas Nipperdey traced the "shadowlines" along which German culture was shaped by political power and political interests, despite Germany's brilliant achievements in art and science in the years before 1918.[91] His survey of 1994 is characterized by an exacting sense of justice, and he seeks to avoid a one-sided sketch of Imperial German society's negative traits; therefore he repeatedly names as the worst of methodological sins the "false perspective" of a simplifying prehistory to 1933.[92] Despite these reservations, aimed not so much at the facts themselves as at the interpretation of facts, he tallies off the deformities of Imperial Germany's political culture: nationalism as a national goal and an end in itself, militarism, anti-modern tendencies, apoliticism as fundamental to German culture, and anti-Semitism.[93] Of the authors whom Nipperdey briefly portrays with regard to the ideological foundations of *völkisch* and anti-modern cultural criticism, none are missing from Warburg's core acquisitions for his library nor from his archive collections: Paul de Lagarde, Julius Langbehn, Count Gobineau, Houston Stewart Chamberlain.[94]

Though it is justified to stress the ambivalence of these tendencies, it is one thing to trace shadowlines today and another thing to have captured and identified them at the time they were most effective; one thing to "resist the witch-hunt that collects anti-Jewish and anti-liberal quotations"[95] and at the same time to call the most important *völkisch* and racist publications dangerous, another thing to have culled them from newspapers and publications as they appeared. Certainly Warburg himself, a contemporary and a German professor, an infallible idealist, partook of the ideological ambivalence of his time—indeed letters preserved in the correspondence copybook for 1915–18 sometimes strike a hateful and chauvinist tone, as Chernow thoroughly shows.[96] We must however ask whether Warburg's militant language might not be explained by a collective rather than an individual madness. Once we recognize that such entanglements are constitutive for bourgeois existence in any modern society, Warburg's judgments in certain well-documented instances are astonishingly objective. This objectivity—this "matter-of-factness"—is extended equally to people and to events, and it gives rise to an extraordinary tension that cannot easily be resolved. This is illustrated by the case of Gustav Schmoller, documented twice over in the archive.

Gustav Schmoller (1838–1917; ennobled 1908), the "Pope of the historical school of economics,"[97] published a polemic against the Jews in the *Jahrbuch für Gesetzgebung, Verwaltung und Volkswirtschaft* ("Schmoller's Annual") in December 1916 shortly before his death.[98] The pretext was his review of Hugo Preuß's book *Das deutsche Volk und die Politik* and of Hans Delbrück's lecture "On Government and the People's Will." His thesis, repeated in the noon edition of the *Berliner Zeitung* of 27 December 1916 and subsequently much discussed in the media, was that "the great ideal of political and legal emancipation can only be completed at the same rate as the nation's consciousness accommodates itself to the law as it stands."[99] The controversy continued in the press in January 1917. The *Berliner Neueste Nachrichtungen* of 17 January 1917 reported that after sustained public criticism of his remarks Schmoller had "taken up the pen in the *Tägliche Rundschau* in order to set forth his views on German Jews." Jews in influential positions were hindering the "Germans and Christians" and there was also the problem of usury in rural areas. There were both Nathans and Shylocks among the Jews.[100] "Schmoller's opportunism" in the "Jewish question" was critically remarked upon in the *Berliner Tageblatt*, the *Breslauer Zeitung* and elsewhere. Many newspapers reported on the respected economist's stance without themselves taking a stand. All of these newspaper cuttings are from the Goldschmidt service in Berlin, which Warburg employed in such matters. Further cuttings and excerpts pasted onto cards can be found in *Zettelkasten* 36, "Jews,"[101] among them the report of a medal awarded to Schmoller. Warburg may well have felt he must follow the case more closely because of the great respect generally granted to Schmoller, which lent weight to his hitherto unpublicized sympathy with anti-Semitic tendencies; or because of the much-used clichés of the extorting Jew and Jewish nepotism,[102] adduced as facile explanations. In retrospect the *Breslauer Zeitung*'s assessment of Schmoller's remarks as opportunist seems on the mark; even centrist politics not only became inured to and accepted the endemic anti-Semitism, but went so far as to express sympathy, and to see the validity of laws as dependent on the *Volksbewußtsein*. Even Thomas Nipperdey would have to recognize Warburg's acuity in recognizing these decisive symptoms.[103]

Schmoller died in Bad Harzburg in June 1917, aged seventy-nine. In November 1917 Warburg was offered the chance to buy Schmoller's library. He wrote to his brother Max: "I enclose an offer which reached me from Baer, concerning Schmoller's library. I hold that as a trading city and above all a future university city as well, Hamburg cannot afford not to acquire this library. Mayor von Melle has his reservations, as I have learned from a conversation with Rathgen—he is worried that the library contains too many 'dry statistics.' Naturally that is nonsense; it holds Schmoller's whole world, which gave rise to our own modern sociopolitical way of thinking. The Commercial Library should also take over a part of it."[104] This objective assessment and vote in favor are clearly not influenced by the controversy of barely a year before. A conscientious recording agent has here tried to assemble the clues and proofs that will give a name to a shadow and a threat: toward the end of his life, one of the Wilhelmine era's most important economists had given way to the pressure of wartime and the temptation to cozy up to populist anti-Semitic opinion. In Warburg's eyes this did not diminish his life's achievement.

Spiritual Crisis

A letter of 22 May 1918 is addressed to Eva von Eckardt, later a long-term member of staff at the Kulturwissenchaftliche Bibliothek; Warburg is clearly responding to her request to use the library.[105] The letter makes clear how Warburg saw his own position and that of his research instrument in these troubled times:

> I am happy to offer you the services of my library. In the next few days I shall send you the book by Rupin[106] and another by Herz, *Rasse und Kultur*.[107] I do not possess the books by Zolschau[108] and Melamet.[109] I am entirely in agree-

> ment with your rejection of Trützschler's tract.[110] It is one of those well-intentioned but boundlessly superficial attempts to see the Jewish question as an isolated problem, when really it is but a part of the gigantic and tragic crisis of the spirit which affects all Europe. After all, cultural-historical development lies on the diagonal of that parallelogram of forces whose shorter side is the physical world as it is, whose other and much longer side is the development of the mind. Europe and particularly Germany were however already in a state of materialist idiocy before the war, gazing only at the shorter side of the parallelogram and stupefied by demagogue windbags such as Chamberlain. This has long cheated us of the pleasure of spirituality, trustingly or critically; the proof of whether this war has really helped us at all must be whether Germany will have freed itself from the Philistine blood myth such as Chamberlain's. We must fear however that the cult of this heavy-industry Moloch will capture many other circles. I hold that every one-sided musing of the race problem is a waste of time, because it detracts from the main task: to achieve a reformation of Europe with the help of a new ideological goal. Do you know Carlyle's *Sartor Resartus*?[111]

Clearly Eva von Eckardt's request had touched upon the "Jewish question" and on cultural history in relation to it. Warburg's reply is characteristically split into a detailed review of the literature and a far-reaching and condensed summary of the problem as he saw it. The pivot between the two parts of the letter is the metaphor of a parallelogram of forces, whose shorter side is the body, the physical and material world, the given, whose longer and more important side however is the mind, developing and mobile. Culture and the ways in which it changes over time—"cultural-historical development"—are thus seen to form the diagonal and vector pointing to the future that results from these forces.

This image (it can hardly be called a concept) of culture not only still contains the idea of development as movement "onward and upward" without explicitly saying so; it is above all dynamic in the sense that culture is understood as the product of a "process of confrontation," an *Auseinandersetzungsprozess* as Warburg would say later. His idealist view that what develops and changes is a priori more significant than the given, comes without explanation and may in part be explained by the intellectual's powerlessness. In this metaphor "materialism" stands for the over-emphasis of what is physical, and this in turn stands for racism such as popularized by Houston Stewart Chamberlain. The "blood myth" of the superiority of the master race, the cult of the "heavy-industry Moloch": the "race problem" is in itself only the symptom of a crisis. For Warburg, only a new reformation could end the European crisis that, as a spiritual crisis, had discharged its destructive energies into the catastrophe of the World War. For Warburg the touchstone of whether the war had been justified lay in jettisoning the "master race" ideology, as he had argued in his essay two years earlier. The blood sacrifice that could wash away the blood myth: both war and racism are draped here in a terminology that shows industrialized war and Jew-hating in the guise of scientific biology for what they also are, regardless of all modernizing: rituals of banishment, magical practices which yet create those monsters they are meant to ward off.

Waves of intense anti-Semitic propaganda followed the end of the war, whereby the German defeat, profiteering from the war economy, the results of the Versailles Treaty and the economic situation of Germany after the war were blamed on "the Jews," particularly the banks and other big business: in short everything came to pass as Max Warburg had foreseen, put down in his essay and then struck out again.[112] Already during the war in 1916, Alfred Roth had written an essay with Theodor Fritsch in which they attacked the "Rathenau-Ballin system." This agitation fell on fertile ground because tensions and contrasts had been uncommonly exacerbated by the war just lost, between the poor and those made destitute on the one hand, and the rich and the profiteers on the other.[113] The largest and most important association with anti-Semitic and *völkisch* aims was founded by 1919; this was the Deutschvölkischer Schutz- und Trutzbund.[114] At times the group had as many as 200,000 members organized into 20 district associations and 600 active branches. This essentially bourgeois association had not quite 40 percent academics in its membership. The director and leading figure in the Trutzbund was Alfred Roth, closely associated with Theodor Fritsch. One of the group's main activities was anti-Semitic rabble-rousing: leaflets, stickers, and tracts sometimes reached enormous print runs. After only three years, in June 1922, the Trutzbund was forbidden almost throughout Germany, following the murder of

Walther Rathenau: several of its members had taken part in the attack. As with all such groups there had already been internal quarrels; now it dissolved and members joined other parties such as the NSDAP. Although by 1924 the political situation in the young republic had stabilized and it seemed that the rug had been pulled out from under the feet of right-wing radicalism, the "unprecedented" hate campaigns had left "deep marks in the mentality and in the political culture."[115]

Also after the war came Aby Warburg's breakdown, the final eruption of his psychosis. Both Carl-Georg Heise and the medical case files show that the threat posed by anti-Semitism had played an important role in it, and perhaps even the decisive one.

5

Scholarly Politics and Current Affairs (1926, 1917)

When in 1924 Warburg returned to Hamburg from the Bellevue sanatorium in Kreuzlingen, he was convalescent rather than "cured." In the meantime Fritz Saxl had continued the work of the Kulturwissenschaftliche Bibliothek and had begun to make the institution more widely accessible. The construction of a new library building was now proposed, planned, and carried out. Warburg would certainly not have been able to continue working without his two comrades Saxl and Gertrud Bing, whose loyalty, tact, and hard work allowed Warburg to bring home his scholarly harvest.

Warburg had spent the years after the war in sanatoria and asylums; in these years the dissolution of the old social order was accompanied by anti-Semitic troubles and attacks on Jewish merchants, even in Hamburg.[1] He had doubtless been protected as far as was possible from bad news,[2] but we know that the murder of Walther Rathenau in 1922 caused him serious mental disturbance and fear. He saw in it a threat to his brother Max and his family, and Max was indeed placed under police protection around the clock at this time.[3] Max Warburg's role as a financial adviser during the treaty negotiations at Versailles had placed him in the public eye perhaps even more than he had been during the war. Yet Aby Warburg cannot have known many details of how the wartime fears that he had shared with his brother Max had come true.

But the Great War was a past that would not lie down—not only in the great change represented by the new republic, but also in many smaller matters. A wide-ranging and unusual document attesting to this is the journal that Warburg and his two colleagues kept from 1926 to 1929.

The Library Journal

> In view of the impending move to a purpose-built home the past and present directors of the library (Prof. Warburg, Dr. Saxl, Frln Dr. Bing) wish to reach an understanding of how the institution can more fittingly be administered. Since these three set out together without regard to personal sensibilities in creating the K.B.W. and since they have determined to work and thrive together without fear or favor, unsparing but solely objective criticism should be made here.
> 3.I.926[4]

From 1926, the moment when the Kulturwissenschaftliche Bibliothek Warburg moved into the new building at Heilwigstraße 116, until Warburg's death in 1929, Warburg, Saxl, and Bing kept a library journal in which they made all kinds of entries by turn. The journal has been consulted and cited in various contexts and has been published since the German appearance of this current work.[5] Read attentively it is far more than a "running commentary" on the day-to-day business of the Kulturwissenschaftliche Bibliothek, although this aspect too is important in understanding how a recently established private research institute is run. With great candor, Warburg and his colleagues exchanged notes on matters concerning staff, visitors, and colleagues, often in connection with questions of academic politics to some degree but from time to time touching also upon larger political questions. The participants set forth and discussed without reservation their opinions, the convictions they held in common, the motives and goals of their actions. In all, nine volumes of this journal of the former Kulturwissenschaftliche Bibliothek are now held in the London Warburg Institute; it was written in old-fashioned, long-lasting ledgers, an amiable adherence to Hamburg mercantile habits also to be seen in Warburg's correspondence copybooks.[6]

The entries begin with four passages by Warburg from January to March 1926, which as yet give no hint of the idea that the journal should be kept by the "directors" in common. The entry by Warburg cited above is from 24 August of that year. Without leaving his colleagues any chance to decline his suggestion, Warburg justified it by explaining that communication had become more difficult now that the library was no longer also his home. This first passage in the first volume is followed by almost daily entries to the end of the year by all three colleagues, as planned at the start. Over the years and from volume to volume it becomes ever clearer that Warburg was the most interested in keeping the journal—Bing and especially Saxl were unable or unwilling to join in to the same extent; Gertrud Bing at least made an effort to heed Warburg when he urged her to write down her experiences regularly, whereas Fritz Saxl only reluctantly contributed very short entries—when he was in Hamburg at all.

Areas Covered

Perhaps the most obvious topic illuminated by the journal can be summed up as *names*. Names of those who saw the library, names of regular or occasional visitors, names of colleagues and staff, names of correspondents, dignitaries from Hamburg and elsewhere, of scholars, students, friends, relatives, and figures from political daily life. Here we see a tightly woven fabric of contacts, close or otherwise, chance acquaintances, and more important ones formed in the Kulturwissenschaftliche Bibliothek or on its behalf, which took it forward as a research institute.[7]

Another area upon which the journals throw light is the internal organization of the library, which is ordinarily described with reference to the well-known "principle of good neighborhood" and to the shelving of books into four large sections (Word-Image-Orientation-Action).[8] The most informative entries in this context are those by Gertrud Bing, for instance from 29 November 1926:

> Morning, checked call numbers 2nd floor. Afternoon discussion with Dr. Noack about shelving in the philosophy section. All philosophy subsections having to do with other disciplines have been removed and reshelved as apparatus with their relevant disciplines. E.g., philosophy of religion with religion, natural philosophy with cosmology, ethics with law. Thus the philosophy section now consists systematically only of works concerned with thought as such, the three distinct

> sections being: phenomenology and logic (objective), to which can be added discussions of knowledge and scientific method, psychology, which can be shelved together with the psychological holdings of the former shelves for symbols (subjective view of the topic), to which belong world-views, education, collective formation of types (e.g., the "dandy"), and lastly symbology, philosophy of meaning and signs, which stands midway between the subjective and objective aspects. This has given rise to a new section, law. In principle this shelving continues a tendency which had already been at work in the BW whereby e.g. aesthetics and philosophy of history have already been removed and reshelved within their disciplines. Thus philosophy has now been defined as discipline in itself and set alongside rather than above the other disciplines as being itself a "symbolic form," i.e., is ranked equally with religion and art, as fits the ideas of the B.W.[9]

Obviously the "good neighbor policy" had its material side as well. The short report entered by Warburg of a family meeting at Kösterberg in Blankenese on 21 August 1927 illustrates this.

> Beautiful weather for a late summer afternoon yesterday; in the long hall at Kösterberg, set Paul's mind at rest concerning our project with G.B.'s help. Max was there for a while with Gisela, Anita, and also Renate. Paul concerned that we have not prepared guarantees for expanding the institute, wishes to know our internal safeguards against excessive costs. He asks therefore whether we have to acquire all the books we need or whether they might not be had on loan from elsewhere (to a greater extent than at present). [. . .] Responded to this objection, that it is precisely the acquisition of a book and its physical presence, its proximity with other books, that created the particular encyclopedic totality and growth potential—and that this depends on a unified system for intersecting, orbiting, or tangentially touching areas of inquiry, which can only be concretely realized in such a *problem-oriented* library [*Problembibliothek*].[10]

In this regard Warburg's education and instinct had found their "confirmation" in the open-shelf seminar libraries in Strasbourg.[11] His phrase speaking of "physical presence" leads directly to what is truly special to the Warburg library, to thought exemplified, materialized, and made physical—in an extraordinary and uncompromising manner. As the journal documents, new insights into European cultural history in these years often led to back-breaking bouts moving furniture or books around. For instance, Bing jotted down "Photo boxes in hall—old house—require that much be changed in the room, which in the end"; and Warburg finished the sentence "was accomplished as all worked together."[12]

Fritz Saxl expressed these thoughts rather more conventionally. In a 1930 collection of sketches and essays about German research institutes he began his contribution with the words, "The Bibliothek Warburg is as much a library as it is a research institution. It serves to examine *one* problem; firstly *presenting* the problem which it wishes to address, in the way it selects, acquires, and holds books and pictorial material; and secondly *publishing* the results of research concerned with this problem. The problem is that of the survival or after-life of antiquity."[13] The clarity with which this program could be expressed in 1930 is the result of years of intense discussions during which questions and problems formulated by Warburg were translated into the form of an institution. Thus the phrase "survival or afterlife of antiquity" as used in the Bibliothek Warburg was clearly owed to Gertrud Bing, who as we learn from the journal for 1928 had rejected Warburg's suggested term "Renaissance" as too narrow.[14]

The transformation into an (almost) public academic institution was multifaceted. It included, for instance, teaching. Fritz Saxl remarks on his experience on 14 July 1927: "After class I spent a long time with H. Heydenreich, who had been much impressed and told me about the struggles in the soul of anyone who has been enthused by Panofsky and by yourself in turn. He also confirmed that the way the library is organized is the best and perhaps the only guide to your thought. He told me that only since he has himself worked in shelving does he know what it is that you want, or he begins to understand."[15] Here is made visible the exciting situation of truly excellent academic teaching, and the lucky set of circumstances in Hamburg during these years, when an enthusiast could be gripped for a second time and brought back to the solid ground of fact.

The busy lecture schedule was also part of how the K.B.W. became a full institution and was, in a sense, part of its public relations. An entry from 1927 with the heading "New plans" records how Saxl's Elsheimer lecture took form: "Elsheimer's views of Italy and guide descriptions. Lecture to the Friends of the Kunsthalle in the series German and Italian Art. Is Elsheimer the first painter to interpret German Romantic ideas about Italy? In what ways does he differ from Romantic landscape painters?" Warburg's comment: "superb idea."[16] In the summer of 1927 followed Saxl's report. "Elsheimer lecture on 28th and 29th. To circa 400 people on both occasions. Refrained entirely from 'art history.' Elsheimer as leading figure in the struggle to create a new unity from Northern richness and melancholy (acedia), and Southern grandeur and clarity, a guide to the fierce seriousness with which he conducted this struggle." Warburg: "Max Adolph very much satisfied with Saxl's lecture." Saxl continued: "It was your suggestion that made me look closely at the Acedia theme. The Rubens letter is indeed as important as you had at once recognized, and Panofsky and myself had not. Proof of this can be found in an Elsheimer picture 'The Realm of Athena' in Cambridge; painter at his easel, scholars with book and globe, and in the foreground Athena mistress of the arts, not as a radiant Classical goddess but seated, face in her hand, therefore Pallas-Melencolia." Warburg: "Marvelous! Where is the reproduction?"[17]

There are at least as many such exchanges regarding the objects and objectives of the Kulturwissenschaftliche Bibliothek's research as there are entries concerned with organizational matters. Warburg's ruminations on his great project of the 1920s, the "Bilderatlas," take up a great deal of room, as was to be expected; there are also notes on the conception and planning of exhibitions, as well as commentary on political events of the day.

In its deeply unconventional fashion, as a unique textual genre practically beyond compare, the journal offers an insight into what Peter Gay has described as Weimar culture.[18] For the daily entries occupy exactly that space where the largely subjective—that is, the different scholarly temperaments of the three contributors—meshes into the objective and permanent structure of an institution in the making.

Becoming an Institution

The Bibliothek Warburg as an institution shared a whole series of desires and self-images with other institutes in the humanities or social sciences (to name but one example, the notion that it was an observatory or a laboratory).[19] The feeling that Fritz K. Ringer vividly described of researching at a time of crisis was also present in the Kulturwissenschaftliche Bibliothek.[20] We further know from the journal entries (as from Warburg's writings) that the crisis was not seen as one that could be definitively overcome. The sober emphasis on practical application, on the single delineated question, and on the detail, was tenaciously opposed to everything fashionable (and much that had long been established). Aby Warburg had himself achieved this general application of acts with very specific biographical roots, by starting work as early as 1904 on making an institution from his research library, his methodology, and his way of framing questions. In this respect the continuing existence of his foundation as the Warburg Institute is proof of how successful his efforts were.

In view of Warburg's strategies, it is illuminating to take a brief look at legal and sociological theories of the institution. A few points to keep in mind here: institutions can of course be anything from the largest to the smallest units, from states down to research institutes (Herbert Spencer recognized six kinds of institutions),[21] but their common origin and characteristic feature is the need for and (as Helmut Schelsky says) the continued existence of social systems that mediate between the individual's subjectivity and society's objectivity. This continued existence can furthermore only be guaranteed by tacit or explicit social recognition and is confronted and eventually conquered by historical change, or in the sociological context by social change.

The particular features of the Kulturwissenschaftliche Bibliothek as an institution become more evident when we compare it with other foundations of the 1920s. Our point of departure can be a work compiled in 1930 in Hamburg on German research institutes, their history, organization, and goals.[22] A cursory comparison of K.W.B. with two institutes founded around the same time—shortly after the First World War—reveals striking similarities as well as marked differences; these are the Foreign Policy Institute (Institut für Auswärtige Politik, Hamburg 1919/24) and the Institute for Social Research (Institut für Sozialforschung, Frankfurt 1922/24). All three institutions owe their existence to the initiative of private individuals who were reacting not least to the turbulent times after the First World War, although the roots of the Kulturwissenschaftliche Bibliothek go further back. Also common to all three institutions is that they clearly show what Maurice Hauriou called an *idée directrice;*[23] he was one of the first theoreticians of what his 1925 essay called "Institution and foundation," and identified this *idée* as indispensable for every viable institution. Only this idea generates an institution's activities, and it cannot be directly equated to "purpose" or "function." For Hauriou, it is that guiding idea that the institute "embodies" as well as "personifies." Warburg chose the phrasing "the idea that commands us."

There is much to suggest that the staying power of an *idée directrice,* and thus of an institution, stands in direct correlation to the urgency of a task. In 1970 Helmut Schelsky elaborated upon this relation of institution to task in a projection of Bronislaw Malinowski's systemic models ("How does culture function?").[24] That such a dynamic was present at the founding of the three institutes here in question is attested by the following statements. Friedrich Pollock said of the founding of the Marxist Frankfurt Institute for Social Research that in the years after the First World War, "scholarship was not thoroughly prepared and was overburdened with day-to-day work; for a while [scholarship] had to abandon the field to pseudo-science, phrase-making, and political demagoguery."[25] One impetus for the founding of the Foreign Policy Institute came when "delegations of the warring powers" in Paris and Versailles came to realize that "none of them had a clear view of how law could be applied in the mutual relations of nations and peoples."[26] Albrecht Mendelssohn Bartholdy said it more forcefully in his 1924 speech at the founding ceremony: "It was great suffering, and after the suffering [it was] a great labor, which compelled us throughout these years of preparation."[27] The "somewhat itinerant origins" of the Foreign Policy Institute before its official foundation were in the Warburg family home at Kösterberg in Blankenese—among the most important of the founders was Carl Melchior, who had been a consultant at the negotiations in Paris and Versailles and was a shareholder in the M. M. Warburg bank.

In 1905 it was "insight into the necessity of a better training for our young art historians"[28] that moved Aby Warburg to think of founding an institute. Yet this "insight" also had a political background, in that it did not trust that German universities could provide what Warburg thought of as good training. "Better training" was, however, already only part of what Warburg characterized in writing to his brother Max in retrospect in 1928: "I shall never forget—as I have often said—that when I asked you for support in my struggle against state-sponsored German triumphalist exhibitionism, you and Father gave me unlimited moral support and splendid financial credit, although I was an unofficial, isolated, and unproven intellectual."[29] It is almost irrelevant whether the connection between a better and different training, and the struggle against "German triumphalist exhibitionism" (*deutschen Herrlichkeitsexhibitionismus*) were already established at the turn of the century or whether they came later, in postwar retrospect. An entry in the library journal of 23 March 1927 documents once more Warburg's motives for making cultural science into an institution, in such terms that we can hardly doubt this fundamental long-term intention: "13 March Prof. DDr. Jeremias[30] wrote us a very flattering letter offering his collaboration in questions of Babylonian astrology (very useful, under any conditions) and asking for our publications." Warburg answered the theologian politely and suspected materialist motives behind the offer. He closes the brief entry, "Who was it who, after somebody had told him about the K.B.W., had said, 'this is a rich man's hobby-horse'? This is the opinion I expect and which from principle I always counter by saying, 'This is not a treasure-house but an instrument for everybody, created some 25 years ago because of a feeling for Germany's spiritual crisis etc.'"[31]

It is striking how far the Kulturwissenschaftliche Bibliothek remained largely in the private sphere even as it became an institution, especially when compared with the other two institutes.[32] For the Kulturwissenschaftliche Bibliothek we can apply Adolf von Harnack's principle for research sponsorship, which he had formulated for the Kaiser-Wilhelm-Gesellschaft (today the Max-Planck-Gesellschaft), founded in 1911, that "the Kaiser-Wilhelm-Gesellschaft should not create institutes and seek the right man for them, but first find the right man and then create the institute around him."[33] To a limited extent this was also true of Hamburg's Foreign Policy Institute, which bore the stamp of Albrecht Mendelssohn Bartholdy's personality; like Aby Warburg this specialist in the law of nations had a fundamentally patriarchal outlook but made allowances for the process of research and scholarship, and conducted his institute as a team concern. The Kulturwissenschaftliche Bibliothek and the Foreign Policy Institute had a great deal in common: their founding impulses "against German triumphalist exhibitionism" and "for dialogue among nations and against war as a political tool"; the founding spirits, Max and Aby Warburg and Carl Melchior; and not least the donors, the German and American

Warburgs. This was true to such an extent that in his memoirs of Hamburg in the 1920s the émigré economic historian Alfred Vagts, who had been a member of the Foreign Policy Institute, wrote that "the Institute was thus a second Warburg Institute, not to the extent of Aby Warburg's of course, but certainly an expression of the old banking house's patronage."[34]

In contrast to the Institute for Social Research, which although privately financed was institutionally incorporated into the University of Frankfurt, and to the Foreign Policy Institute in Hamburg, which the senate of the city had established in 1924 as one of its autonomous organs, the Kulturwissenschaftliche Bibliothek remained in private ownership within the family. Niklas Luhmann's bold assertion that "institutions exist so that consensus can successfully be overestimated"[35] applies exactly to the K.B.W. and to Aby Warburg's strategy of forming an institution with neither charter nor brief—on the one hand an act of will, on the other hand "embodied" in books, bricks, and mortar and only "compelled" by an idea, as Warburg put it in the journal. It seems that neither Warburg nor the family expected it to become an institute in the legal sense—in 1924 Max wrote to Aby Warburg: "Finally we must think in the long term about establishing a fund or a series of annuities, so that the budget can be assured beyond the lifetime of the present benefactors; for I cannot think that I would ever want the library to go to the state or to the university."[36] Nevertheless there was a preliminary session of the "trustees" in January 1928, after it had been resolved that the library would not have to pay property tax.[37] A formal contract among the five brothers, whereby the K.B.W. was owned by each of them equally, followed in August 1929. In 1927 a board of trustees had been established even though there was no foundation to which this board was formally attached. This was not a matter of keeping wealth within the family, but rather of protecting an idea or ideal from state intervention—and from state budgetary constraints, as has been remarked.[38] Warburg was, however, all the more concerned to give his library the status (or one might say the appearance) of a public institution. So much becomes clear from a letter of October 1926 to the rector of the university, Rudolf Laun: Warburg was planning a short celebration for the "handover to the public—to the university and educated readers" and in this letter of invitation he called the K.B.W. a "social institution."[39] The true extent of the mission and the *idée directrice* in Warburg's concept of art historical cultural science can be seen in the letter to his brother already cited. He reports on a favorable review of the K.B.W.'s 1926 publications in the "reactionary" *Süddeutsche Monatshefte* by Johannes Geffcken, rector of the university at Rostock: "If the K.B.W. can find favor in such a place, which is by no means free from internal resistance, it is in keeping with the struggle for the rights of German Jewry, as I believe it should best be fought: to prepare to teach well the Germans of tomorrow, or even of the day after, to make them recognize (whether or not they will say so during our own lifetime) that their elder brother Shem has their best interests at heart, is a more productive expense of spirit than the conceptually empty call to arms against anti-Semitism."[40]

The paradoxes and problems of a concealed battle against anti-Semitism's destructive energies could hardly be more obvious than in this formulation of so wide-ranging a task.

Atmospherics

Certainly the practical problems of developing and strengthening the research institute are at the forefront of the exchanges in the journal. What had however not previously been perceived is how, alongside this, we can see cultural science and the institute seeking a place on the political map of the Weimar Republic, by necessity as much as by design. There are plentiful landmarks on this map; a place had to be found within a spectrum that stretched from Social Democracy on one side to *völkisch*-national groups on the other. The most important category here is not party politics nor how one approaches them: Warburg's German patriotism is just as evident as the acute sense that he shared with Gertrud Bing for the *Herrenmensch,* the German triumphalist "type."

There are two observations about this type, the first by Gertrud Bing on 17 March 1927: "Prof. Wolfgang Stammler (son of old Stammler) from Greifswald; Saxl knows about him because of a good piece of his on the *danse macabre.* He arrived and, since Saxl was not here, I showed him around. [. . .] Much interested in Rembrandt's oath upon the sword and in Baroque theatre, gave me some good bibliographic advice. Monocle, dueling scars, shaven nape, but nevertheless pleasant conversationalist and clearly clever and industrious. Cousin to Dornseiff."[41] This acute observation with one glance remarks and attributes all the clues that reveal social origin, group affiliation, and political tendency. A second report by Warburg goes beyond mere observation. He has been troubled by an evening encounter in the reading room:

> There was a dreadful dilettante called Meyer in the reading room this evening (nobody at the lectern, Alber in soft shoes), he wants to write about Giorgione because he (author of plays) is so amazed that Giorgione caught the plague when infected by his lover. He wants to write a tragedy on the theme suggesting that Giorgione perhaps wanted this to happen etc. . . . a silly brute, wanted to offer a new interpretation of "The Astronomers," didn't think Hartlaub good enough, and asked whether there were books about Giorgione. (!) I pointed him to Ludwig Justi and Häcker's *History of the Great Epidemics in the Middle Ages,* which will soon get rid of his astonishment over just one case. Also referred him to the indifference of the Decameron narrators, which, being an endlessly arrogant blond beast, he listened to with badly feigned politeness. Devil take it, to have such a fellow in the library, with no respect for the book.[42]

This was an attitude that Warburg and his colleagues shared, whatever may have divided them in other regards. They combined a rigorous research ethic with an exact awareness for political circumstances, utterances, and actions, and for the varieties of worldview. This can be seen in a short written dialogue between Warburg and Saxl about Otto Franke's lecture "Cosmic Thought in Chinese Philosophy and the Chinese State,"[43] which was to be published in 1928. Warburg noted on 27 February 1927 that he "liked Franke's lecture uncommonly well, with its reasoned analysis and synthesis of material which is so hard to master."[44] Saxl replied on the same day:

> First feedback to Franke about the conclusion of his lecture. In my view we will publish all kinds of cultural commentary even if it seems plain wrong (only the Occident encourages individuality, the Orient destroys it) but we will not publish remarks on current affairs. E.g., that "presently in Central Europe one is once more chasing the phantom of supranational mutuality. Yet current events show that today one is further from such mutuality than for millennia." Quite apart

> from the fact that we don't think so (cf. Idea vincit)[45] it would be most unwise to publish this, first because of the effect it may have overseas—people would obviously think that such are our politics, since it will be the first such that we've ever published—and second because the volume will appear in two years and we can hardly stretch "current events" over years.[46]

Warburg comments, "In my view an editorial caveat in a footnote will suffice."[47] A glance at the published lecture confirms that Saxl had persuaded the author to phrase these thoughts rather differently, although they stayed in the text, critical of the hopes projected onto the blessings of a world state. It is conceivable that this criticism comes in connection with Germany's entry into the League of Nations (1926) and should indeed be understood as "current affairs." There was however no "editorial caveat" appended.[48]

The Kulturwissenschaftliche Bibliothek's "position" was intended to be unwaveringly objective first and last, although this could not always be unbendingly maintained. As Warburg put it, "we are not here so that one faction or another might take hold of us: we must remain on the weather divide, even when the wind rises."[49] Nevertheless in 1928 the K.B.W. premises were used for broadly political ends, in a way that led Warburg to explain himself to Gertrud Bing, who had expressed her doubts.

> Our colleague Bing has voiced her doubts about two ways in which the K.B.W. has entered current events, 1.) by receiving German students from abroad 2.) by offering K.B.W. premises as offices for the whips for tomorrow's elections.[50] To point 1. Germans abroad are a consolidation of the European, to whom I offer the right to use the K.B.W.—as I have frequently said—only to the extent that they do not hew to racial-*völkisch* ideals but rather regard Germanness as a purely intellectual quality, as do I. There is not the least risk that the K.B.W. might become involved in activist intellectual politics that has any somatic basis: rather do we (B. A. Müller for example) wish to help transform the question of Germanness into a study of other countries as well. This is a worthwhile endeavor and remains subject to

> close self-scrutiny, which shall not shirk from shutting our doors if need be. I thus see no threat to the K.B.W.'s inner or outward objectivity in my conduct. To point 2. I understand the objections rather better here, but we must consider that within the parties the whips include everybody from Eiffe[51] to Erich Warburg and that we are mostly concerned to shake awake the sleeping horde of non-voters. In whose eyes shall this do us harm? Those of the Social Democrats? I have the greatest respect for the Social Democratic movement as such, and as a result have sent a wreath to the late mayor Stolten's funeral with a card bearing "respectful thanks"—I had learned to respect him in turn as a colleague in war-work from the outset. But have the current party chieftains ever shown that they have grasped the K.B.W.'s mission as idealist in their sense, *Excelsior*? Does Herr Götze the Schools Inspector come to visit? Where is Senator Krause, who once took my missionary sermons so much to heart, at Senator de Chapeaurouge's gathering? It is certain that if I do not allow them to telephone from the K.B.W. tomorrow, we will not woo nor win another understanding listener for our audience. Nevertheless I cannot deny that my colleague's concerns have an irreducible, basic relevance.[52]

"Objectivity" was again the most important criterion for a decision on how to handle political events and groups, although as Bing made mercilessly clear, Warburg's idea of objectivity sometimes seems generous. When Warburg expressed his satisfaction at the election results—"Since the result was a strong surge of support for the Democratic Party, securing a center-liberal government, I do not regret having made ourselves available for the election"[53]—Bing comments, "In a matter of principle, success is no justification!"[54] The serene certainty was that cultural science itself could effect enlightenment and thus work politically (as a "Social Democracy of the mind"), but only if used as a set of tools of distancing: yet at the end of the 1920s this certainty came under pressure from an ever more polarized reality.

"Objectivity" (*Sachlichkeit*) was the K.B.W.'s shibboleth, and Warburg's motto for the journal as well; "unsparing but solely objective criticism should be made here. 3.I.926."[55] "Objectivity" was cited again and again, sometimes ironically, as both corrective and invocation. Thus when Gertrud Bing reported on the daily running of the very busy reading room, where she had also noticed some "disorderliness in small things," she added: "Ceterum censeo: Bing also requests a spell of leave from the K.B.W. in order to attain *NEUE SACHLICHKEIT* (NEW OBJECTIVITY)!"[56] This programmatic addendum, with its emphatic trust in the victorious idea,[57] is the objectifying distance of scholarly discipline. "We should go to our work and do justice to the 'demands of the day'";[58] Max Weber's paean to sobriety was also embraced at the Kulturwissenschaftliche Bibliothek, and would always restore the balance between sometimes contradictory efforts in political life and the "politics of mind" (Geistespolitik).

That Warburg was marked by the experience of the First World War, and that he stayed faithful to this experience in his own particular, symbolic way, is illustrated by a tiny detail that yokes together motives and attitudes touching on politics and on research activity, the emotional realm and historical viewpoint. Among the many (often one-sided) character sketches of those who came and went at the K.B.W., three make especial mention of a token that was clearly multiply overdetermined for Warburg. On 30 May 1927 he writes: "Winter's lectures not a success; he failed in his attempt to see Käthchen of Hamburg through new eyes in the broad syntheses and antitheses of large-scale war art, for the material was too thin and meager. Nevertheless the way Panofsky took to his heels was grotesque. One should at least have enough human decency to listen politely to this man, who has proven his ability and has a great deal to say that is perceptive—he still wears his iron watch chain from the war, and this too is a pleasing trait. He could surely take criticism as well."[59] On 12 September 1927 Warburg writes about Oscar von Miller, who was in Hamburg to talk about plans for an exhibition on the history of astrology for the Deutsches Museum in Munich: "Von Miller is marvelously affable in the way he tells stories; unsparing sarcasm sounds like barroom banter from his lips. I was pleased that he too wears the steel watch chain."[60]

The steel wartime watch chain is here perceived as a token that can bridge all possible gaps. It is clear from the context that Warburg also wore this watch chain, as can be seen in a portrait photograph from 1925.[61] It points back to the first days of the First World War, when the transformation to a wartime economy occasioned a series of drives aimed at securing war loans and financing war aid. These drives were mostly organized by women's groups; among them was the campaign "I gave gold for iron,"[62] which had first taken place in the 1813 Napoleonic wars of liberation and later became proverbial. This campaign was revived in Frankfurt late in 1914: "The organizers chose the name consciously to recall the example of Prussian sacrifice and patriotism one hundred years ago."[63] Patriotic fervor was strengthened through this campaign and others, as was the civilian population's feeling of solidarity with the soldiers in sacrifice for their country.[64] Warburg's own war experience, the creation of index cards related to the war, was as Carl Georg Heise reported just such a civilian sacrifice in a different key; he also worked with war relief agencies from the start.[65] The high cost and the futility of this patriotic sacrifice are symbolized in the iron watch chain, worn in place of the golden chain of the bourgeois paterfamilias. By keeping faith with this visible reminder even during the "golden" twenties, Warburg formed ties to other men who had "proved themselves." As a young man Warburg had hoped to show "that representatives of my kind are well suited, in accordance with their talents, to insert themselves as useful links in the chain of present-day cultural and political developments."[66] In the watch chain this early metaphor becomes a symbol, with all the characteristics that Warburg's own work on symbol and sacrifice had elaborated.[67] The patriotic iron watch chain symbolizes inclusion and personal sacrifice, as it creates historical distancing within memory: a memento of that background against which Warburg wished "Germanness" to be seen "as a purely intellectual quality."

A Misappropriated Letter

In late 1926 an Orientalists' congress took place in Hamburg, which Aby Warburg took as the opportunity to hold a lecture on 30 September in the library reading room, where a wealth of pictorial materials had also been assembled for an exhibition on astrology and astromancy; there are notes in the library journal on this and on work related to the third edition of Franz Boll's book of the same title, *Sternglaube und Sterndeutung,* just published in its third edition by Teubner in Leipzig. Yet in the hectic days leading up to the congress a particularly hateful reality suddenly breaks into the industrious labors and the bustle of preparation. Warburg notes, "24 September 926 pictures supplemented and put in order. Fräulein Bing slightly afflicted by jaundice. — Heard from Max M. that Fritsch has published a private letter of mine

Aby Warburg with his watch chain. Universität Hamburg, Kunstgeschichtliches Seminar, Warburg-Archiv.

to Hans Hertz[68] from November 1917 in the *Hammer* of March 1926, and has submitted it to the appeal court as proof of my 'mentality.' The letter must be understood in its context. I suppose that it was stolen from the late Hans Hertz after his death."[69] On the following day Warburg wrote, again mixed in with notes on current projects, "25 September 926 apropos this business with the letter, have looked in vain for the *Reichssturmfahne* and *Thürmer* from 1917. Some comments about Felix in the *Hammer*. Display boards in the reading room progressing very well. Saxl has deduced the identity of the moon nymphs from the Spanish manuscript with Urb. Vat. Looked in vain for dossier with clippings on anti-Semitism."[70] After the end of the Orientalists' congress there is a note of 2 October 1926: "Have meanwhile been in contact with Wilhelm Hertz in Munich,[71] concerning the letter of mine that his wretched sister-in-law passed on to the anti-Semites."[72] On 18 October Warburg notes, "My presence at the Fritsch-Warburg trial counts for nothing with the court"[73] and on 23 October, "Took a stroll with Fräulein Dr. Herschel. Learned a great deal about the trial. Afternoon Erich: also about the trial."[74] Already on 22 October Warburg comments on the sentence passed: "22.X.1926. Fritsch trial: he has been sentenced to four months' imprisonment. At last!"[75]

These sparse comments are barely noticeable among the comprehensive passages mostly concerned with the German Orientalists' congress; at first glance they are incomprehensible, puzzling, and apparently unconnected to the more purposeful entries. Warburg saw his lecture to the Orientalists as a summa of his research with Saxl on the migration of astrological images and on European astrological superstition; with hindsight it seems a bad omen that just as they were preparing to present this work, Warburg should be embroiled in an anti-Semitic attack that concerned him personally and centered on a purloined private letter.

Warburg only learned very late of the publication of this confidential letter, in September 1926; its publication earlier in the year arose from the lengthy suits for libel and slander that Max M. Warburg had brought against Theodor Fritsch. Theodor Fritsch (1852–1933) had compiled the *Handbuch zur Judenfrage* which first came out in 1887 as "Catechism for anti-Semites" and was extraordinarily widely distributed.[76] He was also editor of *Der Hammer*, an anti-Semitic scandal sheet published fortnightly from 1902 onward by the Hammer-Verlag in Leipzig.[77] Theodor Fritsch was among those notorious *völkisch* professional anti-Semites whose publications consisted entirely of tirades against the Jews. His lawyer had submitted the letter in evidence at the trial and Fritsch published it in full in his March 1926 edition, under the title "A Revealing Letter":

> Prof. Dr. A. Warburg
> Hamburg 20, 1st November 1917
> 114 Heilwigstraße, Telephone VI, 3340
>
> My dear Hertz!—Warm thanks for bringing to my attention [the article] which much amused me, since one sees thereby what sort of miserable lies the press is forced to invent if they wish to pin anything on us. My sister-in-law, my brother Dr. Fritz Warburg's wife, is a Warburg by birth (of the Swedish branch). Nobody in our family is in any way related to the Liebermann family. It being wartime we must say nothing about the conversation that my brother Fritz had with Protopopov. These swine know that. It is however a fact that Protopopov must have had thoughts of peace and suggested conditions for a truce, this was in the nature of his talks with my brother. I do not think I go too far in claiming that *these talks were the detonator that caused Anglicized Russia to overthrow its old government. Please maintain strict discretion on this.* Conversely you are entirely free to make use of this correction about our family and indeed I wish you to do so. Were we to ask that the newspaper or papers publish a correction, that would hardly work. These German slanderers must sink much lower before we fight back. I am only troubled that such callous, idiotic, and dangerous journalists can parade themselves as patriots in this Luther anniversary year without some true German man coming forward who dares to write the book on the newspaperman's free conscience, against all capitalism to the left and the right.
>
> I am happy to hear such good news of yourself and your family and hope to be able to admire the children's outfits at some point. We are well, although I am horribly busy. Our eldest daughter is studying assiduously in the ladies' college in Rothenburg o. Tauber.
>
> Fondest greetings from Mary and myself,
> Yours sincerely and in friendship
> Warburg.[78] (italics in original)

This "revealing" letter seems simply to complicate the puzzle further for today's reader, yet there are telling words and turns of phrase, recognizable as Warburg's style and diction even without the further indications in the journal. The two documents cited thus require interpretation and placement in their context, both politically and in terms of the history of scholarship. Such a presentation is however problematized by the two timescales at work here: between the letter of 1 November 1917 and the journal entry of autumn 1926 comes a dividing line, in many senses of the word. The years 1917 and 1918 were a historical turning point in world history and also in a very personal way for Warburg. Nevertheless Warburg's letter in *Der Hammer* conjures shadows from a past that was always present to a German Jew. When a politically unambiguous letter was published for slanderous purposes, it may in 1926 have seemed the last rumbles of a passing storm: with hindsight it seems otherwise.

The Warburg-Fritsch Trial

The charge of libel that Max M. Warburg brought against Theodor Fritsch in August 1923 led to a trial (the second such) that lasted for years and came before several different courts, until finally it ended with Fritsch's conviction.[79] The charge was prompted by a polemical article Fritsch had published in *Der Hammer* in May 1923 under the anagrammatical *nom de plume* F. Roderich Stoltheim. The article was titled "The Secret Kaiser" and was also distributed as a pamphlet; it portrayed Max M. Warburg as a war profiteer and as primarily responsible for "the events of the last ten years,"[80] with a backdrop of a tenuous and convoluted theory about an international conspiracy between Jewish bankers and financiers. A second article in this number was "Who is to blame for the defeat?" addressing Warburg's talks in Stockholm with Alexander Protopopov (July 1916), intended to sound out the chances of a separate truce between Germany and Russia. The results for Germany were America's entry into the war, German defeat, and finally the Treaty of Versailles, and *Der Hammer* traced all of these events to the direct or indirect influence of the American or German Warburgs.

After several adjournments the plaint brought by Warburg and his attorney Carl Melchior (also a shareholder at the bank) led in December 1924 to Fritsch's conviction by a Hamburg jury; he was sentenced to three months' imprisonment and required to publish the verdict at his own expense in seven newspapers.[81] He appealed his sentence. The appeal was heard on 25 January 1926 before the Hamburg district court. This verdict was considerably less harsh and was printed in full in *Der Hammer* of March 1926: a fine of 1000 marks, and publication of the verdict. Max M. Warburg then lodged an appeal against this ruling with the high court, rejected on 15 April 1926. At the same time the district court's finding was overturned and the case was recommended to this court for review. This new trial ended on 17 September with a sentence of four months' imprisonment for Theodor Fritsch. Once sentence was handed down, he appealed on 22 October for a further review. A last article in *Der Hammer* of May 1927 reports that a revision of the Hamburg district court had allowed him the option of avoiding imprisonment by good conduct. "The offender is paroled until 1 May 1929. If by 1 October 1927 he pays a fine of 1000 marks and also conducts himself peaceably until that date, he shall be spared his sentence."

Fritsch had claimed (falsely) that in 1916 Max Warburg was entrusted with negotiations for a separate truce with Russia, and thus the episode Aby Warburg referred to in his letter to Hans Hertz became a focus of the Hamburg district court's attention in passing sentence. The article in *Der Hammer* had remarked of the Stockholm talks that any German diplomat could have secured a truce, and that "the Jewish banker Max Warburg came home having achieved nothing. The courts must bring light to bear on this darkest point of Germany's wartime history." The court's sentence addressed this passage at length, saying that it presented *Der Hammer*'s *völkisch* readership with harmful "Jewish mismanagement" that they were to think was maliciously motivated. The sentence further remarks, "The author also made the error of saying that the plaintiff took part in the Stockholm conference, although in fact it was his brother Dr. Fritz Warburg. The accused has not brought forth even a scrap of evidence that there was any professional misconduct. The defendant did however submit a letter from another member of the Warburg family, Prof. Warburg, to a certain Hertz in Bremen, wherein Professor Warburg expresses the view that the Stockholm negotiations were the 'detonator' that caused Anglicized Russia to overthrow its old government. If this private opinion of Professor Warburg's is correct, this would not imply any misconduct by the German negotiator, since at the time the outbreak of the Russian Revolution was universally seen as convenient for Germany." The court found that the accused had taken Warburg's participation in the negotiations to imply that they had been deliberately mishandled, that this was a frivolous claim, and that it was a punishable offence.[82]

What is remarkable in the judge's summation here is the detachment with which he assesses the letter as "evidence"—a detachment one could almost call agreeable, if it had not recurred as astonishing indifference and even insouciance in his summing-up, for which he was later rebuked in the appeal hearing:

> This court thus reaches a considerably milder verdict in this case than the previous court. The accused is 73 years old and has been active in the *völkisch* movement for over 40 years. This court finds that the accused holds one-sided opinions. Long habit and old age have strengthened the accused in opinions and feelings that he accepts uncritically, and he is thus unjust and immoderate toward Jewry and the Jews. In the matter under discussion the accused succumbed to the temptation to express his distaste for Jews in a manner exceeding the allowed limits. There is no sentence so severe that it would constrain the accused from holding or from expressing this opinion. The purpose of passing sentence can only be to hold him to greater caution in his *völkisch* activities. [. . . A] fine of 1000 marks therefore seems appropriate.

The verdict makes clear to what extent anti-Semitic rants were seen in a certain context as "normal" and unchangeable, even as not unjustified and certainly not actionable. "One-sided," "long habit," "distaste," "allowed limits": the conciliatory choice of words speaks volumes. In this context, to submit a stolen private letter as evidence does not even provoke a reprimand.

The submission of the letter was also reported in *Der Hammer:* "A high point of the trial came when a letter was read from Professor Dr. Abraham Moritz Warburg, a brother of the plaintiff, which allowed a searching look at the Jewish 'mentality,' especially their view of the 'goyim.' Meanwhile the letter has been published many times, e.g., in the *Deutsches Tageblatt* and in the tireless Alfred Roth's *Reichssturmfahne*[. . . .] It deserves mention in the context of this article because of this striking effect it had on all who heard it, including representatives of the press and the court itself."[83] This comes from an article titled "The Warburg-Fritsch Trial in the German Press" signed by

"Lynkeus"; when he read this passage, Warburg knew that his letter had been published not just in a splinter group's scandal sheet (of which the issues for 1914–30 are still held at the Warburg Institute) but in widely read *völkisch* daily newspapers, and in September 1926 he vainly tried to find a copy of the relevant issue of the *Reichssturmfahne*. From Fritsch's article he took the word "mentality," a term that points directly to the dilemma of wresting Jewish identity from endemic anti-Semitism: "my 'mentality.'"

As Ulrich Rauff has shown, the history of the word "mentality" and its usage is not simply the career of a—sometimes nebulous—term in historical scholarship such as Jacques Le Goff's reconstructive approach; in a decidedly political strand, it is also the history of a "battle-cry."[84] During the Dreyfus affair in France both camps in the dispute ("Church, fatherland, and the army's honor on one side, truth and justice on the other"[85]) used *mentalité* and disputed the use others made of it. The term's imprecision, its synthetic rather than analytical quality, make it a suitable instrument for excluding others just as much as for creating group identity within a shared social culture—as do its undertones of passivity and fatalism. Fritsch twisted the term for invective's sake, putting it together with "Jewish" to make the descriptor "mentality" into a vehicle for what had filled the pages of *Der Hammer* month after month, for decades: concentrated tirades of hatred, accusations, pseudo-scholarly versions of history and hallucinated phantasms of all things Jewish.

Once More: War

As such *Der Hammer* can be compared to the *Türmer*, where the article which prompted Warburg's letter to Hans Hertz was published. In index-card box 36, "Jews," is a separate heading for "Fritz" Warburg, concerning the episode that led to the 1917 letter. A clipping from the *Türmer* shows what it was that Warburg put right for Hans Hertz:

> We have learned that when the Russian delegate who was supposed to take charge of the peace negotiations in Stockholm returned home with nothing accomplished, the conservative press there asked in outrage why it was that Germany had sent the Jew Warburg if it seriously intended to enter negotiations. Herr Warburg is married to a sister of Max Liebermann. Clearly there are ways to place a man

> known and trusted by the Liebermann-Cassirer-Meier-Graefe gang where his recommendation will count for much, and whoever knows the true value of family loyalty as a Jewish virtue, knows too that such ways are well used. Karl Storck.[86]

The pointed innuendo and hateful insinuations of this article explain Warburg's asperity in his verdict on such journalism, in calling its exponents "swine."

There can be no doubt that when Fritz Warburg held talks with a Russian delegation in Stockholm as an unofficial go-between, this episode was blown up out of all proportion by the anti-Semites. Fritz Warburg was in Stockholm as a consultant to the German embassy, and without himself knowing quite how or why, was drawn into overtures made to the vice-president of the Russian duma Alexander Protopopov to discuss the possibility of a separate truce between Russia and Germany. In fact, the possibility of a separate truce collapsed when Germany declared Poland's independence in November 1916. Fritz Warburg did not learn what a complicated foreign-policy intrigue he had been embroiled in until after the war.[87] Aby Warburg's assessment that these talks were the "detonator" that set off the February Revolution thus seems much exaggerated.

Warburg's most provocative phrases are to be found, though, in the second half of the letter, when he talks of "German slanderers [who] must sink much lower" and of "callous, idiotic, and dangerous journalists." He sets a distance between himself and the conservative, *völkisch* brand of chauvinist patriotism, and for the anti-Semites this proves him to be what they always claimed, an outsider and a traitor. Warburg's political convictions and his research interests came together at this moment; one crux was the function and effect of the media in political and ideological conflict, and another was Luther, the "true German man" whose example Warburg evokes in his letter. Warburg's "passionate interest in politics,"[88] as well as his work on "pictorial vehicles" (*Bildervehikel*) and "pictorial slogans" (*Schlagbilder*) is formulated in his 1920 essay, "Pagan-Antique Prophecy in Words and Images in the Age of Luther."

During the First World War Warburg was busy with three large projects: he was interpreting and archiving all printed matter that dealt with the war itself, he was working on astrology in words and images, and he was studying the Reformation.[89] It is now agreed that these three areas of research informed one another, and that the experience of documenting the war made Warburg more alert to the media characteristics of Reformation broadsheets. In all these areas his heroic attention to detail is in polar opposition to the flair for making connections he showed at the same time, and that paradoxically makes insight possible even while hindering it. It is from this position that Warburg writes in the introduction to his essay "Pagan-Antique Prophecy": "That age when logic and magic blossomed, like trope and metaphor, in Jean Paul's words, 'grafted to a single stem,' is inherently timeless: by showing such a polarity in action, the historian of civilization furnishes new grounds for a more profoundly positive critique of a historiography that rests on a purely chronological theory of development."[90] These conjectured anthropological constants underpin the reversal that Warburg described thus in a letter: "disregarding what it might tell us about Luther and his age, an examination of the pictures relating to monsters and omens and their history is the only way to comprehend how imagined atrocities function in this current war. But who can persuade journalists that historical psychology is relevant to present concerns?"[91]

The two timelines intertwine in many ways in Warburg's essay "Pagan-Antique Prophecy." Warburg weaves together past and present not least by deploying vivid pictorial language in a masterly fashion (and seems to relish the challenge of Jean Paul's view that language was only "a dictionary of withered metaphors"). He shows that astrologers in the Reformation era had politically manipulated belief in the stars' influence on the course of history and on the fate of the individual, and presents this belief in "influence" as a timelessly present mixture of fear and anger, a distinctive constant that can form explosively at any point in history. Reactions to the lecture and to its printed version show that others agreed with Warburg in seeing this belief as representative of human destructive potential as such, a potential that he and others mistakenly identified with the "irrational." Gombrich writes that Warburg acted "in common with his time and milieu"[92] in confronting this irrational potential with the figure of Luther, who had lived through the panic over apocalyptic floods yet understood the difference between the speculations of pseudoscientific astrology and real dangers and threats. Warburg cites a Martin Luther whose clear judgment is grounded in a realistic viewpoint, and who ridicules "the astrologers [. . .] who had talked of a deluge or great flood, which was to come in the year 1524, but which did not come to pass; however, in the following 25th year, the peasants rose up in arms. Of which not one astrologer had a single word to say."[93] Warburg though is not concerned to decontextualize Luther historically, as Gombrich seems to say, for he showed that Luther's worldview also had a place for incarnate evil in the literal sense, "for however firmly Luther may have rejected the anthropomorphic planetary spirits, the foul fiend himself remained a vivid and indubitable presence."[94]

Nevertheless Warburg's Luther is like "Cranach's Luther"[95] a figure to be used for projections, a "demonic man" who has a role to play in "the tragic history of freedom of thought of the modern European."[96] The threat of the "irrational" consisted of two aspects of one single substance, each aspect the distorted reflection of the other so that they form an irreconcilable, complementary whole. This was the "dialectic of assimilation"[97] that Liebeschütz discusses—a dialectic whose mechanism was, however, a trap. The "self-chosen place" had to be fought for, and was threatened externally at least as much as internally. "As a Jew I had to wage a bitter campaign on two fronts,"[98] Warburg wrote in 1917 to Lore Strack, the widow of a fellow-student, about his university days in Bonn. In his study "Pagan-Antique Prophecy" Warburg concentrated on Luther and Melanchthon and on their differing attitudes to astrology and "mythological fatalism," thereby sketching a picture that has been much altered since. Yet he recognized the internal contradictions of their personalities, their internal and external conflicts, and this picture of Luther in particular was not only different from that of the majority of his peers, who celebrated Luther as a national hero,[99] it has also been confirmed by later research, when Luther's contradictions no longer had to be disguised.[100]

The Humanist Message of Liberation

A similar case is Warburg's reading of Dürer's master engraving *Melencolia I* as a "consoling, humanist message of liberation."[101] "The truly creative act—that which gives Dürer's *Melencolia I* its consoling, humanistic message of liberation from the fear of Saturn—can be understood only if we recognize that the artist has taken a magical and mythical logic and made it spiritual and intellectual. The malignant, child-devouring planetary god, whose cosmic contest with another planetary ruler seals the subject's fate, is humanized and metamorphosed by Dürer into the image of the thinking, working human being."[102] As a reviewer in the 1920s remarked, *Melencolia I* seems an unusual addition to the "pictorial slogans" that Warburg discusses. A recent and thorough survey of Warburg's interpretation as "entirely isolated in its optimism"[103] in the long history of interpreting this engraving could, however, have paid closer attention to the context within which Warburg developed his reading. His portrait of Luther is just as much symbolic as it is acutely historically aware, and similarly Warburg's iconographic interpretation of each detail of *Melencolia I* leads onward to a general interpretation which leaves each of these details far behind,[104] seeing an apotropaic "consoling, humanistic message of liberation." We do not need to seek the "symptoms of the times" that form Warburg's reading in "the simultaneous development of psychoanalysis with its sensitivity for the threats to human reason."[105] The context of Warburg's *Melencolia* interpretation is political, and it is concerned with the danger that reason might be *manipulated,* regardless of other threats.

Warburg's exegesis of the engraving shows structural similarities to Hartmut Böhme's conclusions in his interpretation of the print describing the intellectual's place today.[106] We are, however, no longer so willing as was Warburg in his essay to trust that the "thinking subject" should also act reasonably—what Warburg called the "thinking, working human being"[107] has since shocked and perturbed us. Warburg's formulation is at once straightforward and militant, "the new ideal of the liberating, conscious energy of the modern individual: man the worker."[108] This is a sober paraphrase of "Renaissance man," which describes the precarious existence of a humanist, scholar, or in a more modern term, the intellectual. Read in these terms, we hear a different tone in the often-quoted "conceptual space of rationality" (*Denkraum*) that "the modern scientist" must try to "struggle for"[109] and that must be "won back." The warlike metaphors might be meant much more literally, and the *conceptual space* might also refer to something more concrete than a mental or intellectual position. Warburg recruits Luther and Dürer once more as his comrades, in a battle that began with his background and biography but that had acquired a larger political significance for Warburg, the cultural historian.

Warburg himself puts "his" Luther into a biographical context, writing to Anna Warburg, the wife of his brother Fritz, about a lecture given on 15 November 1917 to the Hamburg Historical Society, which the *Hamburgischer Correspondent* reported to have been called "Reformation Prophecy in Words and Images in the Age of Luther."[110] Warburg writes, "Very few people present understood the main idea, yet they were the ones who count," and continues, "My approach to Luther is nothing new: although I hardly count as a by-the-book Lutheran, I nevertheless owe him a great deal for my protest against Orthodox Judaism, which wished to enslave me with its idiotic justification by works; as a young man (15–18) I often found the strength I needed in his fearlessness."[111] It is not the "whole Luther" who is invoked here, and certainly not Lutheranism; it is the Luther who had said, "Though the world were full of devils," the courageous and bellicose Luther thanks to whose example Warburg dared to be bold.

Certainly Warburg found periods of cease-fire in his "war on two fronts," but he had to wait until late in life for anything resembling peace. "I have kept the faith" was the motto for later life, which Warburg wrote, in Greek, in his journal on his forty-fourth birthday in 1910.[112] This verse from the Bible (II Timothy 4:7) runs in full: "I have fought a good fight, I have finished my course, I have kept the faith" (King James Version). One could hardly think of a motto more ambiguous, symbol-laden, forthright, and ironically broken.

A Safe Stronghold, a Mighty Fortress

Warburg's research interests can be related in many ways to his Hamburg origin, his religion, and his intellectual disposition. He took whatever was useful for the creation of cultural science from art history, from the study of religion, from Classical studies and from psychology, and he made a serviceable instrument with which to address problems and questions he had developed at an early stage. It has also been remarked that Warburg's writings can be read as though they were a single text, the chapters of one book.[113] Some of these chapters have a subtext, not openly articulated, upon which the archive and private communications shed light.

Following Warburg himself, his early religious and psychological conflict has recently been traced alongside its consequences, as a constant that runs through his whole work. These inquiries were the result of a fundamental dissatisfaction with a distanced, historicizing study of art history.[114] Warburg asked about the memory encoded into pictures; he asked about the social and psychological function of antique forms, about the mediality of tapestry and broadsheets, about the relationship of fine art to applied art, about language and images—to name but a few key words. The strength of his methods and his research may be that we can (and should) know how these questions are connected to the scholar's own life, and in this case we need to look at the connections between life and work in the way Hans Liebeschütz has proposed. Theodor Fritsch submitted a letter in the 1917 trial that shows in an exemplary manner how Warburg's research was connected to the present day, and this in turn shows that racist anti-Semitism forms a dark background that must be included in our view of Warburg's work.

Warburg worked to include art historians in academic institutions; he worked to found Hamburg University, and worked for his Kulturwissenschaftliche Bibliothek above all. The library journal not least shows that all endeavors were in part an answer to the challenge that anti-Semitism posed and that he saw clearly—as not all did. From about 1904 he began to change his "arsenal" into a "laboratory," and the building dedicated in 1926 made into bricks and mortar, a safe house, an institution with a public role, what had until then been located between the private realm and the public sphere.

It might not be too far-fetched to see these bricks and mortar in relation to the tower of wisdom behind Dürer's *Melencolia*, which Warburg never called anything more than a "wall."[115] It might be more fruitful to see in them a modern fortress, offering protection, breathing room, and an arsenal to reason, threatened from all sides.[116] Warburg's activism and organizational work in the politics of culture was alien neither to his interest in cultural science nor to his art historical research. Both respond equally to a challenge that was experienced on a personal level but—perceptively—interpreted in a broader political context.[117] Anti-Semitism remains a shadowy opponent here: in many ways it was difficult to confront it, not least because such a confrontation could only have been demeaning. Put simply, Warburg's double answer to a dual provocation was that an art historian must work to show how pictures and texts take effect, must understand how they are transmitted in the realm of human "pure unreason,"[118] and this work is necessary to the enlightenment project. Only thus can the antidote be found in the poison, a topos frequently taken up since the eighteenth century and going back to Antiquity. And this work needs to be fostered and encouraged, for only slowly and with difficulty does it lead to any practical result. It can only survive when it becomes an institution, finds a home, and has an effect on the public. Walter M. Solmitz was a student and fellow at the K.B.W. in Hamburg from 1927 to 1933 and was later (1939/40) with the Warburg Institute in London as a refugee. Looking back, he wrote of the library that "it was a very fine feeling to be able to say, 'Our Warburg is a bulwark'[119]—but we should not feel ourselves to be safe, and should not mistake the *genius loci* for the *locus genii*." He thus captures exactly the political pragmatism that was born both of experience and idealism.

6

The Abstraction of Science and the Concreteness of Religion

In August 1926 Fritz Saxl wrote a long letter to Paul M. Warburg reporting on the past two years, during which Warburg had once again established himself in Hamburg as a scholar. The heart of the letter is a detailed description of the circumstances surrounding Warburg's research on Rembrandt.[1] Saxl calls the synthesis that Warburg achieved while preparing the Rembrandt lecture "a miracle." Reading the text of the lecture shows that when dealing with new material that he had not already been ruminating for decades, Warburg was able to express his theoretical assumptions and methodological procedure with unprecedented clarity. The Rembrandt lecture already formulates the theoretical and methodological basis of the great picture-atlas project.[2]

"What you call the spirit of the age is really no more than the spirit of the worthy historian in which the age reflects itself": Warburg began the lecture by saying that these words from Goethe's *Faust* should be fixed above the desk of every scholar who engages with the problems of cultural history. He goes on to say that historicism can take either of two paths out of this dilemma, one direct and one indirect, "to counter this accusation." The direct way is to bring together documents from all aspects of an historical period (figurative art and drama, religious practice, and literature) and let them throw light on one another. The historian can "thereby eliminate the self as the main source of error from the investigation of these connections between word, action and image."[3] The second, indirect way is to use "an objective constant in the heritage of antiquity" to reveal "the subjective record in the mirror of different epochs, even when these believe themselves to be entirely objective." This record will allow us to "use comparative psychology to observe how time selects and changes, and read this as the supra-personal function of an internally consistent evolutionary process that is to a great extent sociologically conditioned."[4] Warburg expounds this dual strategy in his Rembrandt lecture, and it provides the theoretical framework for the picture-atlas project *Mnemosyne,* which began to take clearer shape at the time. In both cases it is true that while Warburg's texts claim that their goals are determined by the immanent demands of scholarship, a political background is also at work that does not only explain Warburg's urgency in some of his arguments but also makes clear what Warburg's "historicism" argues in favor of, and what it argues against.

Warburg's Rembrandt Lecture

As Saxl reported, the lecture had a long and difficult gestation. Warburg first had numerous photographs taken in Amsterdam, which proved expensive and logistically challenging, and then bought books in all possible relevant fields:

> The first year's acquisitions were very numerous. One felt that the hand on the tiller was not yet entirely confident, but that some measure of convalescent strength could be seen in these purchases. Among these acquisitions was above all an entire library of Dutch books on the 17th century; not a library purchased at once, but one bought bit by bit and that seemed to be very odd at first. Along with a great deal about Rembrandt, there was much on pageantry, much history, much art history etc. At the end of the year we had a wonderful Dutch library, a toolkit for addressing problems of cultural history from Rembrandt's time such as no other library in Germany has assembled.[5]

On 29 May 1926 Warburg gave that lecture in the reading room of the Kulturwissenschaftliche Bibliothek on Rembrandt's use of Italian antiquity.[6] The impetus may have come from Fritz Saxl,[7] the true Rembrandt specialist, who had already published an article on Rembrandt

Foyer of the Kulturwissenschaftliche Bibliothek Warburg
with Rembrandt's draft for *Oath of Claudius Civilis* (greatly enlarged)
above the reading room entrance, 1926. Universität Hamburg,
Kunstgeschichtliches Seminar, Warburg-Archiv.

in 1924[8] and taught a seminar on Rembrandt in 1926,[9] and who would go on to publish (1939) and lecture (1941) on iconographic questions in Rembrandt's paintings.[10] Certainly the "iconologists" have tended to work on Rembrandt a good deal, among them Wolfgang Stechow and William Heckscher. Erwin Panofsky had also lectured on Rembrandt and Jewry a few years before, in 1920, although this lecture was only published posthumously in 1973.[11]

Warburg's Rembrandt lecture concentrated on three works on themes from classical mythology and history, *The Rape of Proserpina,*[12] *The Conspiracy of Claudius Civilis,*[13] and the engraving *Medea.*[14] His central question was, "Which elements of the classical heritage interested the age of Rembrandt so intensely that they molded the style of its artistic creations?"[15] Gombrich has shown that although he had hardly worked on Rembrandt before, Warburg very quickly assimilated what was for him new material with great concentration and brought it to bear on his methodological questions. All three works under examination diverged from traditional composition, and the lecture leads to an ever stronger argument for understanding Rembrandt's works through this difference from Italian tradition.

Warburg made Rembrandt's deliberate detachment the center of his lecture: the clear, rational, yet also ethically grounded choice between the mode of (hollow) pathos that Warburg saw exemplified in the prints of Antonio Tempesta of which Rembrandt made use, and the mode of ethical seriousness, the portrayal in monumental art of the significant, morally fraught moment. Warburg doubly interprets Rembrandt's reception of Italy and antiquity (which also came to him via the festival and the pageant); the pictures themselves always show "the moment of reflection before action rather than action itself"[16] in compositionally and iconographically innovative ways. The artist Rembrandt had also paused to reflect, and in this moment of thought and choice had taken from all the available modes of representation those that could meet his need for detachment.

Gombrich shows that in this lecture Warburg had emphasized the "element of personal choice and responsibility in the face of tradition."[17] At least three plates for Warburg's picture-atlas *Mnemosyne* also date to 1926 and should be seen in the context of the lecture: these are plates 71–73, which document homage through lifting the lord on a shield, the conspiracy of Claudius Civilis, and Medea, with about twenty pictures for each theme. These plates probably date to after the lecture, as we can see from an entry in the library journal. "27 August 926: picture-atlas on Claudius Civilis."[18]

Gombrich remarks not unfairly that Warburg "adapted [Rembrandt's art] to his ways of thinking"[19] and that his lecture presented a highly subjective interpretation. This however is the rule rather than the exception in the context of the uncommonly intense reception of Rembrandt at the time,[20] which was mostly nonacademic and against which we have to set Warburg's contribution. The cult of genius surrounding Rembrandt seems practically to have demanded high-flown and superlative speech, especially in popularizing, nonspecialist literature and in lectures; this can be heard even in Panofsky's 1920 text on Rembrandt. The tradition of Rembrandt studies at work here can be traced back first and foremost to the work of Wilhelm Bode, who as

Rembrandt van Rijn, *Oath of Claudius Civilis,* drawing, 1661. Photo by Martina Bienenstien. Graphische Sammlung, Munich.

long ago as the 1880s had pronounced Rembrandt to be the exemplary Nordic artist. Even in his treatment of Netherlandish painting in its entirety, which no longer politically characterizes Rembrandt's painting as "above all *national* and *of the people,*" Bode starts out by saying, "In Germany, nowadays, people like to claim Rembrandt as a German. True it is that he comes of a pure Teutonic stock, and that his art is thoroughly Teutonic. It is altogether the most powerful expression of Teutonic culture, which has no more perfect representative among its artists."[21] Starting as it does from racial and *völkisch* criteria, this characterization of Rembrandt's art refers indirectly to the anonymous 1890 book *Rembrandt the Teacher, by a German* (*Rembrandt als Erzieher. Von einem Deutschen*) which Bode had favorably reviewed in the *Preussische Jahrbücher* in March of 1890, albeit with some reservations.[22]

Rembrandt the Teacher

Warburg certainly knew about the widespread political connotations of Rembrandt's image: in 1926, the year of his lecture, the Kulturwissenschaftliche Bibliothek purchased half its holdings of works by and about August Julius Langbehn (1851–1907),[23] the "Rembrandt German" and notorious author of the equally notorious anonymous work of 1890, *Rembrandt the Teacher.*[24] There are sixteen such books in the library, and although some of them appeared before 1926, none were acquired before this date; the remaining eight volumes were bought later, the last in 1934. It is typical for Warburg's working methods that he should "incorporate" into his library elements pertaining to any project once undertaken—in this case the coveted copy of *Claudius Civilis* from Stockholm forms one extreme,[25] and the small collection of works on *Rembrandt the Teacher* forms the other. On the one hand the morally fraught, venerated picture, on the other the "enemy one must know."[26]

Langbehn himself admitted that he had not chosen Rembrandt as the protagonist of his book out of any particular fondness for the artist:[27] he rather used the name Rembrandt to put a "label" on his free association and pseudo-mystical diatribe. This would tie in with the established ideological and political image of Rembrandt, which in turn would immediately evoke the associations he wanted. Langbehn also liked to see himself as a doctor prescribing the necessary medicine—Rembrandt—to the German people.[28] Langbehn's book is hard to characterize, being organized into *Leitgedanken* ("trains of thought") that bring Rembrandt's example to bear on all kinds of "decadent" phenomena in Germany. There are sections on Rembrandt as a teacher for I. German art, II. German scholarship, III. German politics, IV. German education, V. German humanity.[29] Langbehn's book is primarily and programmatically antimodern; it is markedly reactionary, *völkisch,* anti-Semitic and anti-intellectual. Bernd Behrendt has most recently marshaled telling quotes on such themes as "the Artificial Age," mystic religion, pan-German racist nationalism, "Jewry," "the social question," criticism of contemporary culture, anti-Naturalism and anti-Impressionism, anti-rationalism, anti-industrialism, and anti-metropolitanism.[30]

The book was hugely successful and went through twelve printings in five-and-a-half months.[31] Over the years it had more than seventy printings and was reviewed many times, often enthusiastically; it was also frequently revised by Langbehn himself and after his death by his "squire" Benedikt Momme Nissen. With hindsight such success is barely explicable, and can only be stated. The success of *völkisch* anti-Semitism could yet be explained along these lines: "Germany at the end of the nineteenth century was the European country in which the drive to secularization had been most rapidly successful, and it can be seen as a huge laboratory for the social irrationalism which we now understand was a product of failed secularism."[32] Otto Modersohn enthusiastically took up *Rembrandt the Teacher* in the spirit in which it had been written, as did Cornelius Gurlitt, who reviewed the book several times; so did Hans Thoma and, more moderately, Wilhelm Bode.[33] "When we open the Rembrandt book for the first time, a fume comes from it as though from a dark cave or a steam bath. If we persevere then we come through the other side, washed, massaged and clean."[34] Quite so: the "text without language" indeed gives off some kind of fume.[35] If there is any cleansing at work then it is that in the innumerable minds on whom the book had its effect, we recognize those whom Warburg sought to treat with his own antidote of enlightenment.[36]

"From Langbehn and Chamberlain Back to Kant and Fichte"[37]

Warburg's lecture can be read as a riposte to Langbehn's distortion, which stylizes Rembrandt as a prophet of introspection: "Rembrandt's inwardness is far-reaching. One might say that in many of his paintings he is more prophet than poet; he seeks spirit more on the dark side of being than on its light side. He has a large measure of true religiosity, that deeply German quality. He shows us Bible stories as we had imagined them when we were children; he speaks for the people in artistic matters, and what artist would wish, or could wish, to be more than this?"[38] Warburg by contrast sees Rembrandt as a hesitant genius—as, for instance, in his description of Proserpina: "But the most telling change concerns the horses; they no longer gallop in the showy grand manner—every lock of their mane befitting a *dux*. Instead they sweep into the abyss of the underworld. [. . .] Rembrandt's new matter-of-factness [*neue Sachlichkeit*] overcame the hollow classical *pathos formula* which, deriving from fifteenth-century Italy, dominated the superlatives of Europe's gesture-language."[39] In this respect Warburg compares Rembrandt to Dürer, whom he also sees as having resisted Italian pathos formulae.[40]

Two phrases are striking in this passage on the *Rape of Proserpina*,[41] characteristic of the new language in which Warburg speaks out against the "Rembrandt German," and characteristic of the different world for which he speaks. When he refers to the expressive content of the manes in Antonio Tempesta's engraving of the Rape,[42] he sees an attitude in these "accessories in motion" which he characterizes as "every lock of their mane befitting a *dux*." We might think that we hear a mild sarcasm; the ideology of the *Führer* had long been at large and is equally spoofed here.[43] He confronts it with "Rembrandt's new objectivity," a matter-of-fact attitude that was also a leitmotif for the Kulturwissenschaftliche Bibliothek[44] and as characterization, an ideal in conscious opposition to dark, inward, "Germanic" prophecy. Where so-called Homeland Art (*Heimatkunst*) stood for all those reactionary values that defined themselves as anti-values,[45] the term "New Objectivity" (*Neue Sachlichkeit*), first used by Gustav Hartlaub in 1923, stood for modernity, for internationalism and a productive affirmation of the industrial age.[46] Warburg's choice of words reflects an awareness of the threatening situation in politics and the politics of the art world. *Völkisch* pan-Germanism appropriated tradition, and he thus confronted it on its own ground, questioning what the Nordic element was, whether its iconography truly had been taken independently from folk art, in short asking the sophisticated questions that professional art history asks in analyzing a picture.

Langbehn addresses Rembrandt's use of the classical tradition under the heading "Modernity versus antiquity." Here we read,

> Since Rembrandt's art so thoroughly forbears Greek serenity, Greek moderation, and Greek calm, in Greek terms it is perhaps the strongest barbarism there ever has been; but this art is also the finest barbarism there ever has been. Therefore

> since we are barbarians and always shall be, we Germans should take it as a pattern for *German* art and teachings. The bright morning star of Greek art is countered by the twilit night sky of Nordic art, and it is hard to decide which of these heavens is the higher: day has its charms just as does night. Phenomena come and go in the heavens above us just as they do in the heavens within us; it is the dance of the Graces—which does not end.[47]

Langbehn here steers clear of any facts, instead tossing about sundry metaphors while also introducing "barbarism" as a virtue and a value.[48] Warburg counters this with Rembrandt's "bitter sobriety," and with his own:

> Rembrandt's "Claudius Civilis" symbolizes the refusal of a genius to be tempted into Romanizing rhetoric or theatrical posturing, either by the memories of other words and images from classical tales about one's own early past or by the tangible immediacy of tableaus and plays. The fact that the bitter sobriety of this picture of revenge did not find favor with the gentlemen of the Town Hall only goes to prove that then, just as at any other time or in any other country in Europe, those who want their art to serve the festive mood of certain occasions are reluctant to face the demanding challenge of a stirring experience.[49]

In this last sentence "then, just as at any other time or in any other country in Europe" Warburg recalls the challenge that public political art holds for the client and the artist,[50] and recalls his own battle over the mural paintings in the newly built Hamburg city hall in 1907.[51]

At this juncture the relevance to current events becomes explicit, while Warburg trusts the strength of argument to reveal the insight that historical study makes possible:

> Those artists who demand of their public that they should respond to a desperate concentration of mental energies in the face of an uncertain, dangerous future, and that they should feel compassion for the eternal problem of Hamlet, the agonies of conscience between reflex-movement and re-

> flective behavior—whether these are embedded in the moral appeal of Medea or of Claudius Civilis, transformed into ethical cult images—such artists will always have to risk being ousted by the purveyors of a triumphant acceptance of the present day and age. But the day of resurrection in the circle of seekers dawned, as it did for the hesitant Medea thanks to Lessing, so also for Rembrandt's Claudius Civilis.[52]

And yet Warburg agrees with cultural criticism of his time in his concluding, pessimistic remark: "Every age has the renaissance of antiquity it deserves."[53] The two "doctors," Langbehn and Warburg, are quite different from one another, yet from time to time we hear curious resonances between their texts, as when in the pictorial strategy of seventeenth-century painters, or in metaphor, the polarization of light and dark is described as a cosmic principle. Warburg's insistence on a moment of reflection and responsible choice does not acknowledge that this moment can be exploited, and has been exploited, to transform "phobic" reactions into consciously counter-rational action. As Elie Kedourie points out, "Kant argued powerfully that conscience is the final arbiter of morality. But he did not allow for the paradoxical and dangerous possibility that self-legislation, restrained by nothing but itself, can adopt evil as its own good."[54]

In 1926 Warburg was busy with another project alongside his research on Rembrandt, the design of a stamp that would be a token of autonomy and would fulfill the demands he had formulated while working on Cladius Civilis.[55] The two projects, research and design, seem unrelated at first, but finally took shape in the library's public work. Warburg brought them together in a summary of the year 1926, which he wrote down at the end of the year. "The central problem, 'realist style or symbolic style,' is the *tertium comparationis* which connects my stamp with Claudius Civilis. We can show how the sublime classical style of a token of sovereignty is usurped by the emblem of currency value that has its own dynamic. In Italy the classical has become a trademark [fasces] and this lays bare their mania for power: set against this Strohmeyer's 'Idea Vincit'[56] is the protest of the 'unpractical' idea."[57] In this balancing summation Warburg effortlessly relates the question of style—at the time art history's single central question as a discipline—to those realms concerned with content, and ultimately with political action.

Neumann's Rembrandt

We might ask whether Langbehn was really to be taken seriously as an opponent in 1926, since the apogee of his influence had passed with the end of the nineteenth century. There is some truth in this but Carl Neumann, author of the most important Rembrandt monograph of the time, summed up Langbehn's influence as follows:

> To me the book seems deceptive because it confuses two different systems of thought and two different purposes. The author was not a disciplined mind, or a strong personality capable of exercising judgment; he was rather a good listener who heard the several slogans of opposition and instinctively brought them together; his enormous success can perhaps be explained because he had brought under one banner so many divisions that had until then skirmished indifferently. No matter that his command was unlikely and even unfitted, it was an effective onslaught. Many now believe that the book has sunk into deserved oblivion. I do not share this opinion. The book was very influential and if we no longer speak of it much, this is only because so much of its thought has passed into common currency and is now taken for granted. The author was right about many things, and although his premises often seem odd to us, we nevertheless accept the conclusions[. . . .] Alongside the painter as dedicated artist and the reformer of the Church, we were shown a German bringing us his message and mission, which was to stir us more deeply than the rest of mankind. *Rembrandt the Teacher* is not a work of art history. Yet the study of art would profit from listening to what the book sincerely has to say, and by taking Rembrandt's example to heart so that it enriches our art and our life.[58]

Neumann's verdict on Langbehn could hardly be clearer. Intellectually and academically the book is worthless for Rembrandt scholarship, but its ideology of the German, *völkisch*, Germanic Rembrandt had struck home with the majority of readers, as Neumann believed. The political tenets of Neumann's Rembrandt monograph become yet clearer in the section on Simmel's Rembrandt, a monograph that had appeared in

1916 and that in his revision of the second printing in 1922 Neumann criticized strongly in detail and in concept.[59] He grants that the philosopher is "ingenious" and has "dialectical virtuosity" but he demands "real facts" in a way that he had not from Langbehn:

> It is not just the author who works in the dark: the reader also loses the thread, for a cocoon of thought shrouds the subject and seeks to anchor its web on far-flung philosophical concepts. We lose sight of reality. Further to this is a particular cast of mind in today's reader. The terrible events of recent history have bred indifference to reality and fact. So much that we thought real has become a dream and melted into air. This indifference to or even contempt for facts and data makes it easy to fly from truth rather than coming to terms with it. And thus the rabble-rousers come, who instead of concrete truths offer a "philosophy" of things, of history, of art, of biography—a philosophy of Rembrandt.[60]

Warburg would have agreed in principle with this criticism of Simmel. In a conversational letter to his friend Schwedeler-Meyer he wrote about Georg Simmel (probably apropos the work on Rembrandt), "Simmel is so clever that he comes out the other side, and becomes stupid. I can't actually read him, but am nevertheless convinced that he is a very fine mind. Gundolf has a much healthier appetite for facts and his work on Goethe breaks new ground."[61] This glancing criticism, however, shows how Warburg's view differed from Neumann's: he does not object to the ingenious, the erudite, the speculative—unlike Neumann he does not decry intellectualism. Neumann forgives Langbehn those same faults for which he denounces Simmel as a "rabble-rouser," and this shows the ulterior motives of a scholarship draped in a mantle of "factuality." Here too we might see the primary cause for Warburg's insistence that the scholar's subjectivity must be excluded from cultural science as a source of error.

In January 1927, Warburg drafted a long letter to Neumann, in which he attempted to enlarge the "Teutonic" Rembrandt with aspects which he had uncovered:

> Trusting in your understanding and consideration as a colleague I shall sketch out for you my viewpoint; it is that the

> classical heritage functions as a memory for Europe's mentality, and as I see it we can no more take sides for or against the classical world than a doctor may distinguish between "clean or unclean ailments." To confront the classical heritage is thus to see the symptom of a *necessitas* that exists apart from the individual, and that intervenes in our every attempt consciously to orient our intellect; once we realize this, we have reached that Archimedean point where we need no longer concern ourselves with the binary choices of practical, ethical aesthetics. This is not to preach a passivity that would idolize and revere the classical heritage: quite the opposite, national character can only prove itself to be tempered steel when it has confronted pagan culture in the full knowledge of how alien it is. Details of body and place are only sides in the parallelogram of forces; in my view it is the historian's task to find how the diagonals of this parallelogram lie, and to test their stability. We thus return—indirectly—to Jacob Burckhardt: there is a psychic parallelogram whose two sides are the Germanic, oblivious of the self, a restless drive for freedom in the infinite, and the restless submission to established classical forms. Its diagonal is the object of awed gratitude, which is the peculiar justification for your exemplary style of scrupulous criticism.[62]

In a remark referring to our contemporary concerns, Hans Belting has pointed out that "it is not for nothing that we talk so gladly about the presence of the Other, since it exonerates us."[63] We know from Börries von Münchhausen's letter that at that time, to talk of the "Other" was to talk of Jews, who made possible that particularly virulent nineteenth-century construction of the "Germanic" and all that came with it—such as Rembrandt. When Warburg proffers the "alterity of pagan culture" as an objective measure of specific, national qualities, this may have been in the existential hope of exoneration.

Absent Images

All during his lifetime, Aby Warburg watched and recorded the movement of anti-Semitism and the spread of *völkisch* racism. Although he only acknowledged a political side to himself after the First World War had begun,[64] the archive material speaks quite clearly long before this date. We can see traces of a silent struggle in the published works as well, even if his answers to questions of art history and history of culture always aim to generalize. However, Warburg never addressed the theme of anti-Semitism and Jew-hating as a pictorial tradition, nor as far as we can tell did he ever collect any meaningful amount of material on this theme. There are only scattered individual images depicting anti-Jewish themes in the Warburg Institute's archive and in its collection of photographs assembled in the Hamburg era—for instance, the legend of Jewish desecration of the Host or ritual murders, both central to this theme. We need have no doubts in concluding that Warburg and the Kulturwissenschaftliche Bibliothek did not systematically collect such material.

Considering the particular historical and personal conditions under which Warburg lived and worked and that we have so far explored, this void is not merely explicable: it is entirely logical given his attempt to resolve counter-Enlightenment paradoxes by means of his great institutional project of cultural science. This void can be explained as a blind spot that was not Warburg's alone, for although there was an anti-Semitic tradition in texts and pictures related to Saturn in the planetary iconography of humors, this was not examined in any publication issuing from the Kulturwissenschaftliche Bibliothek or its circle. The same texts and pictures that Warburg studied in his essay on pagan-antique prophecy, and which Fritz Saxl and Erwin Panofsky examined in their work on Saturn, could also be used to study the negative image of Jews, as Eric Zafran showed in a 1979 article for the *Journal of the Warburg and Courtauld Institutes.*[65]

We can record a few exceptions relevant to the question of whether anti-Semitism truly was an active force in Warburg's life and work; these are three works from the fifteenth century that show Jews profaning the Host, included in the picture-atlas *Mnemosyne.* They are a predella by Paolo Uccello (1397–1475) in Urbino, whose six scenes show a desecration of the Host and the punishment of the culprits[66]—on plate 28/29—and two woodcuts on the same theme from a German and an Italian incunabula on plate 79. Quantitatively, they hardly count for anything among the total volume of a thousand or so reproductions.[67] Presumably, however, the context of the material within the picture-atlas can tell us what value he saw in them in relation to his large-scale and last project.

Picture-atlas Mnemosyne, plate 28/29. Foto Warburg Institute, London.

Picture-Atlas

In the late 1920s the new library building and sustained work alongside Fritz Saxl and Gertrud Bing had made it possible for Warburg to embark upon a synthesis of his life's work in the picture-atlas. Warburg died while at work on this, and the *Mnemosyne* remained a fragment. It has nevertheless been a particular focus of research interest for some time now, and the subject of several publications.[68] In 1929 Warburg wrote an "Introduction to the picture-atlas *Mnemosyne*," put into typescript by Gertrud Bing, which was first published in 1992.[69] An edition of the plates for the picture-atlas and their accompanying texts has appeared since the German edition of the present work.[70] It is not immediately clear what the *Mnemosyne* actually is; attempts to characterize it have mostly been metaphorical, and span from a "symphony,"[71] through a rhetorically schooled assembly of *loci classici*,[72] to "constellations."[73] By contrast we know a fair amount about the project's genesis and its several metamorphoses in the years after 1924. Gombrich reports that it was Fritz Saxl who introduced to Warburg those metal frames with black burlap stretched over them, on which pictures could easily be fixed for display and just as easily removed.[74] Rows and clusters of pictures could thereby be assembled, altered, and rearranged according to any conceivable principle. Warburg enthusiastically took to this visual aid, using it for the various exhibitions that took place in the Kulturwissenschaftliche Bibliothek in the 1920s as well as for his lectures. In this phase up to 1925, there is as yet no talk of an atlas, a work with plates. The new tool's potential for demonstrating the methods of cultural science must have become ever more apparent though. At least in the Warburg library, the technology available to art historical lectures did not even extend to double projection,[75] which has since become indispensable for showing comparative evidence to accompany one's art historical argument. Compared to this, the possibility of displaying twenty or more reproductions alongside one another was a new way of looking, one that allowed the speaker to present the widest possible range of arguments and thematic topics.[76] It was well suited for exhibitions, such as were tested out on a smaller scale in the library, planned for the Deutsches Museum and installed for the Hamburg planetarium: but it was less suited to lectures since, as Gombrich remarks in passing,[77] the reproductions were then too small—hence the idea of a work with plates and accompanying text. The library journals are once again of great importance for the chronology of the picture-atlas's development: they mention nine different stages of work on the assemblage between March 1928 and October 1929.[78] In May 1928 and in the latter months of 1929, weeks before Warburg's death, all of the screens were photographed. There are copious files of notes for the project, containing numerous variant titles for the whole project[79] and for individual plates.[80] For the last series of assemblages, which Warburg worked on until his death, Peter van Huisstede has suggested a division into five broad groups: introduction (A, B, C); antiquity (1–8); the period from antiquity to the Renaissance (20–27); Renaissance (28/29–64); conclusion (70–79). Where the "themes" of individual plates cannot be confidently identified from Warburg's writings or lectures they are still uncertain, since these themes are situated at very different levels of investigation and abstraction. The extreme breadth of possible contextualization for a given theme becomes obvious when we look at plates 28/29 and plate 79.

Host Desecration

On Easter Sunday 1290 a Jew was arrested in Paris on the charge of having profaned the Host in the Rue des Jardins. In 1294 this case gave rise to an elaborate narrative in a Ghent chronicle, which reported that a Jew had obtained the Host from his housemaid and, together with other Jews, attacked it with knives and other weapons. The Host supposedly broke into three pieces and bled ceaselessly. At this, many of the Jews assembled there were said to have converted. When the Host was then cooked in a cauldron it did not dissolve but changed to flesh and blood. Thereupon, more of the Jews were converted.[81]

This story bears all the marks of a genre of legends connected to the Eucharistic controversy, which became especially numerous after the Feast of Corpus Christi was introduced in 1264.[82] Impressed by the miracle of the Host at the Mass in Bolsena, Urban IV saw to it that this new liturgical festival was introduced for the Church at large. In the course of the thirteenth century a great number of miracles are reported about Hosts which bleed, turn to flesh, or transform themselves either into a crucifix or into a child, and these are mostly seen in the context of the Fourth Lateran Council's decision (1215) to make Catholic dogma of the doctrines of transubstantiation and the Real Presence of Christ's body in the Eucharist. The same council decreed that Jews and Saracens were obliged to wear distinct clothing.[83] When the first records of a Jew profaning the Host came from Paris at the end of the century, this gave rise to legends that spread through chronicles in Germany, in Central and Southern Europe, acquiring new motifs and details along the way—the Jewish culprit becomes, for instance, a moneylender—and which resulted in numerous accusations, trials, and executions, and subsequently in the expulsion of Jews from their communities. In the mid-fifteenth century a mystery play dramatizing Jew-

Anonymous. *Desecration of the Host.* Woodcut from *Rappresentazione d'un Miracolo del Corpo di Christo,* Florence, ca. 1500. *Left:* Jewish usurers take possession of a Host; *right:* Jews jab and cook the Host. Universität Hamburg, Kunstgeschichtliches Seminar, Warburg-Archiv.

ish profanation of the Host was written. This drama is preserved in three slightly different variants in French, English, and Italian.[84] The Italian version of the play is the most significant text for Paolo Uccello's predella with a few details added from other sources. A version printed in Florence in 1498 contains the woodcut that was used for plate 79.[85] A Host profanation supposed to have taken place in Sternberg in Mecklenburg in 1492 was reported in several broadsheets of the same year,[86] among them the Lübeck print that also provided an illustration for plate 79.

The fourteenth century was the apogee of blood libel and resultant persecutions of the Jews. Following the great epidemics, Jews were persecuted, killed, and expelled from towns everywhere except in Austria and Bohemia. After these excesses blood libel became rarer for a while, until in the fifteenth century it once again reached its previous level; seven desecrations of the Host and nineteen ritual murders, spread all across Europe geographically and often had repercussions well beyond the locality where they supposedly had taken place. The new media of woodcut, broadsheet, and printed books furthermore brought a new way of broadcasting such cases; already familiar accusations could be conjured up at any time and thus attained a new currency since they could be put into pictures in such a versatile medium.[87] In the sixteenth century, charges brought for alleged profanations of the Host were hardly ever successful in court. Unlike the charge of ritual murder Host desecration was not revived for anti-Semitic propaganda purposes in the nineteenth century. Nevertheless the memory of this accusation against the Jews never died away: as late as the inflation crisis of 1922 an emergency banknote was issued in Sternberg showing the 1492 woodcut with the inscription "2) The Jews of the town of Sternberg desecrate the Host. 20 July 1492."[88]

In the Warburg archive there are only two documents on the profanation of the Host, and it does not seem to have been an especially important theme. Warburg was interested in the origin and meaning of a particularly widely distributed folio, describing in twelve scenes and a long text a charge of Host desecration against Jews in Passau, their trial, execution, and expulsion.[89] A newspaper cutting from 1912 with the title "A medieval prosecution" reports about a young man who had vomited after taking Communion and was thus accused of blasphemy in court of law; he was sentenced but later pardoned.[90] The reproduction of the woodcut on plate 79 in the picture-atlas showing the Jews of Sternberg probably comes from the 1927 *Jüdisches Lexikon,* where it illustrates the entry on "Desecration of the Host."[91] There can be little doubt that the facts summed up here also informed the way images related to this theme were placed in the picture-atlas.

Cassoni

Paolo Uccello's predella from Urbino is surrounded on plate 28/29 by reproductions related to it on several levels. Pictures 1 and 2 are reproductions from painted wedding chests (cassoni), showing a tournament and a horse race. Picture 3 is a facsimile from Apollonio di Giovanni's studio ledger, pictures 4 and 5 are a detail—an apothecary—and full view of a further cassone showing a particular moment of the Feast of Saint John in Florence. Picture 6 shows a roundel in the Palazzo del Tè

Anonymous, "Sterneberch Van den bosen ioden volget hyr ein gheschicht Dar to van den sulven eyn merklik ghedicht" (Of the evil Jews a tale now is told; also on the same a memorable poem) woodcut. Lübeck: Matthäus Brandis, 1494. Universität Hamburg, Kunstgeschichtliches Seminar, Warburg-Archiv.

from Giulio Romano's decoration scheme for the Camera dei Venti, which also shows an apothecary (a *Serpentario*). Next come Saint George slaying the dragon by Paolo Uccello, from the London National Gallery, picture 7, and Uccello's cassone of a hunting scene, from the Ashmolean Museum, picture 8, followed by six further reproductions of works by Uccello. Pictures 9–11 show three views from the battle of San Romano in which Florence defeated Siena. Pictures 12–14 each reproduce two scenes from the predella, although the second and third pairs of scenes come out of sequence. The three last pictures, 15–17, show the rape of the Sabine women and the reconciliation of the Sabines and Romans, from a cassone in the Harewood Collection, along with the Adimari wedding, on a cassone in the Accademia in Florence. We thus have six cassoni in seven pictures, all reproduced in Paul Schubring's annotated edition on the genre,[92] and nine further reproductions of paintings on wood or frescoes, eight of them by Paolo Uccello's hand. Since Warburg's time, these cassoni have almost without exception been attributed to the workshop of Apollonio di Giovanni,[93] so his decision to show a page from the studio ledger in this plate of the picture-atlas seems almost prophetic; Schubring had published this ledger with Warburg's annotations.[94] The material assembled here is from the mid-fifteenth century and mostly Florentine, except for the *Serpentario,* today attributed to Agostino da Mozzanega,[95] and concentrates first on a particular genre, painted wedding chests from the early Florentine Renaissance, and second on the work of Paolo Uccello. Apart from the predella itself, all the works reproduced here are discussed in greater detail in Warburg's published works, even if only in footnotes.

As we examine the pictures and their themes at the iconographic level we should not disregard this concentration on a particular period, a particular artist, and a particular genre in applied art. This said, we must also ask whether the assemblage as a whole might also be read iconographically. Other than the seller of remedies against snakebite, no theme appears more than once; given that the fresco of the *Serpentario* from the Palazzo del Tè is of relatively late date, this picture can be called a commentary on the cassone showing the Feast of Saint John. George slaying the dragon is the only saint depicted in the assemblage; especially as the dragon is a wingless lindworm, we might align this picture with the theme of snakebite or we might say that it shows a fight with a fabulous creature and as such belongs alongside the hunt scene, which is where we find it. The remaining pictures have in common that they depict social transactions that all bring numerous people together in group activities with a greater or lesser degree of ritual. Tournament, horse race, and *palio;* a hunt, a battle, a Eucharistic procession, an execution; public festivals and a wedding procession—these can only be connected insofar as they visualize social organization both concretely and symbolically. Processions and pageants, blood sport and mounted battle as pictorial themes also form social occasions whereby the group—in this context, urban society—becomes aware of itself as a coherent unit.

The cassoni assembled on plate 28/29 are connected with festival and pageantry in two ways—first as objects incorporated into the wedding ritual itself, and second as pictorial records of past self-representation. In "On Imprese Amorose" Warburg remarks that "the cassone has the far more prosaic function of storing the costly trousseau of a bourgeois bride: it is a symbol *dell'amore possessivo nuziale* [marital proprietary love]. This is the love that takes delight in seeing the lavish garments and jewels of the wedding guests commemorated on the gaily painted sarcophagus that marks the demise of *passione sentimentale.*"[96] Warburg's thesis that the cassoni painters' decorative arts give pictorial form to the festive, energetic joie de vivre of tourney, procession, and *rappresentazioni* is disputed in Ernst Gombrich's essay on Apollonio di Giovanni,[97] but the thesis has lately been convincingly confirmed by Götz Pochat, who has shown just such a relationship to historical reality for four of the cassoni reproduced in Warburg's picture-atlas.[98]

One conjecture on the function of the Feast of Corpus Christi in the context of late medieval and early modern towns has been that in such processions, urban society presented itself as a corporation, as at one and the same time a unit and socially differentiated.[99] We might vary this interpretation and use the category of "society as figuration"[100] to read the assemblage including Uccello's depiction of the Host desecration. Though we may know more now than Warburg had known about Florentine painters of cassoni and about Apollonio di Giovanni's work,[101] later research has only recently caught up with the questions he had asked.

"The Wound in the Wall"

Seen in the light of these questions the narrative scenes of Paolo Uccello's predella of 1467–69 have one telling detail. The legend is divided into six scenes, although these are not given in their proper sequence as assembled in the picture-atlas—the fifth and sixth scenes have been placed before the third and fourth. A woman brings a Host to the moneylender; placed in a pan in the moneylender's house, the Host begins to the Jewish family's astonishment to bleed so copiously that the blood runs through an opening in the wall of the house and out into the street, where the night watch becomes aware of the miracle and breaks down the door. The Host is returned to the altar in a solemn procession in which the pope also takes part. The woman who had brought the Host to the Jews is about to be hanged when an angel appears to prove her innocence. The family of the Jewish moneylender is burnt in an auto-da-fé—including the children. A dying woman lies on a bier, around which angels and devils compete for her soul.

Paolo Uccello, Predella with scenes of a profanation of the Host for the Corpus Christi brotherhood's altar of the Holy Sacrament, oil on panel, 42 x 351 cm, Urbino, Palazzo Ducale, Galleria Nazionale delle Marche.

At the pawnshop

The discovery of the desecration of the Host

Eucharistic procession

The rescue of the Christian woman

Auto-da-fé of the Jewish family

The death of the Christian woman

Marilyn Lavin has painstakingly explained the details of the narrative and the painting's iconography, using textual and pictorial sources and the circumstances of the confraternity's commission to Uccello and later to Joos van Ghent for the alter-piece. She shows that Joos van Ghent's *Communion of the Apostles* (1473) addresses the theme of "Jewish and Christian"[102] alongside the theme of the Eucharist. The story Uccello tells is the story of how Jews in Italy begin to be marginalized and persecuted within a society that confirms its own coherence through the Eucharistic procession shown in the third scene. Like Marilyn Lavin, Stephen Greenblatt in a lecture held in 1995 on the altar of the Corpus Christi confraternity in Urbino read the interplay of its two parts, Joos van Ghent's altarpiece showing the communion of the apostles and Uccello's predella.[103] He focused on the opposition between the Christians' "most venerated object," the Host, and their "most despised object," the Jew. Among other polarities visualized on the altar is that of the pure and in some ways abstract wafer, which God incarnate gave to his disciples as his body, and the carnal, bleeding Host revealed to the skeptical realist Jews in the legend told below, in the predella. The bleeding opening in the wall is a painterly invention by Uccello, and we may read it as the "wound in the wall," the treacherous point at which the "mode of representation" threatens to break down. The Jew is an exemplar of the individual, as well as of a particular type, and he is confronted by ecclesiastical and military groups; he is used to legitimate such social formations and to confirm dogma. Jews are sacrificed so that the sacramental act may be believed. Greenblatt's reading of the altar may perhaps overload the metaphorical structure,[104] but we can ask whether it does not also offer a way to read the atlas assemblage. Here the Urbino predella would be the treacherous wound that, for the first time in Warburg's life, depicted the Jew as victim in the midst of the festive bustle of life; an aporia among his interests, which seemed in the years around 1900, when he was planning to publish the ledger of Apollonio's workshop,[105] to be safely distant from the happenings of the time.

This is one possible reading among others, perhaps equally justified. Warfare and the way it is sublimated as sport, magical control of hostile powers, control over space by means of perspective—all these aspects of the pictures assembled here are also important. The commentary that Warburg never wrote is unlikely to have emphasized the anti-Semitic content of the predella. It is, however, conspicuously there.

Serious Issues

The last plates of the picture-atlas, 77, 78, and 79, are markedly different from the rest of the work. This is not primarily because Warburg here places contemporary material, photographs, alongside historical pictures—for Gombrich a "selection of images which could not but strike a note of whimsicality"[106]—but rather because in plates 78 and 79 a particular contemporary event is discussed in pictures. This is the signing of the Lateran Pact between Mussolini's Italy and the Catholic Church under Pope Pius XI on 11 February 1929; Warburg was in Rome at the time and witnessed the event. By this concordat (plate 78) the Church renounced its claims to secular power and was in return recognized as the state religion, compensatory payments to the Church were fixed, as were the present state borders of the Vatican City. Warburg seems to have seen the Catholic Church's changed priorities as symbolically very significant, much more than historical facts might justify. He "was in Saint Peter's Square when the pope blessed the crowd

Picture-atlas *Mnemosyne*, plate 78. Foto Warburg Institute, London.

after this act of renunciation, which he interpreted as a turning-point in history. The contrast between the crude symbols of power displayed by the Fascists and the withdrawal of the pope to the confines of a merely symbolic domain became for him another link in the long chain of mankind's road toward enlightenment."[107]

The pictures in plate 78 are solely concerned with the signing of the pact and its consequences, while in contrast plate 79 places the treaty in the context of historical images. Warburg specifically acquired from various picture agencies the contemporary press photographs on

Picture-atlas *Mnemosyne,* plate 79. Foto Warburg Institute, London.

plate 79, which show a "Eucharistic procession" in Saint Peter's Square on 29 July 1929. The procession is shown in various shots that focus either on the crowd of spectators, on the pope and clerical participants, or in two pictures on the Italian army and Papal Swiss guard. A photograph that has been included from a newspaper cutting captures the signing of the Locarno Treaty (1925 in London).[108]

An illustrated page from the *Hamburger Fremdenblatt* is also included; the largest picture on this spread from the edition of 30 July 1929 showed the pope in procession.[109] We still have Warburg's description of these assemblages of news photos from an address to a group of graduating doctoral students, when he took the opportunity to examine their pictorial content. An additional clipping shows a news photograph of a train crash: a priest is giving the Sacrament to a dying man. Another contemporary item related to papal Rome is the reproduction of a book from 1918 on the papal army.

The remaining pictures provide historical depth and background to the news pictures. Three reproductions show the *Cathedra Petri,* in a photograph from 1867,[110] then in a frontal view where the ivory inlay and the whole design are clearly visible,[111] finally as Bernini installed it in Saint Peter's. Immediately beneath this is a reproduction of Raphael's fresco of the Mass of Bolsena, from the Stanza d'Eliodoro in the Vatican. Below and to the left of the mass is the personification of Hope from Giotto's grisailles in the Arena chapel at Padua, with the inscription "Speranza," and next to that Botticelli's last communion of Saint Jerome. The woodcuts showing the profanation of the Host are in the bottom row, on either side of the picture of marching Italian soldiers. Two pictures on obviously non-European themes are in the top row, between the pictures of the papal throne and the London treaty signing. The photograph on the left shows preparations for a ritual suicide (hara-kiri or seppuku) in Japan; to the right is reproduced a drawing on Japanese corporal punishment showing severed arms and a severed head. Gombrich's thematic summary of plates 78 and 79 is that "[n]ews photographs of the signing of the Concordat with Mussolini were juxtaposed with renderings of the Mass and of the Eucharist to remind viewers of the seriousness of the issues involved."[112]

Unlike plate 28/29 there can be hardly any doubt about the actual thematic focus of these last plates: the pictures of the Eucharistic procession and of the Mass of Bolsena, the two pictures showing the last communion of Saint Jerome and of the crash victim, and the two depictions of Host desecration, all bring into focus the Sacrament and above all the Sacrifice of the Mass. This Sacrifice is supposed to supplant all blood sacrifice, and yet in the history of Christianity has repeatedly required such human sacrifice in its turn. As the history of Host profanation charges shows, to not see and yet to believe in the Eucharist's redemptive presence is at the problematic core of European Christian culture.

The arrangement of images on the plate itself suggests that we should see the fresco in the Stanza d'Eliodoro as the focus,[113] like the central text in a glossed manuscript. The scene is hieratically composed within the lunette; the painting is given in a large reproduction; the fresco itself is compositionally oriented to the altar; the Host is elevated. All of this effects a further centering, which shows all the other images to be at many different levels commentaries on the central picture. Recent research has emphasized that an important feature of the fresco is the moment of timelessness in the Miracle of the Mass, allowing Raphael to depict the times of 1263 and 1511 alongside one another.[114] The clergy and congregation on the left belong, like the priest,

Raphael, *The Mass of Bolsena,* fresco. Vatican, Stanza d'Eliodoro.

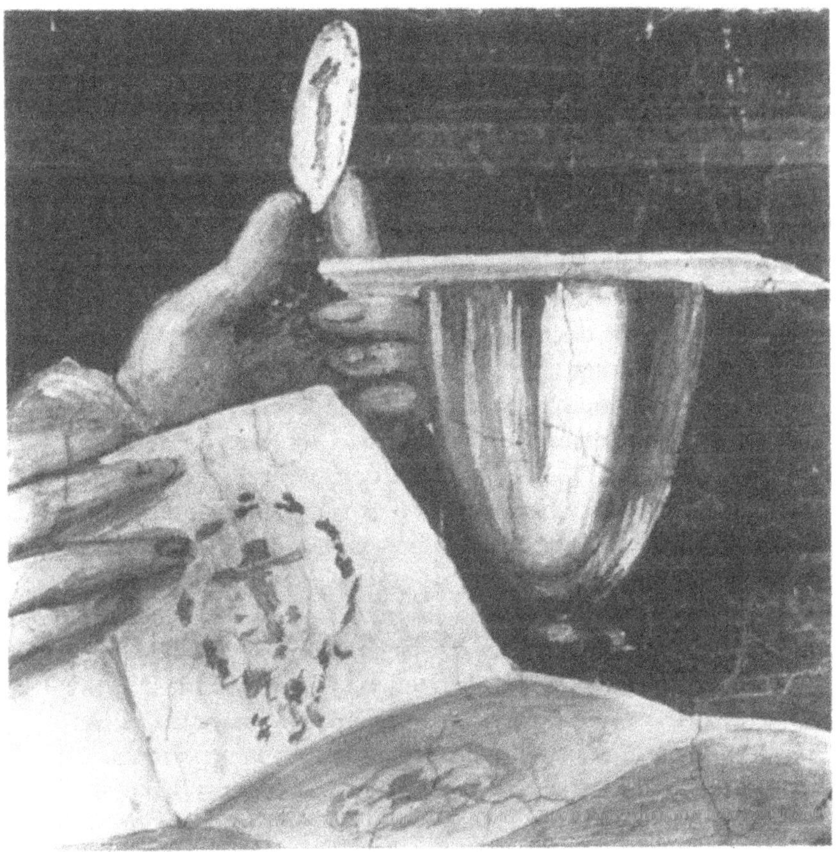

Raphael, *The Mass of Bolsena,* fresco (detail: The bleeding Host). Vatican, Stanza d'Eliodoro.

to the age of Urban IV, while the pope is shown as Julius II, whose retinue and Swiss Guard at the lower right are shown in contemporary sixteenth-century costume. As we look at the picture we too are drawn into this timeless episode by the figures, one on either side, who look back at us.

Warburg's commentary-in-pictures addresses this moment of timelessness and along with this, a further implication of temporal duplication: on the left, the gesture of the woman looking upward is repeated in Giotto's personification of Hope; on the right, the clipping of the Swiss Guard in procession repeats the guardsmen in the fresco. The pictorial commentary thus also emphasizes a polarity in Raphael's

Mass of Bolsena, showing two aspects of the bloody miracle of the Mass—the Church in its historical military representation and the personified hope of redemption mediated by the priesthood, in which we might catch sight of the "Nympha" exalted to pious spirituality.[115] It is not merely in Raphael's fresco that we see how this miracle of the Mass materializes rather than spiritualizes the Real Presence of Christ.[116] The same miracle, the appearance of a bloody cross on the Host, can clearly be seen repeated in the Italian woodcut illustrating the mystery play of the Host desecration. Warburg spoke of this "concreteness of religion" in his address to the doctoral graduates on 30 July 1929: "It is not with a mind to submitting to that dogma, but to understand the present state of the psychological conflict which is essentially due to the tension between the concreteness of religion and the abstraction of science, that we need, here in the North of Europe, a receiving station that registers the give and take between the past and present and that can thus assist us in containing the chaos of unreason by means of a filter system of retrospective reflection."[117] Practically every word in this closing passage of his speech to the young art historians can be found paralleled in Warburg's published works, particularly the construction of a polarity between concreteness and abstraction; thus he remarked in 1917, in a letter written while he was at work on the essay "Pagan-Antique Prophecy in the Age of Luther": "I had known in general that Luther was to be placed between practical magic and abstract symbolism, yet had not known it in my personal being."[118]

The library journal of 1927 documents a long and complicated discussion of the role of astrology in the sixteenth century, including the comment that "Saxl rightly pointed to Levy-Brühl on primitive thought,"[119] at the end of which Warburg remarks, "Thus at the end of the era stands the belief in witches, and the dispute on the metaphorical distance in the Eucharist: *significat* or *est.*"[120] Yet in this late text there is an "or" interpolated between the two extremes, which seems not to produce an "either-or" but rather shows that Warburg now considers both possibilities, the religious, magical, practical, and concrete just as much as the abstract, symbolic, and scientific, as real opportunities at the time to contain "chaos."

In 1931 Edgar Wind lectured at the Aesthetic Congress in Hamburg on "Warburg's Concept of Cultural Science and its Significance for Aesthetics,"[121] and closely examined Warburg's concept of the symbol and its origin in Friedrich Theodor Vischer's symbol theory.[122] Warburg's and Vischer's central example was the Eucharistic controversy, the question of whether the words "Hoc est corpus meum" are to be understood as trope or as metaphor. Wind says that for Vischer and Warburg, the two divergent views are "the magical view that binds image and meaning into one, and the logical view that separates the comparison and explicitly introduces an *as if.* The first view cannot do without religious cult practices. It needs the priest, whose words have the magical power to effect the alteration in substance."[123] A third conception of the symbol, which Vischer called the conditional view, "arises when one does not actually believe in the magic immanent in the image, yet remains under its sway."[124]

There have been many studies of Warburg's concept of the symbol, not least in the context of the fruitful contact between Warburg and Wind in the late 1920s. These have emphasized Warburg's belief that images (*Scheinbilder*) had a mediating role whereby the powers of chaos could for a while at least be controlled as form.[125] "For even harmonious compromise is the product of a conflict in which the whole man participates, with his religious urge to corporality and intellectual striving for enlightenment, his urge to possess and his desire to hold the world at arm's length."[126] Thus the "metaphorical distance" is the precondition for any possibility of self-enlightenment, and salvation from the urge to sacrifice oneself and others.

On 10 and 13 August 1928 Warburg noted down several variant descriptions of his concept of the symbol, under the heading "The nature of the symbol" in the library journal: "To contain the fluid Infinite by setting imaginary, pictorial, or symbolic limits, in the course of which the creative worker remembers expressive values stored up and given shape by social tradition; his capacity for such memory functions as an objective, personal organ, selecting and *purposefully exaggerating.*" He adds, "cf. Vischer, the symbol. (heathen passion—Christian passion in the Mediterranean basin—the mint) Greek clarity—Jewish intuition—abhorrence of 'the Law.'"[127] The "creative designer" (*der Gestalter*) stands at the center of this description: certainly this means the artist first and foremost, but the choice of words allows a broadening of the term to include all "creative designers" inasmuch as social processes are creative as well.

Seen from this perspective of the theory of symbols and from Warburg's concept of the function and meaning of metaphor, Raphael's classicizing, hieratic version of the Feast of Corpus Christi and its foundational legend visually contemplates this concept of symbol and metaphor. As a young man Warburg had heavily underscored his copy of *The Birth of Tragedy* where Nietzsche writes, "For the true poet the metaphor is not a rhetorical figure but a representative image that really hovers before him in place of a concept."[128] Raphael shows magical cult practice standing between the hope of redemption and a claim to power; if the bloody and substitutive sacrifice could be believed, it could prevent further bloodshed and further sacrifice, at a time when the Catholic Church had finally given up its claims to power.

This then would explain the function on plate 79 of the reproductions of Japanese suicide ritual and corporal punishment in a greater context of sacrifice and self-sacrifice. A further definition is made possible by an undated newspaper clipping from the *Frankfurter Zeitung* in Warburg's dossier on "Religion."[129] Here Ludwig Rieß of Berlin gives a thorough account of Japanese religious tradition under the heading "Nogi's suicide and Japanese political religion."[130] He writes that animism and the ritual suicide of servants to "accompany" their dead lords had gradually been suppressed by Buddhism, but had then been revived as a "political religion" as Japan became a nation and dominant in East Asia. The occasion for this comprehensive account was the sensational ritual suicide of the Japanese field marshal Kiten Nogi, who along with his wife committed hara-kiri at the funeral of the Emperor Mutsuhito on 12 September 1912. One might assume that the two images with Japanese themes refer to this notion of reverse development, of nineteenth-century nationalism politically functionalizing and reviving a sacrificial ritual that had already become obsolete—a picture of "political religion." It is not merely that the context reveals structural similarities with the revival of the blood libel, an atavism that nationalism reactivated in a similar way and in a comparable situation; this also explains in the context of the whole plate the meaning of the hara-kiri tableau, which refers back to the sixteenth century in Japan. It recalls the decisive step that the Catholic Church had recently taken in renouncing worldly power (and military force) and also calls to mind the possibility that such a civilizing measure, once accomplished, might yet be reversed. The pictures of Host profanation have the same thematic bearing on the Church's renunciation of violence: in relinquishing force it had also allowed the possibility that the Jews' sacrificial role could no longer be religiously legitimated, that their blood would no longer be shed to give content and reality to the miracle of transubstantiation.

"The Daily Jews"

In an unnumbered *Zettelkasten* in the Warburg Institute archive is a section that seems to have served as a traveling box-file during the visit to Rome in 1928/29; it contains some of the last testimony to Warburg's tireless watch for anti-Semitic agitation.[131] Ephemera of all kinds went into the file, ordered by assorted rubrics that clearly were added to as needed: Hotel, plaster-of-Paris, libraries, sport, air travel, political news, Curia, and so forth. The section on "The daily Jews" (*Tages Juden*) contains solely material on racist or anti-Semitic activity. Among this is a pamphlet,[132] *Invitation to Subscribe to Jacob Brafmann: The Book of the Kahal.*[133] The editor, Siegfried Passarge (1867–1958) was one of the most fanatical racists and anti-Semites in Hamburg academia.[134] In 1925 he had published a book called *The Development of the Character of Peoples*, saturated with racist and anti-Semitic ideology, which the library immediately acquired.[135] In the box-file there is also a satirically phrased newspaper cutting about a new law in Turkey, whereby foreigners (Levantines) born in Turkey had to take Turkish citizenship. A Levantine woman reportedly founded a travel trust for pregnant Levantine women, so that they might give birth to their children outside Turkey and thus save the Levantine "breed" (*Sammelrasse*) from extinction.[136]

The last two news clippings concern the NSDAP and those of its activities of which the courts took notice. National Socialist "rowdies" had attacked passersby at night in Bremen in September 1928, beaten them brutally, and then vanished into the darkness shouting anti-Semitic insults. Among the victims of the attack was an Italian merchant. One of the assailants was recognized as a well-known city Nazi.[137] A trial took place in June 1929 to pass sentence on this "premeditated bodily harm in connection with unprecedented anti-Semitic attacks." The assailants were—as usual—only lightly punished.[138] The two liberal newspapers, reporting about half a year after the events, state that the streets of Germany were becoming lethally dangerous for anybody who looked "Jewish" and that the courts sentence such cases lightly; they are in fact reporting on the slow retreat of civil society, on the spread of violence and anarchy that relies on tacit approval from the bourgeoisie. A professor of geography at Hamburg University, the very institution Warburg had worked long and hard to help found, was using Brafmann's works, long exposed as forgeries, to peddle his racist ideology under academic disguise. We cannot be far wrong if we assume that this open, shameless, and militant anti-Semitism, its inroads into the very institutions which were intended to stem the tide of violence and lies, represented for Warburg that "chaos" of which he spoke to the doctoral graduates. Perhaps not chaos in its entirety, but certainly its most dangerous part. "The daily Jews": in Warburg's documentation anti-Semitism, part of that ever more accepted racial hatred, had become everyday life for Jews. From his first reports to his mother, to the "madhouse," and on to this matter-of-fact ordering between "Hotel" and "Kurie," he had traveled a very long road.

In his lecture on Rembrandt, Warburg had said of the Amsterdam city council's rejection of *Claudius Civilis*, "We shall see that in the matter of the murals for the lunettes of the city hall—today the Palais—in Amsterdam, Tempesta's line in monumental elegance triumphed over Rembrandt's inward, patriotically pitched, desperate detachment [*Sachlichkeit*]."[139] This "inward, patriotically pitched, desperate detachment" is without doubt also a self-description—perhaps that first and foremost. Warburg had hoped to make room for such objectivity and to give it form in the institution he had founded. As a German patriot, he failed, was failed—but his institute lives on and preserves in its archive all that we can know about the reasons for its foundation.

Conclusion

In his 1918 lecture "Science as a Vocation" Max Weber explained the academic career as follows: "Academic life is a wild gamble. If young scholars come to ask advice about becoming a lecturer, the responsibility of encouragement is almost unbearable. If he is a Jew, one of course says *lasciate ogni speranza.*" Admittedly things were not much better for anybody else (and Weber also found that women need not even consider this gamble, "of course") but this verdict—delivered at a well-attended student event—leaves not the shadow of a doubt as to its finality: Jews were not welcome in German academia. As he pronounced it Weber made it clear that he did not share this opinion, and we know that just a little later it no longer applied quite so strictly at the "young" universities (such as Hamburg and Frankfurt am Main).

To come forward at all as a Jewish academic and scholar under such circumstances can be understood as a sign of self-confidence, and of a great confidence in the stability of that historical process believed to lead to complete social emancipation for Jewish citizens. Yet to assume that the obstacles so vividly described would not leave marks on those who had to overcome them seems to me entirely naïve. The question remains what form their response took, and what effects it had on their scholarship. The role the construction of "the Jew" was to play in this response can only be investigated in individual cases and for individual scholarly achievements.

Even when we have done so, the question remains of how important we should consider the findings of our investigation, and here our motives and aims as historians play a deciding role. Whoever holds that there is an objective process inherent to scholarship that specifically cuts away all that is conditional and period-specific, will reckon that personal motives for scholarly accomplishment (in this case, the reaction to anti-Semitism) are less important: what counts is the result. Whoever believes that the human sciences cannot do otherwise than construct what they claim to analyze at a distance, will argue that motives for inquiry must be heeded. The present study has been written with this assumption—I might say, with this burden. I can now see Warburg's research on European culture with new eyes, having (re-)constructed his art history and cultural science as a strategy of defense against what he once called the "clipped tones of the noble pale-face."

In her 1958 lecture on Warburg, Gertrud Bing said, "He had none of that pride in Jewish tradition which had always been a feature of the Orthodox and which even liberal Jews later developed under pressure from anti-Semitism, and he sharply condemned it wherever he encountered it."[1] Bing did not judge this attitude, which today would certainly meet with incomprehension and rejection. It seems to me important that Warburg (and many others) be seen to have *achieved* their rejection of a clear-cut identity, something to which everyone in Imperial Germany was expected to subscribe, especially during wartime. It is this achievement that allowed him to see the fractures and contradictions of European civilization with acute clarity.

Appendix

The documents in this appendix can be found in the archive of the Warburg Institute, London; this institute also holds copyright for the letters and writings published in translation here for the first time.

Two letters from Aby Warburg to his mother, 1887 from Bonn and 1889 from Strasbourg

26.1.87

Dear Mama!

Today I received your letter of Tuesday; and Dr. Unger has also just now told me what was in Papa's letter. According to Dr. Unger, there are about 10 observant Jewish families hereabouts, but not one of them would be willing to have a guest eat with them regularly, or if they were, it would be much like at Rothschilds'; but if something can be found, which Dr. Unger thinks most unlikely, then we shall see what can be done. I will not eat at Rothschilds any longer; I shall get by somehow or other, or shall fall in with whatever choice you might suggest.

Were it not that I knew that my lifetime success, or lack thereof, depends on this, I would not have demanded of you that which you think so dangerous to grant; it seems that you trust Dr. Unger enough for him to be able to undertake my cause with you, yet—although I do not know what he wrote—he can hardly have told you anything that you have not already heard from me, yet you wished to hear from an objective witness that I am indeed unhappy;

When you write, dearest Mama, about the things that will go by the board through eating differently, I must tell you that you are doing me an injustice. I am not at all ashamed to be a Jew, on the contrary I am trying to show others that representatives of my kind are well suited, in accordance with their talents, to insert themselves as useful links in the chain of present-day cultural and political developments; but just because I want to do that I must strive to shake off whatever will not fit organically into my activity. I want to act as I am; I want to be regarded by people for what I am. In any case my striving is honest and the will is there. If I am wrong—well, I shall at least have acted in what seemed to me the right way; but I am too old and have in other respects been standing on my own feet for too long to be able, out of consideration for people who are very dear to me, to go on doing something which is in the most glaring contrast to what I think.

I hope to show you one day that I am capable of achieving something in my self-chosen place.

I thank you both for understanding my position, more than I can say; only in this way can our relationship remain a sincere one; and that is my heart's desire.

Your truly loving
Aby.

[added later by Max A. Warburg for E. Gombrich: "important: whole letter"]
25.XI.89

Dear Mama!
I am writing only today, because I had to prepare some work for Ziegler's philosophy seminar, which took place yesterday morning. Now that this (which was on Kant's prolegomena to the Critique of Pure Reason) has passed off successfully, I have enough of my mind free to be able to turn my thoughts to you.

I felt that it was hard work and arduous thinking: I find Kant very difficult to understand anyway; and of course it is even harder to reproduce his thoughts with a hint of critical scrutiny. I am glad that Prof. Ziegler was happy with my work. Such recognition does me good from time to time. I feel quite certain of what I am doing and what I can leave out, but I have not yet achieved a disdain for opposition that is not academic. I am still governed by the rather lamentable wish to enjoy the tacit respect of everybody with whom I have to do, as I go about my business (which I know to be quite respectable). I find though at every turn that our so well beloved German people, with the blessing of the authorities, choose to see every Jew as above all a foreign interloper with dubious manners, which depresses me. To be sure, I must also emphasize that everybody whom I have come to know a little better—students or professors—shows me good faith and goodwill, and they are quite a number of rather nice people.

And yet, and yet! The common folk here are dreadful: I cannot go out during the day without once or twice hearing the comment somewhere behind me: "Thassa Jew!" Or as recently—when I go into the *Germania,* I hear a group of Christian gentlemen entertaining themselves by murmuring and *mauschel*-ing as they play cards: of course in such cases you cannot call anybody to account: it has nothing to do with oneself; but *how* such things can happen at all!—Neither are the debates in the Reichstag committee encouraging: even if there is no official regulation that Jews should not be made reserve officers, the will to recognize an individual's worth is still lacking; and this would be the only real way to achieve some sort of social integration. In all this one notices that of course one is dealing with parvenus of national sentiment who are not yet certain of themselves; "It's got to get better!"

I often entertain the thought of seeking a practical solution to the Jewish question later: does one have the right to keep life at a distance?

My great-grandchildren may become professors, or rather my great-grandnephews, as I shall not marry. Apart from anything else, I must myself be quite pronouncedly Oriental in my own appearance. This at least has the advantage that, if one finds it at all worthwhile, one has to confront oneself completely. This of course does not make life much happier.

Whatever may come, I will work and there's an end to it. Pardon me for singing the ballad of the good Jew at such length! But I do not see why we should not speak out on this point just once.

Greetings to you all
from
your 'blond'.

The Jewish question in the context of Germany's entire policy.

Note on transcription: all text in italics is from the earlier draft and was cut or altered. Emphasis in the original is not reproduced here.

The demands of the moment. The Jewish Question as Framed by German Politics.

The position of the Jews in Germany is of extraordinary significance not just for the Jews themselves, but also for the state as such. *I have therefore written out the following thoughts, spurred by the wish to bring out the importance of this question at a time when great and difficult challenges face Germany. Much may depend on how we approach the Jewish question within Germany; for every country has the Jews which it deserves.* I wrote the following not as a Jew, a German of the Jewish faith, not in a narrowly conceived Jewish sense, but in the interests of a better German policy internally and thus also externally.

All parties in Germany attempt to keep to the truce [*Burgfrieden*], as honestly as they can under the prevailing circumstances. Many quarrels that could be found in any country seem to have been forgotten, and we must do all we can to ensure that this condition becomes permanent. This truce *however* must not be simply a transitory measure taken during wartime; *rather* it must be internalized, i.e., we must use these present difficult times to look within ourselves, to forget as far as we can the prejudices that possessed us up until the war: *here belongs* self-scrutiny for now, lasting self-control for later, are needed, because otherwise the harmony demanded by interests of state will never be attained. All of us, Christians and Jews, must behave thus.

For love of our country we must decisively banish to distant regions long-planted disagreements, for otherwise we will never be able to work together in the interests of the state. This inward turn is a bitter necessity for the success of the state, only then will all those who are able to work put themselves, joyfully and free from envy, at the state's service, and employ their talents where these are most useful; only thus is it possible to make best use of the existing German productive capacities.

The basic tenet of the Germans is to put themselves lovingly at the state's service, in war, as in peace. Our enemies falsely call this militarism. Our strength is that each one of us asks himself how best he can be of value to the state. In this dedication to the state in peacetime, which in wartime leads even to self-sacrifice, lies Germany's strength, and now this ideal of the state, this sense of community, is fought for within Germany. It is not a crusade, not a racial struggle, not a battle for a religion, it is a fight we wage for the security of our fatherland and the free movement of our labor beyond its bounds. We will not let a state such as England dictate to us how far we are permitted to act in the world, for each one of us has put his whole strength at the state's disposal and now demands the full, autonomous development of this state. *With this intent, Germany is always faced with* The question of life and death is this: "How can we make every citizen a useful and joyful fellow combatant in war and in peace?"

The quarrels between the parties *have been discussed often enough. These quarrels* must resurface once more, and they will do so, for political opinions can only take the clear form in the political arena of an honorable dispute. Likewise the conflicts between different worldviews at the intellectual level will endure.

Yet we must forget certain quarrels, i.e., we cannot make them the cause of our contention, if we wish to bring forward the life of the German state to its highest development. These are quarrels of a religious nature. *In the future, e.g., an academic chair must be occupied only by one who is most capable in the field; a given university may no longer require that the teacher be Catholic, or another that he be Protestant. The nobleman's prejudice against the bourgeois must be quashed, although we must certainly grant that thanks to the traditional training for one job that has prevailed in a family through the generations, members of these families are more suited to certain functions than a bourgeois of equal ability, because of the constant engagement of their ancestors; likewise, however, there are many functions in which, given equal talent, the untapped strength of the bourgeoisie is to be preferred to the capacity of a noble family. For all the conflicts between Protestant and Catholic, a feeling of solidarity has always prevailed despite the keenness of the contest, which makes this competition not so inwardly hateful as the fight against the Jews in Germany.* In recent times the feeling of solidarity has calmed the battles of Protestant and Catholic despite their intensity, yet the struggle against Jewry has been waged openly and secretly in a hateful manner.

We are often surprised that the Germans are so unloved and are *so* falsely shouted down as brutal overlords; there is hardly a tendency that has so much advanced this misunderstanding as anti-Semitism, which first found an enduring "scientific" justification in Germany. Nor has it lost strength in Germany; in the last few years it has perhaps lost some of its edge, but now as earlier there are still a great many positions closed in principle to Jews simply because of their faith. Russia and Romania aside, such discrimination and exclusion exists in no other country in the European sphere*!*. One would hardly claim, though, that Jews in Germany, properly selected, might not fulfill the same demands as Jews in other countries! Natural differences should be used for mutual furtherance.

German Jews have often enough proved that they possess the talents for responsible positions, for they, *once baptized* on conversion, are appointed to high posts and acquitted themselves well in these positions. Yet baptism and the acceptance of a new faith, when it does not also demand an inner conviction *hardly ever with an inner conviction for this faith,* demands an unprincipled insincerity *toward oneself* that shows anti-Semitism to be yet worse. This being so the Jews, who refusing baptism without religious conviction *as they must on principle,* had hardly any chance to distinguish themselves in high governmental positions in Germany.

Foreigners have justly been able to claim that Germany is in truth not yet a state wholly subject to the rule of law, because no Jew in Prussian Germany can or could become a reserve officer; no Jew has yet held a high post in the state; the civil service is closed to him with the exception of the judiciary, where, however, a Jew will never become a high court judge and rarely moves above the circuit. *It is nothing less than bizarre that Jews may become judges, but never attorneys for the state.* Every Jew must serve under arms, as must every Christian, and in wartime must fight for his country; like every German he simply fulfils his civic duty, yet he is without exception (in Bavaria, there have been a very few exceptions) refused a position of honor for which, though certainly not all, yet nevertheless many are suited. This is notoriously the case, and all too often described as such to the one-year volunteers by their superior officers, at which it is *thereby* hinted that they should accept baptism. Those who take this unprincipled step then often become officers. *while those of strong principles cannot enjoy this advantage.* Now, in wartime, we have sought to quash this prejudice *at least to begin with* early on, and a number of Jews have been named as reserve officers. *Yet as soon as trench warfare led to the nomination system with all its formalities and enquiries prevailing once more,* the promotions gradually stopped. *And now—in the midst of war—promotions of Jews to reserve officer hardly occur. A number of Jews also became officers in the war of 1870/71, and at that time many Jews returned from the war decorated with the Iron Cross for bravery. That, however, did not at all hinder leading political parties from surrendering themselves and their banners to anti-Semitism a few years later, and up until the outbreak of this war nobody hesitated to keep unbaptized Jews not just from the status of reserve officer but also from the great majority of civic posts and many other positions in Germany, as a matter of principle.*

At first justice was seen to prevail, but then came the census of the Jews, which must disgust every right-thinking man and which, although the military authority conceived it as a way to ward of unjustified accusations, must occasion a split within the army as a whole and—whether or not this is intended—cause unequal treatment and deep resentment.

Also, Even now during the war Jews, even those who are brave and capable, are often being passed over. I hear of the bitterness felt by those who set out filled with joy, love, and enthusiasm and must now look on as comrades who are younger and less capable than themselves are promoted before them, simply because they belong to one of the prescribed faiths. It is not true that this prejudice has been generally quashed in wartime. Yet what should those who have been passed over do? Complain? In wartime? That would make their own position impossible. Everything is written down neatly and apparently justly for the files, and one may glibly demand that parliament point to single cases! How easily the letter of the law is circumvented, if the will is there. Yet an individual's bitter experience has consequences that cause great damage to the state, well beyond the individual case, *namely* the justified *bitterness,* disappointment, and indignation of the parents, siblings, and sons and further, of all those of the same faith, who have given and *often* lost their own for the fight, and who now see that even those who died for their country are, because of their faith, seen as less than equal by those for whom they fought and died!

Not only As well as its military importance, the non-promotion of officers has a very far-reaching effect on the possibility of partaking in civilian life, *namely* not only in the civil administration of the state, but also with regard to advancement in private affairs.

Those who, because they did not want to suffer this unjust state of affairs, *in the past* earlier turned their backs on their fatherland, were not the least worthy Jews. And we will not be able to dismiss these emigrants with the remark, "God be thanked that we are rid of them," for these Jews who left for overseas—and it can be proved that a certain portion of the Jews who play a part in various enemy countries *originally turned their back on* left Germany because they or their ancestors did not wish to live *because of the* with anti-Semitism in Germany—represent *not just a human* a loss, *but also* a loss in men and intelligence which, properly valued, could be of extraordinary use to the fatherland. I will not credit that the German Christian feels *more* more deeply for his country than the German Jew; quite the opposite, the Jews, who despite their discrimination love their country fiercely and voluntarily have put themselves at their country's service for the front or for any other service, are particularly good patriots, because in the moment of danger they forget this discrimination.

I If a man were enough of a philosopher to look on calmly as another anti-Semitic wave *came* grew in Germany after the end of the war and if he were *strong, or rather* strong and decent enough *successfully to battle* to see this wave break and spend its strength, even so this shameful injustice must not be allowed to repeat itself—regardless of ethical reasons—for reasons of state. *It is not however a question of avoiding a shameful injustice to the Jews, a scandal for Germany as after 1870/71, rather this wave of anti-Semitism must be avoided for the interests of state.*

We must see clearly that after the end of the war envy will once more play a much greater role particularly in Germany. Those who made money during the war will have fingers pointed at them and, since there will quite naturally be a few Jews who have become rich because of their peacetime occupations and their abilities, the Jews at large will be cursed and, because of the ease of general association another anti-Semitic movement will take the stage. In truth however the number of Jews who have made large profits from the war is low. Partly this is because exactly that trade which Jews mostly control, as e.g., grain, metal, and fodder, was very early compulsorily confiscated; partly, however, because there are other circles that enjoy much better relations with those organs of the general staff which grant contracts. Therefore it would surely be utterly unjust to make a means of agitation against the Jews in general from the large war profits of a few.

The really large profits are made by agriculture and heavy industry, the chemical industry, etc.; it would be a superficial injustice to say that these profits were too large, but it is certain that partly because of mistakes in distributing contracts and in general measures too much has been earned; those sinful war profiteers who are Germanic through and through naturally have an interest in finding a whipping-boy and divert the general indignation that is already present against Jewish war contractors, in order to divert attention from themselves.

One should indeed proceed in fullest severity against those Jews and Christians who have illegally made themselves rich, yet one must also beware of the injustice of guilt by association.

If we really win those smaller states that surround us to our own side in one way or another, and especially if we wish to contribute to solving the East European problem, then we must learn internal tolerance and practice it in our social life, which would qualify us for such a task in the world at large. We have no right to make Poland independent, to free the oppressed—which means millions of Jews as well—if we do not show in our own land that we are also just to Jews who have for generations shown themselves to be good Germans, for he is not suited to care for other children who is an unjust father to his own.

Every proud German Jew has until now had to tolerate, with a feeling of inner indignation, that his faith and his lineage close many doors to him. Laws are of no help here, the only help is upright dealing, conviction, and if we wish to cultivate good dealings then we must fight an honest inward struggle—and for this the time of the truce is well suited—which will lead to the decision that we will never again be governed by prejudice, but from civic solidarity will be just toward one and all! Only he who practices justice in the smallest matter of everyday life has the right to high respect, and only the nation that makes this justice its motive in everyday matters can earn recognition in the world! And the form such justice takes and must take in daily life is freedom from prejudice, decency, morality that is good because it is just.

For interests of state, every single person must be assessed for his value and used accordingly. That must be the goal. Even the English, who in other matters have social sense of caste, have reached this realization for the life of their state, and *have* drawn great benefit for their state from applying it. It must be the government's task to educate for justice those functionaries and officers who are still caught up in old prejudices, and to break their passive obstruction of the will that comes from a higher instance.

The law of tolerance would have to be preached in the schools. These days many schools are real breeding-grounds for anti-Semitism. Schools still exist, in particular private schools, that *simply* refuse to take pupils of the Jewish faith; not just schools of religious character that have a reason not to accept Jewish pupils on principle as a matter of course. Tales are told in class, and lessons are taught, that must make every Jew feel hurt. Here pressure must be applied. For only then can one demand of the Jews that they feel no bitterness. The current customs have driven them for the most part into opposition. Although the Jewish religion teaches the Jews to be conservative, to work for the government at all times, to pray for blessings on the ruler, the exclusion of Jews from many activities and the rejection that can only be briefly touched upon here has driven them to opposition. This is why we find so many Jews on the parliamentary left: the parties of the right would simply not accept them. If Jews in Germany were truly treated *well* justly, then their coreligionists in foreign parts, who are spread across the whole world (there are 11 millions

Jews living) would work for Germany. We should not underestimate the propaganda that could thus be made for Germany.

The English have always understood how to be the protectors of the Jews and have thus gained the sympathy of Jews around the world, which has also shown practical results for the life of the state. However arrogant the Englishman may be in his club, however great the gulf between rich and poor in England, the Englishman has discovered certain basic social and human attitudes that we in Germany do not yet possess.

In *all the* all great civilized countries *that are fighting us,* except Russia, we find Jews as ministers, as high-ranking officers and in influential positions—not in Germany!

The Jews want, just like the Christians, to put themselves entirely at the service of the state, yet in the moment when they strive for the positions due to them, the doors are closed to them, the consequence is that bitterness on the part of the Jews which has been described, a waste of the nation's strength of which account is not taken in Germany, an injustice that repeats itself in daily life in Germany, whereby Germany is herself humiliated and diminished in the eyes of the world so that the German is said, not without cause here, to know neither benevolence nor justice.

The German government should thus take all steps to spread reason to all circles, so that not only is the unheard-of injustice of anti-Semitism recognized, but also the German state's interest in crushing this movement is made clear.

The German Reich must be agreed; the truce between Protestant, Catholic, and Jew must not be superficial, but must continue after the war as honorable and lasting! It can only last when everyone tries starting today—in the army especially—to be just toward his fellow soldier, regardless of which faith!

Rather than discussing the uncertain future, the following demands of the moment urge themselves upon all who fight at the front or behind the lines; to practice true, deep tolerance, above all those who have the power to decide the fate of their subordinates. Much that must be changed is rightly delayed until the war is over. That officers should think again, and think anew, cannot wait so long; here the word is: *hic rhodos, hic salta!* Now or never! Yet sins are still committed in the army now, while we are at war. The purpose of my *indictment* tract is to point this out to all those who must take corrective action for interests of the Empire.

The military personnel who are to be promoted are determined to perform their very best, and demand promotion only insofar as the authorities appointed by the state approve this after expert examination. The state therefore needs merely to ensure that the military authorities can implement objective military examination, as is their duty, so that the promotion of properly selected personnel of nonconformist religion can proceed automatically; previously the objective examination according to military criteria has been disrupted by the necessity of spiritual opinion on the mysteries of this world and the next being subject to military approval. Whoever wants to be promoted, *must* should join the Christian church, *thereby* whereby, and this corrupts both morally and objectively, no value as such is placed on whether baptism is the expression of innermost conviction; rather, conversion is made as easy as possible for these persons, so that their inner religious condition is utterly ignored, only the certificate of baptism is demanded and the persons concerned are then promoted without further ado. Those however who will not undertake religious mummery in order to win worldly advantage, are seen thenceforward as "common folks."

The state must now be firm, during the war and thereafter, that it is no longer admissible to treat Jews who are faithful to their religion worse than those who are compliant; for in order to make the full weight of its political authority felt internally and externally, it must itself have a clear conscience, as a rational and well-governed state under the rule of law. After the war its own people will pitilessly ask, "How, my state, did you handle your human resources? Did you not besmirch the great will to sacrifice by intruding in personal matters of conscience, and where men were ready to give their all, did you not deny them this joy?"

Only Jews who are true to their faith would have any influence on the Jews in the East; but they will only wish to undertake the thorny and thankless task of acting as filter for the Eastern Jews when they are strengthened by the awareness that they are supported in this inner cultural mission by an unconditional rule of law. Read the session transcripts of the Reichstag from not two months before the outbreak of the Great War, when Gothein unflinchingly and bravely tackled this unconstitutional state of affairs, and you will hear indirectly from the then–minister of war von Falkenhayn's reply that he and his predecessors in the ministerial post felt that state of affairs to be painful, not just "pro forma." A stream of our nation's blood shed in this sacrificial war must wash away this uncouth blot on the German army's pristine shield.

For those to whom the full equality of Jews in the army still seems an impossibility, it may be instructive to consider how Frederick the Great treated bourgeois officers in comparison to the nobles. Once forced to accept the bourgeois into the army as officers during wartime, he hoped to *get rid of* root them out after the end of the war. Many an officer may privately think the same of Jews today. And what would the German army be, if we had not officers from the bourgeoisie? And how many more worthy officers we would have had at the outbreak of war, if the Jews had also been properly selected and made officers!

If once we succeed in carrying through this change in the army, then comes the more difficult task for Germany that will set our country a task at the global level and the proper solution of which will improve and elevate its position in the world: namely the general solution to the Jewish question. The Jewish question is by its nature international, first because all countries must concern themselves with it, second because when Jews are badly treated in one country their emigration results and other countries are often not affected by this emigration in ways each country of immigration may wish. Is Germany ready and willing to contribute to the solution of the Jewish question? Will Germany take the leading role in this question where Europe is concerned? Anti-Semitism has certainly found stronger expression in Germany than in England and in France, yet we must be clear that in these countries the friendship toward Jews is not unconditional. Even very recently the Dreyfus affair has shown that unusually strong anti-Semitism could flare up in France. In England there has been strict reticence with regard to Jewish immigration in recent years. Laws were passed and in this regard England certainly rather lost the world's goodwill, since she did not flinch from forcibly deporting Russian Jews back to Russia who had sought asylum in England years before because of the atrocious circumstances in Russia.

The 11 million Jews living around the world mostly understand German, and their knowledge of the language might help in launching a movement from Germany that could only *be* work to Germany's own advantage *for it would be in a position* and win her new friends throughout the world. This possibility has never been sufficiently recognized by Germany's leaders. A good work here can *be profitably conjoined* to improve Germany's political reputation. The land that undertakes this problem with scientific thoroughness and a deep sense of justice does not merely contribute to the solution of one of the most difficult tasks, but also attains significant moral stature by tackling this challenge and gains influence in the whole world. Paradoxical though it may sound, Germany could be called upon, just as it has nurtured anti-Semitism scientifically, to find a scientific basis for solving this difficult question.

We cannot solve the problem without taking some account of Zionism, although here we must be clear that the Zionist movement, even if most successful, will only in some decades be able to solve the Jewish question and even then, only to a limited extent.

What does Zionism want? Its goals have never been clearly expressed, for these goals have not always been the same. To create a place of refuge for those who must leave their fatherland because of ill treatment is a worthy goal, as is to give Jews the chance to live according to the precepts of their religion in one place, so as to deepen their creed in a way that they could not in the diaspora.

Yet just as Catholics remain good citizens of their own state when they demand for the Pope a commanding role in the world, likewise the Jews, even if they are interested in or even passionate for Zionism, must be in a position to be good citizens of their own land. The Pope is head of the Catholic church. The Jewish religion is more democratic; there is no high priest who must be treated as such. The wish to bring one's own religion to its purest form can only be fulfilled, so some Zionists believe, when an independent community does not live as a part within the body of a state, but has the chance to live as a closed group in a foreign state.

The German Empire can be of help in realizing this wish, by taking steps in Turkey for the benefit of the Jews. Here must be established from the outset that the separation of the land in question from Turkey is not intended, but rather that this concerns a closed religious state under the sovereignty of the secular state, Turkey.

Germany's general course in answering the Jewish question can be only briefly hinted at here, but must be touched upon to show, even briefly, the course open to us if we justly solve the Jewish question here at home for humane reasons and in the interest of the state. If we respond to the demand of the moment, then we contribute to making good those sins committed over the centuries so commonly that the sinful was forgotten!

I know that in writing these lines I lay myself open to accusation.

It will be said that at this moment it is not fit to speak of mistakes that the army has made and continues to make, but I find that when a body is so generally healthy as is our military body, it can endure being alerted to such mistakes, for only thus is healing possible.

I will also be accused of demanding a disproportionate favoritism toward the Jews once the war is over. This is not at all the case. One may test the Jews for their capability and strength of character much more thoroughly than the rest. By no means do I demand exaggerated consideration; to the contrary, if anti-Semitism is to be banished for good, we certainly must not overdo it. Yet if once this war is over we are to take up the economic struggle, we need aid from the most capable, and also the most capable of the Jews, and we need the sympathy of Jews around the world if we wish to use all means to succeed politically and economically.

I will thus gladly endure the personal charges that will be falsely leveled against me, if only the interests of the German Empire are fulfilled.

I can freely and openly confess this because I am inwardly and outwardly independent and aim for nothing for myself personally; I am only wishing that it be recognized in the German Empire how important is self-scrutiny with regard to the treatment of the Jews. Without false modesty and without undue pride I must warn of this danger, as a German and as a member of a family which can be traced back in both lines in Germany for 300 years, which has also honorably contributed to art, to science, and to philanthropy, and which shed its blood sacrifice in the war of 1870/71 just as in this present war.

November 1916
M.W.

Directives concerning the military promotion of religiously nonconformist persons suggested by one

26. June 6

The central question is twice rooted in the soil of jurisprudence, although its roots may extend further: in state law and the law of human rights. In state law, because this law has the task of formulating how the member of a society may best and most effectively be used, in human rights, because these demand that state deployment confine itself to a minimum regard for personal freedom. The social interest and the natural efforts of each individual, which otherwise must naturally oppose one another implacably in their demands, here meet and join in the matter of "directives," as long as such a compromise is not summarily opposed. For those military personnel who are to be promoted are determined to perform their very best and demand promotion only insofar as the authorities appointed by the state approve this after expert examination. The state therefore needs merely not to hinder the military authorities in implementing the objective military examination that is their duty, so that the promotion of properly selected personnel of nonconformist religion can proceed automatically. Previously, of course, the objective examination from the military point of view has been disrupted by the spiritual opinion on the mysteries of this world and the next and has sheerly destroyed the technocratic results of Prussia's military organization, if it happen that the persons examined have not ceremoniously (through baptism) made the Christian church's faith their own. Thereby, and this corrupts both morally and objectively, nobody insists that only those may convert who have an inmost conviction. Rather conversion is made as easy as possible for these persons, so that inner religious conviction is utterly ignored, only the certificate of baptism is demanded, and the persons concerned are then promoted without further obstacle. Those, however, whose scruples will not allow them to undertake religious mummery in order to win worldly advantage, are seen thenceforward as "lesser folks."

The state must now be firm, during the war and thereafter, that it is no longer admissible to treat Jews who are faithful to their religion worse than those who are compliant; for in order to make the full weight of its political authority felt internally and externally, it must itself have a clear conscience, as a rational and well-governed state under the rule of law. After the war its own people will pitilessly ask, "How, my state, did you handle your human resources? Did you not besmirch the great will to sacrifice by intruding in personal matters of conscience, and where men were ready to give their all, did you not deny them this joy?" The Entente has hypocritically peddled the wares of the French revolution and will continue to do so, yelling that we and our allies subjugate men's conscience, and they have told this to the Jews who will

very shortly come under German rule, who will only become good Germans if they see that for the German state there are indeed "only Germans." Converted Jews will be in an impossible position as regards these fellows of their tribe, for the most difficult problem that awaits Germany is to civilize the Eastern Jews. Only undiluted Jews would have any influence on the Jews in the East; but they will only wish to undertake the thorny and thankless task of acting as a filter for the Eastern Jews when they are strengthened by the awareness that they are supported by an unconditional rule of law. Read the session transcripts of the Reichstag from not two months before the outbreak of the great war, when Gothein unflinchingly and bravely tackled this unconstitutional state of affairs, and you will hear indirectly from the then–minister of war Falkenhayn's reply how he and his predecessors in the ministerial post felt that state of affairs to be painful not just "pro forma." A stream of our nation's blood shed in this war of independence against England must wash away this uncouth blot on the German army's pristine shield.
Reichstag report 1916, S. 8564, 8559 & 9105.

Börries v. Münchhausen to Max M. Warburg

Berlin N.W. 7, Hotel "Der Königshof"
28 May 17

My very esteemed and dear Herr Warburg!
I would have written to you some time ago and thanked you for so kindly sending to me your pamphlet, had I not been waiting each day for an essay for the *Kunstwart* to arrive, which I would have liked to enclose here. Since it has still not arrived today I shall no longer delay in answering your kindness with something in exchange, nor in writing down for you my own thoughts on the Jewish question. As you will see from my book *Juda* (which follows in the posts), this problem has occupied me artistically, yet long ago it also caught my attention politically and humanly. I have often and again spoken of this with my Jewish friends, with brothers-in-arms in my regiment, with high and low, with men and women and have been able to establish the following:

1) The Nature of anti-Semitism:

Anti-Semitism, that is the awareness that Jewry is in many respects very alien to the Aryan nature, and the conscious refusal of Jewry's essential and characteristic traits, is not a sentiment that can be spread as it were by infection, but rather one that anyone will feel who has taken the time to think more deeply about the world in which he finds himself. It is wrong to say that schools are responsible here, or clubs at university; anti-Semitism is merely more forthright and impatient here, because youth in general is impatient and unequivocal. We must not delude ourselves. Each and every Aryan has and will always have the sense of otherness from each and every Jew.

This irrepressible and involuntary feeling can no more be ignored than one can forget, in conversation with a lady, that she is a woman, or while conversing in a foreign language, forget the fact that one is not speaking German. Further, anti-Semitism is a racial feeling and has not the least thing to do with religion. No anti-Semite will feel that the famous writer Ruth—I forget her surname—who converted to Judaism, is a Jewess, any more than this feeling of otherness falls silent in the presence of a Jew converted to Christianity. When the state more or less openly forces Jews to deny their religion and only then opens certain posts to them, then to my mind that is not only an unprecedented infamy, which insults two religions at once, but also and above all a wholly incomprehensible stupidity. No anti-Semite wishes for the baptism of the Jews; one might also say: quite the opposite. In conclusion I repeat: anti-Semitism is a racial feeling, not a religious one, and furthermore it is in no way a feeling of hatred or contempt.

2) In all nations this basic feeling has given rise to feelings and behaviors that decent men of all races can only agree upon. Each word spent on this subject is a waste. Intolerance against other nations, other ages, other languages, other religions, or political convictions is in all circumstances the sign of a narrow mind, and this intolerance can only be justified under one condition, that is when the survival of one's own people, one's own language, religion, etc. seems threatened by the foreign. In this case, everyone has that most basic human right of self-assertion. I have lived in sincere friendship with Jesuits and Frenchmen, until the former tried to convert my children and the latter laid claim to parts of my fatherland. I therefore feel that anti-Semitism is justified as a defensive phenomenon wherever I see German nationhood and German culture in danger of being taken over by Jewry. In my opinion this is especially so as regards the way in which our cultural legacy is handled. Quite apart from the question of whether German culture is higher or lesser than the Jewish, it is for us in the highest degree troubling that our press, our literature, our theater, our art trade has slipped almost completely into the hands of an alien nation that quite obviously cannot feel as Aryans do. On the other hand I do not think that the predominance of Jews in commerce is so dangerous. Here it is not—or not to the same degree—a question of cultural goods, but only of those that have to do with civilization: money and suchlike. An accusation against the Jews is that they are never productive, that they create no values but act only as middlemen, that they are not farmers, craftsmen, workers, sailors, productive artists—that rather they are almost always only reproductive artists and tradesmen. This fact cannot be disputed, but it is a sign of intolerance to take racial characteristics as grounds for an accusation. Furthermore

the Jew has largely attained his majority in these fields thanks to qualities that can only be seen as desirable and that the Germans so often lack: sobriety, ambition, single-minded endeavor, and industry, whereas our nation tends much more to immoderation, idleness, and distractedness.

3) I believe that assimilation is a monstrous, fatal error, which is all the more indefensible because every racial assimilation so far has failed. I am thinking here of the attempts to settle Jewish farmers in Palestine. For several years I have been in close contact with the Jewish farmers' and gardeners' school near Hanover and have repeatedly heard from those who know the conditions, and also from this institution's annual reports, how little comes from these efforts in the long run. In the long run no race can be forcibly changed. Likewise I believe that assimilation by marriage is fatal. Any mixture of the races necessarily destroys what is characteristic in each race; as a German I feel this to be doubly regrettable, since the dark-haired races are always physiologically the stronger, so that the descendants always lose their Germanness to a greater degree than their Jewish-ness. I feel the Semitic trace unmistakably in the third or even fourth generation of my acquaintances, not just in the appearance but in their being. These descendants are almost always inwardly torn, unhappy people, they are lost as members of the Jewish as of the Aryan nation and it seems to me that a real Jew must be just as unhappy for them as a real German. Perhaps other races, such as the Roman, mix more easily with the Semites, just as anti-Semitism seems to be less pronounced in France and Italy than with us; here, though, one must remember that it often needs only a nudge, as with the Dreyfus affair, to escalate the justified feeling of otherness to the most regrettable anti-Semitic excesses.

4) What then is the escape from this dilemma? In my view it can only be strict separation. It is bare injustice to force Jews to become soldiers without giving them the chance also to become officers. Therefore they must either be wholly excluded from the military, or, and this seems to me the most practical path, they must be allowed to form their own regiments with their own officers, regiments that would not be religiously but rather racially oriented. I do not doubt for a moment that in competition with Germans these regiments would perform just as well as our own people. Obedience would be a matter of course in them, whereas my twenty years' experience as a soldier in all manner of regiments has shown me that a Jewish superior of Aryan soldiers always plays an unspeakably thankless role. Regardless of whether he is baptized, often indeed on the basis of sheer suspicion, such a man is always known throughout the regiment as: the Jew; and he may do as he will, but it will always be taken amiss. His strictness is not tolerated, his amiability is seen as fulsome. If he is scrupulous with money, then he will be called penny-pinching, if he is generous, it is thought that he wishes to buy favor; in short I can think of no more horrid position than that of a Jewish officer in an Aryan regiment. Those

corps where baptized Jews have the chance to become officers are also known far and wide, and I believe that every true friend of Jewry must wish to spare these worthy, noble, and decent people such a terrible position.

5) In addition, there is the following consideration: it is always humiliating to strive to be accepted in circles that reject you. After all, I would as a Protestant never force myself into a Catholic regiment, and as a bourgeois citizen or one newly ennobled would think myself despicable if I sought to join the Knights of St. John; given my financial circumstances I would find it ridiculous to be put up for membership in the Union Club. Therefore everybody who is concerned for the welfare of the Jews must advise them not to put themselves in this position. And if it were indeed possible (as it has been in this war) to make a few hundred or a few thousand Jews officers, we merely make a few hundred or a few thousand unhappy people, men who are all the more unhappy the more sensitive, reserved, inwardly worthy they are. I can expect no good at all to come from this. Since, however, the army has nothing to do with our cultural legacy, I do not consider this point at all essential.

You write that you cannot accept that the German Christian feels more deeply for his fatherland than the German Jew. Politically and militarily, certainly not. The Jew is readier to sacrifice, feels more deeply, is more generous in giving than the Aryan, and thus without question has always done more than the German for the state and the community as a whole. However, experience has shown that the Jew is incapable of comprehending the depths of German being and culture, just as the Aryan is incapable of feeling Semitic culture deeply. These words are my verdict on the volume of verse that will follow this letter. Today I would no more write this book than I would write many of the Gypsy songs of my youth, because I have become too much aware that only an artificial attempt at sympathy can result, an imitation, a wrenching of one's own self without really gaining any of the values of the foreign nation. Just as a man would never really be able to write songs in the maiden's voice, the "Frauen-Lieb und-Leben," or as today's lady ballad-makers have never succeeded in a really heroic poem, just as an aristocrat from Niedersachsen cannot write Social Democratic workers' songs—just like these, my Jewish and Gypsy songs are intrinsically impossible. You may thus see, dear Herr Warburg, that I am ruthlessly consistent in my thinking.

I have made a few small notes in the margins of your work and thus enclose it here for you, but respectfully request that you send your valuable pamphlet back once more for my library.

It is infinitely difficult for me to discuss these matters with a Jew, although I could talk quite freely about the differences of our races with a Slav or one of the Romance races. If I am right then the reason for this lies in what I have learned to see as an unusual sensibility, which in the final analysis is exaggerated pride, just as one finds in Catholics when it comes to questions of religion or in Frenchmen when it comes to politics. In your nation's past it has led to the aristocratic concept of the "people of Moses" and finds expression in hundreds of Mosaic, and even more Talmudic, commandments that address the relation of Jews and non-Jews. I hope that I have been able to convince you that my pen has been driven by a passionate love for justice as by a great concern for the cultural legacy of my nation!

Most of all I would like to talk these things over with you face-to-face and thus ask you to let me know when you are next in Berlin and have an evening free for such a conversation.

With assurances of my great respect I remain, esteemed Herr Warburg,

Yours sincerely
Börries v. Münchhausen

Letter from Aby Warburg to Max Warburg about Börries v. Münchhausen

Dear Max!
Just a few marginalia to Herr v. M.'s letter, which I returned to you last night once I had had a copy made. Pity, such self-satisfied narrow-mindedness behind a tactful façade; all in all it is nothing other than the clipped tones of the noble paleface.

To 1): The aristocratic officer will have felt (and still feels) the same sense of otherness, which is acquired rather than natural; albeit that it has different causes in this case, it was nevertheless just as infallible and in earlier times, dominant.

To 2): The noble Germans cannot get used to the fact that they are simply shareholders in the business of culture and not absolute masters. They reserve for themselves the right to throw their Jewish subordinates out at any moment without giving notice, if they happen to think that they are doing any harm or that there are too many of them around. They have not yet heard of the fundamental idea that a common intellectual goal might act upon all parts of the nation and urge them onward to something higher and unknown. The wicked chatter about the unproductivity of the Jews rests on astonishing historical ignorance; in their own country the Jews were herdsmen, farmers, vintners, in short agriculturalists, governed by a caste of priests with a war-leader monarch at the top: a pure culture of Prussia in the Orient.

To 3): Here Chamberlain's destructive influence can be seen at work. Even the idiotic doctrine of the inwardly torn, unhappy bastard is represented. If only these lads actually had some horse sense at least. What do horse-breeders mean when they talk of an English thoroughbred? A mixture of the "Noricum" horse with the Arab breed. The only area in which crossbreeding has been tried and tested we find that the most valued achievement of science is a mixture of Aryan and Semite, and here I should remark that horses are most likely an Asian import.

To 4): Jewish regiments are a desperate measure that would rob our army of its highest ethical effect, which is to make uniformity from diversity.

To 5): Likewise the entirely desperate measure, the decision to treat a whole class of men as suspicious from the outset in order not to upset one's personal lack of breeding. Here it is best to turn the wheel and say that an officer corps that does not see it as its highest duty to examine each person's qualities without reservation and to develop the good qualities with love and care, is basically an unpatriotic, provincial clique and I do not doubt that it will be swept aside as such once the war is over. There is no principled Jew who does not know and feel that the army is more than just one part of the German organism, that rather it embodies the nation's manhood in the highest sense; and no such principled Jew will take account of those noble souls who do not want to be upset. Every attempt to bar the Jews from participation simply means making them the landlords' helots. As far as consideration for Germany's cultural legacy is concerned, Herr v. M. obviously does not know what such minds as Neander Stahl, Lassalle, Marx, or even Riesser, Simson, and Isaac Wolffson (I name only those of great practical significance for Germany in recent years) have done for Germany's higher intellect and unity. I would further like to know what this distinguished poet thinks or thought of Heine. He must have undergone a change of heart caused by his altered attitude to Lilien. Herr v. M. has not studied the matter enough as to be able to draw a real distinction between Galician and German Jewry.

In any case, because of their lack of intellect such types, when they aim at world domination, are hopelessly outclassed by imperialist techniques of liberty as well as by the spiritual militarism of the Catholic church: for these world powers the individual is very much more than a "body" to be counted. One more word on Jewish sensibility: we are a rather decayed aristocracy, but we are no proletarians who can be "dragooned": and we had our seats in the uncanny hotel of the "Three Fates" while v. M.'s dear departed ancestors were most likely still lodged under open skies.

Warmly, yr. A.

I am too good a German to wish that anybody from the Entente got to read v. M.'s letter: a true document of barbarism.

Notes

Preface to the English-Language Edition

1. In Warburg, *Renewal of Pagan Antiquity*, 585–86. Full references for citations and literature are given in the bibliography.
2. Warburg, *Images from the Region of the Pueblo*; Cestelli Guidi and Mann, eds., *Photographs at the Frontier*.
3. "The lecture that follows represents only a provisional sketch for a forthcoming, detailed publication that will contain an iconological study of the sources of the fresco cycle in the Palazzo Schifanoia." See Warburg, *Renewal of Pagan Antiquity*, 563. That publication never materialized.
4. Stimilli, ed., *Ludwig Binswanger–Aby Warburg*.
5. Heckscher, "Genesis of Iconology," 339–62.
6. Wuttke, *Aby M. Warburg*.
7. Woodfield, ed., *Art History as Cultural History*. The collection contains essays by Kathryn Brush, Ernst Gombrich, Peg Katritzky, Kirsten Lippincott, Dorothea McEwan, Matthew Rampley, Aby Warburg, and the present author.
8. Michaud, *Aby Warburg and the Image in Motion*.
9. As is demonstrated in Didi-Huberman, *L'image survivante*.

Introduction

1. "Eine jede Idee tritt als fremder Gast in die Erfahrung und wie sie sich zu realisieren beginnt, ist sie kaum von Phantasie und Phantasterei zu unterscheiden" (Goethe, "Maximen und Reflexionen," 439).
2. Noted under the date 23 July 1929 in *Zettelkasten* 13, "Weltanschau-

ung" with the reference "Goethe, Schultze—Plethon, 46." See also *Tagebuch der K.B.W*, 445.

3. Wuttke, ed., *Kosmopolis*, 33: Letter from Warburg to Ernst Robert Curtius, 5 August 1929, giving advice on how to found a new research institute: "Since I am in no way dependent on any government agency, the K.B.W. could set itself a task which has been called fanciful, and here I always think of Goethe's words in the 'Maxims and Reflections:'" he then cites Goethe, as above.
4. "Büchertrutzkasten"; in Warburg's letter to his brothers. See Stockhausen, *Die Kulturwissenschaftliche Bibliothek Warburg*, 174.
5. Gombrich, *Aby Warburg*, 305. "We have seen that the idea of this threat was identified in Warburg's mind with certain motifs. The emphasis on the 'head-hunting woman' reveals the subsoil of fear that underlies Warburg's fascination with the 'Nympha,' but the same ambivalence (which led him to formulate his philosophy of polarity) may also account for his identification with Perseus, the hero who brandishes the head of Medusa. It would be tempting to follow the chains of associations that may lead from the image of Perseus with his weapon to that of Saturn with his sickle and further on to the myth of the Birth of Venus which stands at the opening of Warburg's career as a scholar; but it is safer to break off at this point than to enter into these dangerous labyrinths where not only laymen can easily get lost."
6. Vom Bruch, *Weltpolitik als Kulturmission*, which contains an extensive bibliography and sources.
7. François Bourricaud in Chevalier, *L'Antisémitisme*, 7: "Une des questions les plus énigmatiques et les plus cruellement embarrassantes que puisse se poser un homme de XXe siècle."
8. Burke in *Aby Warburg*, 39–44; Raulff in Warburg, *Schlangenritual;* Settis, "Kunstgeschichte als vergleichende Kulturwissenschaft"; Steinberg, "Aby Warburg's Kreuzlingen Lecture."
9. By now the methodological tools are surely ready to address this aspect of Warburg's work analytically—and here too Gombrich's view is due for correction. Cf. especially Ortony, ed., *Metaphor and Thought*, which contains numerous insightful essays.
10. See also Warnke, "Aby Warburg," 123: "Warburg's project of cultural history demanded more from a history of art: it should become a field of enquiry in which were prefigured his own phobias, questions, repressions, and fears for the future, and those of his age." Even today this "diagnostic understanding of the artwork" is Warburg's distinctive and as yet unsurpassed contribution to the discipline's discourse.
11. Rathenau, "Staat und Judentum," 189.
12. Meyer, "Aby Warburg in His Early Correspondence," 452.

13. Burckhardt, *Reflections on History,* 34.
14. Ibid., 35, and White, *Metahistory,* chapter 6.
15. Warburg, *Renewal of Pagan Antiquity,* 534–35.
16. Ibid. Here Warburg speaks of "taking our orders from the problem in hand (in the present writer's case, that of the influence of antiquity)."
17. Ibid.
18. Gombrich, *Aby Warburg,* 214–15.
19. Ibid.
20. London, Warburg Institute Archive; collected in *Zettelkasten* 36, "Juden." The institute's archive will henceforth be abbreviated as WIA in the notes.
21. Steinhausen, ed., *Monographien zur deutschen Kulturgeschichte.*
22. Diesener, ed., *Karl Lamprecht weiterdenken,* with several contributions; Schorn-Schütte, *Karl Lamprecht.*
23. On "survival" (*Nachleben*) as a phenomenon see Raulff in Warburg, *Schlangenritual,* 78.
24. Gilbert, "From Art History to the History of Civilization," 390: "There is no doubt that Warburg's unwillingness to find evolution, progress or development in history is in contrast with the normative character which he ascribed to the classical world."
25. Warnke, "Aby Warburg," 123, speaks of Warburg's "diagnostic understanding of the artwork." David Nirenberg rightly questions the unchanging nature of European anti-Semitism in a study of the coexistence of Christians, Jews, and Muslims in medieval Spain: Nirenberg, *Communities of Violence,* especially 3–17.
26. Of particular interest here are Yerushalmi, *Freud's Moses,* and Klein, *Jewish Origins of the Psychoanalytic Movement*; cf. also the excursus on Freud in Kany, *Mnemosyne als Programm,* 219–21, where Kany compares Freud's *Interpretation of Dreams* to Walter Benjamin's work, and Schorske, *Fin-de-Siècle Vienna,* 181–207.
27. Diers, "Professor V. Aby Warburgs Krankenakte."
28. See 111–19.
29. Kany, *Die religionsgeschichtliche Forschung.*
30. A method which thus sets out to search for "clues" can ground itself in Carlo Ginzburg's work "Kunst und soziales Gedächtnis," but also in Warburg's own methods. See also the explication of Kany's *Mnemosyne als Programm.*
31. Grolle, "Die Büste Aby Warburgs," note 17, 169 (Hans Harder Biermann-Ratjen, 1901–69, was a notary in Hamburg from 1929, member of the Free Democratic Party from 1947, city senator for cultural affairs 1953–66).
32. WIA, GC, Gertrud Bing to Senator Biermann-Ratjen, 10 July 1963, 3;

in a transcription made by Silvia Baumgarten and Bettina Götz.

33. WIA, GC, Gertrud Bing to Senator Biermann-Ratjen, 10 July 1963, 2 f.
34. Cf. Broich and Pfister, eds., *Intertextualität*, or Lachmann, *Gedächtnis und Literatur*, 13–50.
35. Vom Bruch, ed., *Kultur und Kulturwissenschaften um 1900.*

Chapter 1

1. "Die Furcht vor Anti-Semitismus nie ganz los geworden," Warburg, *Ausgewählte Schriften und Würdigungen*, 455–64, here 463.
2. Ibid., 463; since Joist Grolle reconstructed the way in which the occasion was organized, it has been evident that Gertrud Bing found this speech arduous and difficult, cf. Grolle "Die Büste Aby Warburgs," 157 f.
3. Gombrich, "The Ambivalence of the Classical Tradition," 135.
4. Diers, "Kreuzlinger Passion."
5. Cf. in contrast, the analysis offered in Steinberg, "Aby Warburg's Kreuzlingen Lecture," 67–87.
6. Gombrich, *Aby Warburg*, 303.
7. Cited by Gertrud Bing in her 1958 lecture (Bing, "Aby M. Warburg," 464).
8. *Worte zur Beisetzung.*
9. Heise, *Persönliche Erinnerungen an Aby Warburg*, 38, on the International Congress of Art Historians.
10. Ibid.
11. Ibid., 12.
12. Ibid., 18.
13. These follow on from the section titled "Racism" in the library: *Catalog of The Warburg Institute Library*, 1:548–51. Some of the works reached the library because Warburg was a member of the Gobineau Society.
14. Gobineau, *Versuch über die Ungleichheit der Menschenracen.*
15. Heise, *Persönliche Erinnerungen an Aby Warburg*, 11.
16. Ibid., 50.
17. Ibid., 51
18. Raulff in Warburg, *Schlangenritual*, 84–92.
19. Heise, *Persönliche Erinnerungen an Aby Warburg*, 52; additional information in Königseder, "Aby Warburg im 'Bellevue.'"
20. Heise, *Persönliche Erinnerungen an Aby Warburg*, 51.
21. Warburg's son Max A. Warburg provided the "biographical scaffolding" for his work; Gombrich, *Aby Warburg*, 5.
22. On the cult of the Renaissance see Buck, *Italienische Renaissance*, and

Buck, ed., *Renaissance und Renaissancismus.*

23. Gombrich, *Aby Warburg*, 11 f.
24. Ibid., 19–20.
25. Ibid., 20; from the "Notizen zum Schlangenritual," 16–18.
26. Ibid., 23.
27. Ibid., 25; see 25–29; 165 f.
28. Ibid., 71–72: "(A) Personal gods whose power makes itself felt in an arbitrary and incalculable way-sacrifices for particular ends. (B) One personal god, ruling steadily, angry but can be reconciled-clearly prescribed and regular sacrifices. (C) Christ, St. Paul: God is love. Rejection of the crudely sensuous aspect of sacrifice: sacrifice and ceremony (the law) eliminated from daily life; what remains is prayer and a few ceremonies, baptism, Eucharist. (D) God is within us: daily work the same as divine service." This fragment of 4 September 1888 antedates by far Weber's study on the Protestant ethic in 1905.
29. Liebeschütz, "Aby Warburg." In the 1920s Liebeschütz had ties to the K.B.W. in Hamburg, and he made a life's work of the study of European civilization and its attitude to Jewry; thereby he necessarily also examined the variously marked anti-Jewish tendencies in philosophy, historiography, and politics. See Liebeschütz, "Das Judentum im Geschichtsbild Jacob Burckhardts"; "Treitschke and Mommsen on Jewry and Judaism"; "Max Weber's Historical Interpretation of Judaism"; *Das Judentum im deutschen Geschichtsbild,* and so forth.
30. Liebeschütz, "Aby Warburg," 226.
31. Ibid., 227.
32. Ibid., 227 f.; cf. also Lippincott, "Aby Warburg, Fritz Saxl," who compares Warburg's and Saxl's radically different ways of working.
33. Liebeschütz, "Aby Warburg," 228.
34. Ibid., 229; see chapter 3 for Warburg's fragment, 55–60.
35. Ibid., 230.
36. Ibid., 232–34.
37. Gay, *Weimar Culture.*
38. Liebeschütz, "Aby Warburg," 230.
39. Gilbert, "From Art History to the History of Civilization," 381. Gilbert remarks of the difficulty of writing this review: "On the one hand, it must explain, why Gombrich was justified in devoting to Aby Warburg, a German art historian who died more than forty years ago, a full-length biography. The significance of Warburg's ideas not only for specialists in art history but for historians in general must be demonstrated. On the other hand, it will have to be made clear that, if the reader remained not fully convinced of Warburg's seminal importance, this is not the fault of the subject of the book but of the treatment it received; despite the light

which it throws on Warburg's ideas and achievements, the book does not place him adequately in the framework of intellectual history." Edgar Wind was of a similar, and even more pronounced, opinion: Wind, "Appendix," 106–13.

40. Gilbert, "From Art History to the History of Civilization," 388.
41. Ibid., 389 f.
42. Ibid., 390.
43. Ibid., 391: "If the Renaissance period has any exemplary value it lies in the material it provides for analysis of the origin and the conditions of cultural achievement."
44. Syamken, "Warburgs Umwege als Hermeneutik More Majorum," 17 f.
45. Deppner, "Bilder als Kommentare."
46. This is indeed made clear in the first paragraph but is thereafter used in the sense of Talmudic Jewish exegesis of the Bible (Symaken, "Warburgs Umwege als Hermeneutik More Majorum," 15).
47. The motto chosen for Syamken's essay can be found in Warburg, *Ausgewählte Schriften und Würdigungen,* 618 and 620.
48. As also noted by Anne Marie Meyer, "Aby Warburg in His Early Correspondence," 445.
49. Warburg, *Schlangenritual,* 63–94.
50. On which see also the further facts adduced by Königseder, "Aby Warburg im 'Bellevue.'"
51. "Lediglich spekulieren läßt sich darüber, ob es tatsächlich 'nur' eine zeitlebens gefährdete Psyche war, die jetzt nachgab-oder ob nicht vielmehr eine überaus komplexe und fragile politisch-ethnisch-religiöse Identität, die sich ebenso in Anlehnung an das politische System des wilhelmischen Deutschland (Stichwort 'Hamburger Kaiserjuden') wie in Absetzung von diesem, in der Identifikation mit dem Judentum wie im Bruch mit der praktizierten Religion gebildet hatte, dem Druck der Verhältnisse nicht mehr standzuhalten vermochte" (Raulff in Warburg, *Schlangenritual,* 63); the "Hamburger Kaiserjuden" is a reference to Tramer, "Die Hamburger Kaiserjuden."
52. Bing, "Aby M. Warburg," 464.
53. Raulff in Warburg, *Schlangenritual,* 67.
54. Ibid., 73.
55. Ibid., 73–78.
56. Ibid., 78.
57. See 25–42.
58. Meyer, "Aby Warburg in His Early Correspondence," 446.
59. Ibid., 447.
60. See 25 f and 165 f.
61. Meyer, "Aby Warburg in His Early Correspondence," 451.

62. Ibid., 452.
63. Steinberg, "Aby Warburg's Kreuzlingen Lecture: A Reading," 68.
64. Ibid., 70.
65. Ibid., 87.
66. Ibid., 105.

Chapter 2

1. Meyer, "Aby Warburg in His Early Correspondence," 447; Gombrich, *Aby Warburg*, 26. The two letters are given in translation in an appendix, see 165–67.
2. Meyer, "Aby Warburg in His Early Correspondence," 447.
3. See Gombrich, *Aby Warburg*, 20.
4. WIA, III.52, "Anti-Semitism," the sketch on the "characterology of the Jews"; cf. 56.
5. Warburg Spinelli, *Die Dringlichkeit des Mitleids*, 43.
6. Chernow, *The Warburgs*, 27–32, draws extensively upon Warburg Spinelli.
7. Warburg Spinelli, *Die Dringlichkeit des Mitleids*, 42.
8. "Deutschland nicht so sehr als Staat, sondern als Gemeinschaft von Menschen" (ibid., 44 f).
9. Eckardt, *Lebenserinnerungen*, 1:202.
10. Ibid., 1:202 f.
11. Ibid., 1:204.
12. Gombrich, *Aby Warburg*, 22–24.
13. Correspondence copybook VI, 304, letter to Lore Strack dated 1 July 1917.
14. "Aber daß so etwas vorkommen kann!"
15. Jarausch, *Deutsche Studenten 1800–1970*, 59–70; the historical chapters of this German study on the history of students in Germany are based on Jarausch, *Students, Society, and Politics*, in English, in which particularly chapters 5 to 7 are of interest here.
16. Jarausch, *Deutsche Studenten 1800–1970*, 62.
17. Ibid.
18. German students' dueling societies required their members to fight one another with fencing sabers; these duels were non-lethal and highly regulated. (Translator's note.) See also Jarausch, *Deutsche Studenten 1800–1970*, 69, and Elias, *Studien über die Deutschen*, 122–24.
19. Jarausch, *Deutsche Studenten 1800–1970*, 68.
20. Elias, *Studien über die Deutschen*, 132 f., 142–51.
21. Jarausch, *Deutsche Studenten 1800–1970*, 67, and Jarausch, *Students,*

Society, and Politics, 270–74.
22. Elias, *Studien über die Deutschen*, 63.
23. See the profile offered in ibid., 62–71.
24. On these statistics cf. Jarausch, *Students, Society, and Politics*, 292–332.
25. Cf. the letter to Lore Strack dated 1 July 1917 in Correspondence copybook VI, 304; weekly meetings with John Hertz, Max L. Strack, Paul Ruben, and others in a wine bar. Meyer, "Aby Warburg in His Early Correspondence," 448, cites from a letter that Warburg sent to his mother from Bonn, mentioning among other matters the bar which he frequented on Tuesdays and Fridays.
26. Meyer, "Aby Warburg in His Early Correspondence," 447; WIA; GC, Warburg to his mother, 26 January 1887.
27. See examples in Meyer, "Aby Warburg in His Early Correspondence," 451 f.
28. Weber, "Science as a Vocation," 14.
29. Ibid.
30. Mosse, *Confronting the Nation*, 121–30; here 121.
31. Cf. Erikson, *Identity and the Life Cycle.*
32. Meyer, "Aby Warburg in His Early Correspondence," 448.
33. Bollenbeck, *Bildung und Kultur*, 160–288.
34. Goethe, *Wilhelm Meister's Years of Apprenticeship*, 2:79.
35. On which cf. Mosse, *Confronting the Nation*, 112 f.
36. Goffmann, *Stigma;* Erikson, *Identity and the Life Cycle.*
37. Hermsen, "Werk und Wirkung Erik H. Eriksons"; Frank, "Erik Homburger Erikson," 164–73.
38. Marquard and Stierle, eds., *Identität.*
39. Gleason, "Identifying Identity."
40. Gergen coined the term "patchwork-identity" in *Saturated Self.*
41. Particularly insightful is the section titled "Assimilation and Dissimilation" in Klein, *Jewish Origins of the Psychoanalytic Movement*, 1–39. See also the brief and instructive summary offered by Meyer, *Jüdische Identität in der Moderne,* especially 10–18.
42. Gombrich, *Aby Warburg*, 238.
43. Giesen, ed., *Nationale und kulturelle Identität.*
44. Hammerstein, *Antisemitismus und deutsche Universitäten 1871–1933.* Much can be learned here from studies of Freud's place in the history of scholarship, Yerushalmi, *Freud's Moses,* and Schorske, *Fin-de-Siècle Vienna.*
45. See Gombrich, *Aby Warburg*, 5.
46. On the Kant seminar see ibid., 55 and 77, although Gombrich did not use this letter for his *Intellectual Biography;* Warburg also attended Theobald Ziegler's seminar on probability theory, see ibid., 55.

47. Kant, "Prolegomena zu einer jeden künftigen Metaphysik."
48. Pulzer, "Die jüdische Beteiligung an der Politik," 169–72, here 170; Paucker, "Zur Problematik einer jüdischen Abwehrstrategie," 508–9; see 80–88.
49. On the history of the term "Jewish question" see Rürup, "Emanzipation und Krise," 1–56.
50. Ibid.
51. The Germania life-insurance company, based in Szczecin/Stettin, had an office building in Strasbourg on the Pont Royal, built in 1888; the building also housed a restaurant, which became a favored haunt for students; see Warburg's letter to his mother dated 7 November 1889, cited by Meyer, "Aby Warburg in His Early Correspondence," 449. In 1921 the building and the restaurant were renamed "Gallia." Student organizations continue to use the premises even today, see Foessel, Marriotte, and Morand, *Strasbourg,* 58 f.
52. Roth, *Juden auf Wanderschaft*; Hoffmann, "'Ostjuden' in Westeuropa."
53. Weltsch, "Die schleichende Krise der jüdischen Identität," 695.
54. Ibid.
55. Gilman *Jewish Self-Hatred,* 190; cf. also Aschheim, *Brothers and Strangers.*
56. Klein, *Jewish Origins of the Psychoanalytic Movement,* 1–39.
57. Volkov, "Die Erfindung einer Tradition."
58. Boehlich, *Der Berliner Antisemitismusstreit,* 7.
59. Gilman, *Jewish Self-Hatred,* 270.
60. Ibid., 72 and passim; see also Daxelmüller, "Das 'Mauscheln.'"
61. Volkov, "Selbstgefälligkeit und Selbsthaß," 1–13; Gilman, *Jewish Self-Hatred*; Loewenberg, "Antisemitismus und jüdischer Selbsthaß," 455–75.
62. In 1879, Heinrich von Treitschke had said in a notorious speech: "There has always been a chasm between the Occidental and the Semitic natures, even since Tacitus lamented the *odium generis humani;* there always will be Jews who are nothing more than German-speaking Orientals." Cited in Boehlich, ed., *Der Berliner Antisemitismusstreit,* 12.
63. Gombrich, *Aby Warburg,* 14: "Warburg's style."
64. *Tagebuch der K.B.W.,* 70: "I do not like the text: it is still in my old cramped eel broth style." ("Der Text . . . gefällt mir nicht: noch im alten gedrängten Aalsuppenstyl geschrieben.")
65. Gombrich, *Aby Warburg,* 14–15.
66. Gilman, *Jewish Self-Hatred,* passim.
67. Weber, *Politische Schriften,* 277, 280 f.
68. Plessner, *Die verspätete Nation.*
69. Rürup, "Emanzipation und Krise," 3 and note 6, 20–27. Nipperdey,

Deutsche Geschichte 1866–1918, 2:290 f.

70. See also Chernow, *The Warburgs,* 14.
71. Max Liebermann von Sonnenberg, 1848–1911. This conservative anti-Semite founded the Deutschsoziale Partei in 1889, in connection with which he spoke in Hamburg. Since 1890 he was a member of the Reichstag.
72. WIA, GC, Moritz Warburg to Warburg, 29 November 1889. The letter only exists in an obviously incomplete copy.
73. "Das Lied vom braven jüdischen Mann." Gottfried August Bürger's "Ballad of the good man," *Das Lied vom braven Mann,* first appeared in the Göttingen Musenalmanach of 1775.
74. Freud, *Interpretation of Dreams,* 151.
75. Yerushalmi, *Freud's Moses,* 64 f. (with sources).
76. Schorske, *Fin-de-Siècle Vienna,* 181–207, stressing Freud's avoidance of political arguments.
77. Toury, "Die bangen Jahre," 164. On parallel developments in Vienna see Schorske, *Fin-de-Siècle Vienna,* 116–80.
78. Cf. Moses, *Die Lösung der Judenfrage,* Warburg Institute library inventory number 1908/7.
79. *Weltmännisch-distinguiert;* Schulz, "Weltbürger und Geldaristokraten," 638.
80. In Eric Warburg's words, "Gar nicht erst ignorieren. So sagt man hier in Hamburg."

Chapter 3

1. Gombrich, *Aby Warburg,* "The Conflict of styles as a Psychological Problem," 147–85.
2. Ibid., 148.
3. Warnke, "Vier Stichworte," 61–68; on the coinage *Pathosformel* see most recently Settis, "Pathos und Ethos."
4. Gombrich, *Aby Warburg,* 96–105.
5. Ibid., 105–27.
6. Ibid., 108.
7. Ibid., "Classical Pathos and Its Dangers," 177–85.
8. Warburg, *Renewal of Pagan Antiquity,* 175.
9. Ibid., 176.
10. Wölfflin, *Kunstgeschichtliche Grundbegriffe,* 8.
11. Gombrich, *Aby Warburg,* 152–59.
12. Warburg, "The Mural Paintings in Hamburg City Hall," in *Renewal of Pagan Antiquity,* 711–16; see also Syamken, "Aby Warburg," 13–21,

and extensive material at WIA, III.77.3–4 and IV.29.

13. Gombrich, *Aby Warburg,* 180, reports Warburg's view of the picture: "on the 'Massacre of the Innocents' fresco, however, the pagan figures have left the zone of archaeological contemplation and run riot on the stage." In this case the zone of archaeological contemplation is depiction in relief (for instance, on a triumphal arch) or *en grisaille.*
14. Cf. Warnke, "Der Leidschatz der Menschheit," 141 f.
15. Warburg, *Renewal of Pagan Antiquity,* 553–58; WIA, III.61.6.1 "Dürer" notes and drafts.
16. Originally published in the *Verhandlungen der achtundvierzigsten Versammlung deutscher Philologen und Schulmänner in Hamburg vom 3. bis 6. Oktober 1905,* Leipzig 1906, 55–60 (Warburg, *Renewal of Pagan Antiquity,* 729).
17. WIA, III.61.6.1 "Dürer" Notes and drafts.
18. Simon, "Dürer und Mantegna 1494"; Schuster, "Zu Dürers Zeichnung 'Der Tod des Orpheus'"; each gives the older literature. A quixotic interpretation is Wind, "'Hercules' and 'Orpheus,'" which sees parodic traits in Dürer's drawing; more recently Posèq, "Left and Right Orientation."
19. Warburg, *Renewal of Pagan Antiquity,* 555. See also Buck, *Der Orpheus-Mythos,* and Ohly, "Die Zerreißung als Strafe für Liebesverrat," especially 570–73, for further pointers on the divergent textual and pictorial traditions; notes 28–30 give the art historical literature on the theme.
20. Warburg, *Renewal of Pagan Antiquity,* 555.
21. Ibid.
22. These phrases are from ibid., 556–58.
23. Jessen, *Heinses Stellung zur bildenden Kunst,* 70–72; Warburg Institute shelfmark CIO 215, and accession number 04/96. The citations are all from Jessen.
24. Wilhelm Heinrich Wackenroder, *Herzensergießungen eines kunstliebenden Klosterbruders* (Effusions of an art-loving monk), an influential work of art criticism from Germany's early Romantic period.
25. WIA, III.61.6.1 "Dürer" notes and drafts, 41.
26. WIA, III.61.6.1 "Dürer" notes and drafts, 41 f.
27. On the "energetic inversion" of the *Pathosformel* of the stricken Orpheus: Posèq, "Left and Right Orientation of a *Pathosformel* in Dürer."
28. Warburg, *Renewal of Pagan Antiquity,* 558.
29. An article (possibly by Warburg himself?) from the *Hamburger Correspondent,* 10 October 1905, noon edition.
30. Cf. introduction, 10 f; WIA, GC, Gertrud Bing to Senator Biermann-Ratjen, 10 July 1963.
31. Cf. Diers, *Warburg aus Briefen,* 137–45.
32. Cf. for instance "Anekdote aus dem letzten preussischen Kriege."

33. WIA, *Zettelkasten* 67.
34. Cf. on this topic Dudley and Novak, eds., *Wild Man Within,* and Midgley, *Beast and Man*; on Warburg's ideas in this area, which were based partly in evolutionary theory and partly in Darwin's psychology of expression, see Gombrich, *Aby Warburg*, 243–46; on Warburg and theories of evolution, Gombrich, "Aby Warburg und der Evolutionismus."
35. See Ohly, "Die Zerreißung als Strafe für Liebesverrat."
36. Cf. WIA, GC, Gertrud Bing to Senator Biermann-Ratjen, 10 July 1963, 2.
37. Cf. Warburg, *Schlangenritual;* in general, and on Freud in particular, Corbey, "Freud's Phylogenetic Narrative," 37–56.
38. Cf. Bitterli, *Die 'Wilden' und die 'Zivilisierten'*; Stocking, *Victorian Anthropology.*
39. Gombrich, *Aby Warburg*, 226.
40. Corbey, "Freud's Phylogenetic Narrative," 54; here see also Theweleit, *Männerphantasien.*
41. "Psychoanalysis is the sickness that it pretends to heal." (*Die Psychoanalyse ist die Krankheit, die sie zu heilen vorgibt.*)
42. Corbey, "Freud's Phylogenetic Narrative," 54.
43. Ibid.
44. Freud, here see Yerushalmi, *Freud's Moses,* and also Schorske, "Freud's Egyptian Dig," 35–40.
45. Nr. 29, Hamburg, 17 July 1892, 4th year in print (editor: E. A. Hübner, 2, Alsterstraße 10).
46. WIA, IV.68.1 "Konitz, Dreyfus"; a small dossier of forty clippings on the Konitz affair. IV.68.3 a further collection of clippings filed under "Kiev. Beilis."
47. WIA, IV.68.9 "Juden Verfolgungen. Russland u. seine Juden."
48. *Zettelkasten* 36, "Juden"; item 036-018444, with notes in Warburg's hand.
49. The library contains thirty-one titles on ritual murder and blood sacrifice, including offprints (shelfmark GMM 440). Nineteen titles were accessed to the K.B.W. before 1929 and ten after 1929. Fourteen further titles were accessed after 1945. Of the nineteen texts acquired before 1929 nine are anti-Semitic texts, five are rebuttals, and five can be classified as scholarly works.
50. Strack, *Das Blut im Glauben und Aberglauben.*
51. Liebeschütz, "Aby Warburg," 229: Warburg "felt a call to interpret the attitude of Jews who had grown to manhood during the twenty years since Prussian Protestants had opened the fight against Jewry with the exhortation to be 'slightly more modest'"; on Liebeschütz, see introduction, 17.

52. WIA, III.52 "Anti-Semitism": Text that the author had crossed out has, where legible, been restored here in italics within brackets.
53. Liebeschütz, "Aby Warburg," 229.
54. Ibid.
55. *Jewish Encyclopedia*, vol. 7, Konitz Affair, columns 552–55; *Jüdisches Lexikon*, vol. 3, Konitz-Affäre, columns 841–44; *Encyclopedia Judaica*, vol. 10, Jerusalem 1971, Konitz. Since the research carried out for this book in the 1990s at least three substantial studies concerning Konitz have been published, all of them in 2002: Groß, *Ritualmord beschuldigungen gegen Juden;* Nonn, *Eine Stadt sucht einen Mörder;* and Smith, *The Butcher's Tale.*
56. See the trial transcripts in the matters of Massloff in 1900 (*Der Prozeß gegen Maßloff und Genossen*) and Lewy in 1901 (*Der Prozeß gegen Moritz Lewy*).
57. Dundes, ed., *Blood Libel Legend*; this volume assembles fourteen essays on the theme, many reprinted from elsewhere. See also Erb, ed., *Die Legende vom Ritualmord.*
58. Erb, ed., *Die Legende vom Ritualmord*, 7.
59. Schroubek, "Zur Tradierung und Diffusion," 17.
60. Ibid., 20.
61. Ibid., 18.
62. Ibid., 19; William of Norwich was supposedly murdered by Jews in 1144.
63. Lichtblau, "Die Debatten über die Ritualmordbeschuldigungen," 267–92; Anselm, "Angst und Angstprojektion," 253–65.
64. On Warburg's theory of social memory and the role of "pagan frenzy" in this context see Gombrich, *Aby Warburg*, and critically, Warnke, "Der Leidschatz der Menschheit," 116–18.
65. Cf. Kany, *Mnemosyne als Programm*, passim.
66. Warburg used Nietzsche, *Die Geburt der Tragödie*, AMH 700, no accession number; he probably owned this copy even when he was a student. Cf. the rich collection of Nietzsche literature, and particularly of Nietzsche criticism from the turn of the century and from the 1920s, *Catalog of The Warburg Institute Library*, 5:429–41; on Warburg's reading of Nietzsche, Pfotenhauer, "Das Nachleben der Antike."
67. Gombrich, *Aby Warburg*, 185, translating a diary entry of 9 December 1905.
68. Ibid., 190–91.
69. Nietzsche, *Birth of Tragedy*, 62.
70. Ibid., 16 and *passim.*
71. Ibid., 45.
72. Nietzsche, *Die Geburt der Tragödie*, 39 and 53 (copy in the Warburg

Institute).

73. Nietzsche, *Birth of Tragedy*, 92.
74. Nietzsche, *Die Geburt der Tragödie*, Warburg's copy in the Warburg Institute; on a fly-sheet at the end of the book.
75. Warburg, *Renewal of Pagan Antiquity*, 251.
76. Lightbown, *Sandro Botticelli*, vol. 2, catalog numbers B35–B38, 47–51; Lightbown, *Sandro Botticelli*, 114–19.
77. Warburg, *Renewal of Pagan Antiquity*, 459.
78. Cf. the somewhat convoluted chapter on this topic in Maikuma, *Der Begriff der Kultur bei Warburg*, 56–90.
79. Nietzsche, *Birth of Tragedy*, 16.
80. Gombrich, *Aby Warburg*, 12.
81. "Damit wir endlich eine künstlerische Kulturgeschichte bekommen." Third and last lecture in a series on Ghirlandaio, held 24, 26, and 28 October 1901; WIA, III.51.1–3, Ghirlandaio lectures, here notebook 3, 39–41.
82. WIA, III.51.3, 39 f.
83. Warburg, *Renewal of Pagan Antiquity*, 223–62.
84. WIA, III.51.1.
85. Warburg, *Renewal of Pagan Antiquity*, 185–221
86. WIA, III.51.1., 1 f.
87. WIA, III.51.1., 4.
88. WIA, III.69.7 "Sassetti I, 1907," 40.
89. WIA, III.69.7, 54.
90. There is an ironic or even self-ironizing note here; WIA, III.69.7, 60.
91. WIA, III.51.3, Ghirlandaio lecture; written on the back of the first sheet.
92. On the concept of the Renaissance, see the literature collected in Warburg's *Zettelkasten*, 4a; cf. also the references given below in note 96.
93. Borsook and Offerhaus, *Francesco Sassetti and Ghirlandaio*; Lavin, *Place of Narrative*, 203–7.
94. Borsook and Offerhaus, *Francesco Sassetti and Ghirlandaio*, 56–58. "Nowhere is there discord between pagan and Christian subject matter, nor does the presence of the Medici and other celebrated Florentines overpower the personal aspirations of Sassetti."
95. WIA, III.69.7, "Sassetti I, 1907," 54.9.
96. See also Buck, *Italienische Renaissance*, and Buck, ed., *Renaissance und Renaissancismus*, which survey the older literature on this subject.
97. WIA, III.69.7, 91–98.
98. "Durch charaktervolle besonnene sich umformende Aufklärung Ausgleichsversuche zwischen Altem und Neuem" (WIA, III.69.7, 54).
99. WIA, III.69.7, "Sassetti I, 1907," titles on 52–55.
100. On which cf. also Diers, *Warburg aus Briefen*, 94–97.

101. WIA, III.69.1–2.
102. The copy at call number DMC 35 has been annotated by Warburg.
103. WIA, GC, Warburg to Mary Warburg, 26 March 1907.
104. There was a further, posthumous edition in 1920, which had been prepared for publication by Weber himself.
105. Weber, *Protestant Ethic,* 140.
106. "[A historical term] must be gradually put together out of the individual parts which are taken from historical reality to make it up" (ibid., 12, et seq.).
107. Ibid., 117.
108. Ibid., 122.
109. See Winckelmann, ed., *Max Weber*; for a more recent reckoning with Weber's errors, Mackinnon, "Calvinism and the Infallible Assurance of Grace," and "Weber's Exploration of Calvinism"; for a thorough account of the original text and its reception, Tyrell, "Worum geht es in der 'Protestantischen Ethik'?"
110. Weber, *Protestant Ethic,* 123.
111. Weber, *Protestant Ethic,* 1; this view is also expressed by Hans Liebeschütz when he writes that "no summary can communicate the pathos of inquiry, transmitted by the dialectic of his sober and completely unartistic, sometimes involved, prose in the original language"; Liebschütz, "Max Weber's Historical Interpretation of Judaism," 41–68.
112. WIA, correspondence copybook II, 1907, No. 159; see also Diers, *Warburg aus Briefen,* 94–97.
113. Weber did, however, refer to the exchange obliquely, albeit without mention of Warburg's name, in a footnote to one of his contributions to the Protestant Ethic debate in his second reply to his critic Karl Fischer: "For example, one perceptive art historian has traced right down to characteristic artistic motifs [. . .]" First published in *Archiv für Sozialwissenschaft und Sozialpolitik* 26 (1908): 275–83. See Chalcraft and Harrington, eds., *Protestant Ethic Debate,* where on p. 49 the anonymous art historian is erroneously identified as Carl Neumann.
114. WIA, III.51.1, 54.
115. Schluchter, *Rationalismus der Weltbeherrschung,* 81.
116. Gombrich, *Aby Warburg,* 168–76; see also Diers, *Warburg aus Briefen,* 96f.; cf. Meyer, *Jüdische Identität in der Moderne,* 19–47.
117. Avarice (*auri sacra fames*) was not "that attitude of mind from which the specifically modern capitalistic spirit as a mass phenomenon is derived," Weber, *Protestant Ethic,* 22. On page 36 he explicitly addresses the differences between *quattrocento* Florence and Pennsylvania in the eighteenth century.
118. WIA, III.69.7, 35.

119. WIA, GC, Warburg to Mary Warburg, 26 March 1907.
120. Gombrich, *Aby Warburg*, 105 f.
121. See 25–42.
122. WIA, III.69.6, "Sassetti Testament, notes," 84.

Chapter 4

1. WIA, III.2.1—*Zettelkästen,* 1, 2, 4, and 17, 27.
2. There are two reports from Warburg himself on his "war collection"; WIA, IV.65.2 "*Die Kriegssammlungen,*" a response to a questionnaire, and WIA, V.3.3.1–3, a report to his brothers.
3. WIA, III.2.1; the numerous handwritten notes are by various hands but never by Warburg himself, cf. Heise, *Persönliche Erinnerungen an Aby Warburg*, 47–48. Apropos the documents on anti-Semitism it is worth noting that at least a part of the "war collection" did not remain in Hamburg, and has thus been preserved.
4. Warburg used the Berlin clipping service of Dr. Max Goldschmidt, Bureau für Zeitungsausschnitte, Berlin N. 4.
5. Jochmann, *Gesellschaftskrise und Judenfeindschaft,* 13–98.
6. Nipperdey and Rürup, "Antisemitismus," 137–50.
7. On the connection of nationalism and anti-Semitism see Estel, "Nationale Identität und Antisemitismus," 63–69; on religion, philosophy, and racial theory in the nineteenth century, recently Olender, *Die Sprachen des Paradieses.*
8. This problem has for instance been formulated in Nipperdey, *Deutsche Geschichte 1866–1918,* 2:289–91, Berding, *Moderner Antisemitismus,* 7–9, and was emphasized also by Nirenberg, *Communities of Violence,* 3–10.
9. Among other things, Schack was president of the Deutschnationaler Handlungsgehilfenverein. WIA, IV.31.3 "*Arische Pracht-Typen,*" clippings.
10. See Settis, "Warburg 'continuatus,'" with a detailed criticism of Stockhausen, *Die Kulturwissenschaftliche Bibliothek Warburg.* Both works also give the older literature and sources on the organisation of the library.
11. *Catalog of The Warburg Institute Library*, vols. 1 and 3.
12. For instance Jochmann, *Gesellschaftskrise und Judenfeindschaft,* 30–170; Toury, "Die bangen Jahre," 164–85; Nipperdey, *Deutsche Geschichte 1866–1918,* 2:289–311.
13. WIA, IV.68.7 "Zionismus"; in a letter which is also printed in Diers, *Warburg aus Briefen,* 56, Warburg describes his attitude to anti-Semitism as that of a "futurist" situated uncomfortably between assimilation and Zionism; anti-Semitism is not his primary opponent, he says.

14. Dr. Max Goldschmidt news clipping service, Berlin (as in note 4); cf. also the letter in correspondence copybook VI, 1915–18, No. 212, 18 April 1916: "Supposedly a 13-year-old boy (John?) was found murdered in Eberswalde some time ago (see *Hammer* 332, 219). Please supply me with the earliest and all subsequent reports."
15. Catalog of the exhibition *Die Macht der Bilder*; Schoeps and Schloer, eds., *Antisemitismus*; Rohrbacher and Schmidt, *Judenbilder*.
16. Particularly Theodor W. Adorno's numerous works examining occultism, astrological superstition, and the "authoritarain personality": Adorno, "Antisemitismus und faschistische Propaganda"; cf. also Simmel, ed., *Antisemitismus*, 12–34.
17. Bock, *Astrologie und Aufklärung*, 23–32; cf. also Frenkel-Brunswick and Sanford, "Die Antisemitische Persönlichkeit," on "the antisemitic personality."
18. Since 1966 also by the Institut für die Geschichte der deutschen Juden at the University of Hamburg in Germany; cf. Freimark, Jankowski, and Lorenz, eds., *Juden in Deutschland*, 13–14.
19. Mosse and Paucker, eds., *Entscheidungsjahr 1932*, Mosse, *Deutsches Judentum*, Mosse, *Juden im Wilhelminischen Deutschland*.
20. As for example in an anonymous pamphlet that reached the K.B.W. from Franz Boll's library: "The antisemitic movement is dead and gone, inasmuch as it was a serious political movement with real goals. Nobody in Germany today thinks to alter the constitution to discriminate against any particular religious belief. The words of two emperors have shown that antisemitic loudmouths have nothing to hope for here" (1881, 1); cf. also Toury, "Die bangen Jahre," 180 f.
21. Berding, *Moderner Antisemitismus in Deutschland*, 9.
22. The most important documents are collected in Boehlich, ed., *Der Berliner Antisemitismusstreit*; an excellent summary can also be found in Belke, *Moritz Lazarus und Heyman Steinthal*, lxi–lxxiii.
23. Cf. Jochmann, "Struktur und Funktion," 411–14, Volkov, *Rise of Popular Antimodernism in Germany*, 220–23.
24. WIA IV.31.2 "Antisemitisches"; the article is dated but there is no place of publication.
25. Boehlich, ed., *Der Berliner Antisemitismusstreit*, 237.
26. Ibid., 5.
27. Ibid.
28. Ibid., 7.
29. Belke, *Moritz Lazarus und Heyman Steinthal*, lxiii.
30. Liebeschütz, "Treitschke and Mommsen on Jewry and Judaism," passim.
31. Ibid., 173 f. On anti-Semitism at the German universities in general, Hammerstein, *Antisemitismus und deutsche Universitäten 1871–1933*.

32. See the documents in Boehlich, ed., *Der Berliner Antisemitismusstreit*; also Lazarus, *Treu und Frei,* especially 53–113 and 115–55.
33. See **56 f.**
34. In the winter of 1927/28 Johannes Geffcken held a lecture at the K.B.W. in the series on theatre and drama, which was later published in *Vorträge der Bibliothek Warburg* 1927/28.
35. Geffcken, "Neues und Neuestes," 324–28. The article is in fact a review of all K.B.W. publications up to the year 1925 and contains no more than three sentences on the Hamburg institution as such.
36. From the letter of thanks to Geffcken, 16 January 1926; WIA, GC, Warburg to F. Geffcken, 1926. Warburg's letter to his brothers is at WIA, V.2.3.3.3.
37. See below, letter to Eva von Eckardt, **92 f.**
38. WIA, IV.67, Reichstag sessions, 1914; transcripts of sessions from 6 to 20 May 1914.
39. Toury, *Die politischen Orientierungen der Juden,* 230; Angress, "Prussia's Army," 39.
40. *Zettelkasten* 118, "Krieg und Kunst" ("War and art") contains a postcard with this motto and a portrait of Wilhelm II, along with a collection of about thirty postcards with portraits of the Kaiser; cf. also Jochmann, *Gesellschaftskrise und Judenfeindschaft,* 99 f.
41. See appendix, **166 f.**
42. Meyer, "Aby Warburg in His Early Correspondence," 450; Chernow, *The Warburgs,* 64; Roeck, *Der junge Aby Warburg,* 81–91.
43. WIA, IV.31.2
44. Paucker, "Zur Problematik einer jüdischen Abwehrstrategie," 508.
45. Ibid., 169 ff.; for a critical political evaluation of the question see Kehr, "Zur Genesis des königlich preußischen Reserveoffiziers," who concludes that "we may rightly call the epoch from 1890 to 1914 Wilhelmine, if this term is taken to mean an attitude that was fundamentally false, a weakness which held that snobbery was strength, arrogant obscurantism was somehow dignified and boasting was good form; here Wilhelm II and his reserve officers were of one accord" (63).
46. Kehr, "Zur Genesis des königlich preußischen Reserveoffiziers," 60; Cecil, "Wilhelm II. und die Juden," 319.
47. Angress, "Prussia's Army"; see also Liebeschütz, "German Politics and Jewish Existence."
48. See appendix, **167–76.**
49. Paucker, "Zur Problematik einer jüdischen Abwehrstrategie in der deutschen Gesellschaft," 518; cf. the summary in Berding, *Moderner Antisemitismus in Deutschland,* 168–70.
50. Cf. Jochmann, *Gesellschaftskrise und Judenfeindschaft,* 101–25.

51. WIA, FC, Max Warburg to Warburg, 13 June 1916.
52. See Jochmann, "Die Ausbreitung des Antisemitismus," 422: "Officers had already made contact with prominent anti-Semites by the end of 1915, in order to obtain the 'ammunition' they required but especially to coordinate their actions and to prepare and carry through their common campaign. This development marks the beginning of cooperation between the officers and the 'squalling anti-Semites' whom they had previously socially rejected." Among the anti-Semites at this conference were Adolf Bartels, Schmidt-Gibichenfels, Theodor Fritsch, the Count Reventlow, the royal privy councillor Lehmann, and Johannes Henningsen.
53. WIA, FC, Max Warburg to Warburg, 23 October 1916.
54. "Richtlinien bei der Beförderung von Militärpersonen unvorschriftmässiger Confession, vorgeschlagen von einem"; WIA, IV.69.1: "Politica, Judenfrage."
55. "[A]ls gemeinsame Arbeit ansehe, wenn Du auch die Hauptsache geleistet hast"; correspondence copybook VI, 1915–18, No. 270 of 25 November 1916.
56. WIA, FC, Max Warburg to Warburg, 25 November 1916.
57. WIA, IV.69.1; cf. appendix, **167–76.**
58. Brenner, *Renaissance of Jewish Culture in Weimar Germany*, 25–28, on Münchausen's work on *Juda* with the artist and illustrator Ephraim Mose Lilien.
59. Mittenzwei, *Der Untergang einer Akademie,* 157–82; Stockhorst, *Fünftausend Köpfe*, 467.
60. WIA, IV.69.1; cf. appendix, **178–82.**
61. See appendix, **182 f.**
62. WIA, FC, Warburg to Max Warburg, 6 June 1917.
63. WIA, FC, Max Warburg to Warburg, 7 June 1917.
64. Chernow, *The Warburgs,* 171 ff. on Max Warburg's other activities in the year 1916.
65. This assessment is also in Chernow, *The Warburgs,* 171–91, though perhaps somewhat more brusquely.
66. Warburg, *Die Judenfrage im Rahmen,* 1; cf. appendix, **168**.
67. Ibid., 4; cf. appendix, **172**.
68. Chernow, *The Warburgs,* 9–12.
69. Warburg, *Die Judenfrage im Rahmen,* nine times in all.
70. Ibid., four times.
71. After the conclusion of the war there would have to be the possibility for a debate on differences of worldviews in a secular state; ibid., 168.
72. Ibid., 169.
73. Ibid., 170.

74. "The 11 million Jews living around the world mostly understand German, and their knowledge of the language might help in launching a movement from Germany which could work to Germany's own advantage and win her new friends throughout the world" (ibid., 175).
75. Ibid., 174.
76. Ibid., 176.
77. Ibid., 174.
78. Convincingly presented by Jochmann, "Die Ausbreitung des Antisemitismus," 425–27.
79. Warburg, *Die Judenfrage im Rahmen,* 175.
80. See Angress, "Prussia's Army."
81. Jochmann, "Die Ausbreitung des Antisemitismus," 427.
82. Ibid.
83. Armin, *Die Juden in den Kriegs-Gesellschaften*; Oppenheimer, *Die Judenstatistik des preußischen Kriegsministeriums.*
84. On the role of statistics and empirical tools in social conflicts in general, cf. Megill, ed., *Rethinking Objectivity,* and Porter, *Trust in Numbers.*
85. Beginning in 1904 with the study by Ruppin, *Die Juden der Gegenwart.*
86. Bureau für Statistik der Juden, *Statistik der Juden,* 5.
87. Angress, "Prussia's Army," 40; see also the conclusions on 40–42.
88. Cf. the letters in correspondence copybook VI, 1915–18, Nos. 79 (6 May 1915 to Wilhelm Waetzold), 97 (23 June 1915 to Röse) and 260 (November 1916 to Fritz Schumacher).
89. Rathenau, "Staat und Judentum," 185–207.
90. Ibid., 206 f.
91. Nipperdey, *Deutsche Geschichte 1866–1918,* 1:812–34.
92. Ibid., 813; cf. also 823 on analyses of illiberalism in Jarausch, *Students, Society, and Politics,* and Stern, *Kulturpessimismus als politische Gefahr.*
93. Nipperdey, *Deutsche Geschichte 1866–1918,* 1:813–18.
94. Cf. the *Catalog of The Warburg Institute Library,* 1:545–66.
95. Nipperdey, *Deutsche Geschichte 1866–1918,* 1:831.
96. Chernow, *The Warburgs,* 174–77.
97. Nipperdey, *Deutsche Geschichte 1866–1918,* 1:370.
98. On Schmoller see also Krüger, *Nationalökonomen im wilhelminischen Deutschland,* vom Bruch, "Weiterführung der Schmollerschen."
99. WIA, IV.69.3 "Schmoller"; the word used for national consciousness was *Volksbewußtsein.*
100. WIA, IV.69.3.
101. WIA, III.2.1 box 36.
102. Rohrbacher and Schmidt, *Judenbilder,* 43–147.
103. Nipperdey, *Deutsche Geschichte 1866–1918,* 1:829: "Finally: many readers who were not themselves *völkisch* nevertheless grew used to seeing

völkisch beliefs as something 'normal.' This might condition them not to respond and not to resist."

104. WIA, FC, Warburg to Max Warburg, 11 November 1917.
105. Eva von Eckardt was the daughter of Warburg's friend Felix von Eckardt, editor of the *Hamburger Fremdenblatt;* in the 1920s she joined the K.B.W.'s staff.
106. Ruppin, *Die Juden der Gegenwart* (Warburg Institute 04/438; GMM 40).
107. Hertz, *Rasse und Kultur* (Warburg Institute 15/207; DHD 25).
108. Zollschan, *Das Rassenproblem* (Warburg Institute 26/119; DHD 50).
109. Melamed, *Die Psychologie des jüdischen Geistes* (2nd ed.; here the 1st ed. must be meant).
110. Trützschler von Falkenstein, *Die Lösung der Judenfrage* (Warburg Institute 17/418; GMM 485).
111. WIA, GC, Warburg to Eva [Isabella] von Eckardt, 22 May 1918.
112. Warburg, *Die Judenfrage im Rahmen,* first version; WIA, IV.69.1; see appendix, 171.
113. Berding, *Moderner Antisemitismus in Deutschland,* 170.
114. Ibid., 178–89.
115. Ibid., 189.

Chapter 5

1. Lorenz, *Die Juden in Hamburg,* 1004–18.
2. In an interview with the present author in January 1995, Mary Warburg's niece Dorothea Hertz spoke of how painful Mary Warburg found it to write harmless letters each week.
3. Königseder, "Aby Warburg im 'Bellevue,'" 87; Krohn, *Die Juden in Hamburg,* 203 f.
4. *Tagebuch der K.B.W.,* 2.
5. Landauer, "The Survival of Antiquity"; Stockhausen, *Die Kulturwissenschaftliche Bibliothek Warburg*; Huisstede, "De Mnemosyne Beeldatlas."
6. Diers, *Warburg aus Briefen,* 189–94. Before the publication of the journal, it had been used for three recent books whose authors each attest to the great value of the source: Carl Landauer called the diary "Possibly the best source for the operation of the library" (Landauer, "The Survival of Antiquity," 302 f.); in his book on the library building in the Heilwigstraße in Hamburg, Tilmann von Stockhausen called it "perhaps the most important but as yet only rarely used source for the history of the Library" (Stockhausen, *Die Kulturwissenschaftliche Bibliothek War-*

burg, 17); Peter van Huisstede's work on the picture-atlas *Mnemosyne* collects numerous entries from the journal indispensable for understanding the project (Huisstede, "De Mnemosyne Beeldatlas" and "Der Mnemosyne-Atlas").

7. Stockhausen, *Die Kulturwissenschaftliche Bibliothek Warburg*, 29, lists names from the library's visitors book, many of which are also found in the journal; cf. Schoell-Glass, "An Episode of Cultural Politics," on Warburg's correspondence with Thomas Mann, recorded in the journal.
8. Stockhausen, *Die Kulturwissenschaftliche Bibliothek Warburg,* 75–90; Settis, "Warburg 'continuatus.'"
9. *Tagebuch der K.B.W.,* 31–32.
10. Ibid., 130.
11. Ibid.
12. Ibid., 121.
13. Saxl, "Die Kulturwissenschaftliche Bibliothek Warburg in Hamburg," 355.
14. Landauer, "The Survival of Antiquity," 97 f.
15. *Tagebuch der K.B.W.,* 118.
16. Ibid., 109.
17. Ibid., 151
18. Gay, *Weimar Culture.*
19. Several such comments in Brauer, Mendelssohn Bartholdy, and Meyer, eds., *Forschungsinstitute*, particularly Erich Rothacker's article on research institutions in the humanities, and Ferdinand Tönnies's article on the social sciences.
20. Ringer, *Decline of the German Mandarins.*
21. Familial, political, industrial-economic, religious, ceremonial, professional; cited in Schelsky, "Zur soziologischen Theorie der Institution," 12.
22. Brauer, Mendelssohn Bartholdy, and Meyer, eds., *Forschungsinstitute.*
23. French philosopher of law, 1856–1929: Schnur, ed., *Die Theorie der Institution.* Hauriou was a friend of the philosophers Georges Dumézil and Jean Jaurès.
24. Schelsky, "Zur soziologischen Theorie der Institution."
25. Pollock, "Das Institut für Sozialforschung," 347.
26. Mendelssohn Bartholdy, "Institut für Auswärtige Politik," 332.
27. Mendelssohn Bartholdy, "Rede zur Eröffnung," 89.
28. Letter to Max M. Warburg of 13 June 1928, cited in Naber, ". . . die Fackel deutsch-jüdischer Geistigkeit weitertragen," 397.
29. Ibid.
30. Dr. h. c. Dr. phil Joachim Jeremias, born 1900, theologian, docent in Leipzig 1925, lecturer in Berlin 1928, Greifswald 1929, professor in

Göttingen 1935; New Testament scholar.

31. *Tagebuch der K.B.W.,* 69 and 70.
32. Cf. also Stockhausen, *Die Kulturwissenschaftliche Bibliothek Warburg,* 24–35.
33. Glum, "Die Kaiser-Wilhelm-Gesellschaft," 360.
34. Vagts, "Albrecht Mendelssohn Bartholdy," 211.
35. Luhmann, "Institutionalisierung—Funktion und Mechanismus," 30.
36. WIA, FC, Max Warburg to Warburg, 24 September 1924.
37. *Tagebuch der K.B.W.,* 173–75; Warburg comments that "Kessal [of the Warburg bank] is busying himself with the form the institution will take," 174.
38. Also in Stockhausen, *Die Kulturwissenschaftliche Bibliothek Warburg.*
39. Letter to Rudolf Laun, 9 June 1926, Staatsarchiv Hamburg.
40. See **78 f.**
41. *Tagebuch der K.B.W.,* 69.
42. Ibid., 164.
43. *Vorträge der Bibliothek Warburg,* vol. 5, 1925–26; Franke, "Der kosmische Gedanke."
44. *Tagebuch der K.B.W.,* 61.
45. A reference to Warburg's project of a print titled *Idea vincit* in the year 1926; *Tagebuch der K.B.W.,* 23–40. See Schoell-Glass, "Idea vincit?" and Michels and Schoell-Glass, "Aby Warburg."
46. *Tagebuch der K.B.W.,* 61.
47. Ibid.
48. Cf. Franke, "Der kosmische Gedanke," here 41 f.
49. *Tagebuch der K.B.W.,* 133–34; Saxl, 23 August 1927: "After a very earnest discussion with Frau Bondi I have declined for the moment to give the Steinthal-Schwesternloge a tour. It would be a tour for a group of Jewish ladies, to broaden their general education and show what Jewish money achieves in a private capacity." Warburg: "Understood, and in agreement."
50. Hamburg civic elections on 19 February 1928.
51. Peter Ernst Eiffe, born 1889, served in the navy in the First World War; 1919 *Freicorps Bahrenfeld,* 1932 joined the NSDAP, Hamburg delegate in Berlin since 1933. See *Das Deutsche Führerlexikon,* 516.
52. *Tagebuch der K.B.W.,* 205.
53. Results: three seats for the NSDAP, sixty seats for the Social Democrats, and twenty-seven for the Communists, between twenty and twenty-two seats for three other parties each. The resulting coalition remained politically moderate.
54. *Tagebuch der K.B.W.,* 206.
55. Ibid., 2.

56. Ibid., 160; Neue Sachlichkeit is the name of one of the modernist movements in 1920s Germany, mainly used in connection with modern architecture.
57. "Idea vincit," the postage stamp and print project, see note 45.
58. Weber, *Science as a Vocation*, 31.
59. *Tagebuch der K.B.W.*, 96–97.
60. Ibid., 146.
61. Recently also in Chernow, *The Warburgs*, opposite page 192, with his son Max Adolph.
62. Roesler, *Die Finanzpolitik des Deutschen Reiches*; on the semantic field of the iron, *das Eiserne*, see Elias, *Studien über die Deutschen*, 272 f.
63. See the catalog of the exhibition *Ein Krieg wird ausgestellt*, 152 f.; cf. also Diers, "Nagelmänner."
64. Cf. Huhn and Rautmann, "'Gold gab ich für Eisen.'"
65. *Tagebuch der K.B.W.*, 205.
66. See **166 f.**
67. Wind, "Warburgs Begriff der Kulturwissenschaft," esp. 408–12.
68. Hans Reinhold Hertz (1881–1918), engineer and ship-builder, cf. Hertz, "Wilhelm Ludwig Hertz," columns 307–8.
69. *Tagebuch der K.B.W.*, 13.
70. Ibid.
71. Wilhelm Arthur Hertz (1878–1945); cf. Hertz, "Wilhelm Ludwig Hertz," columns 307/308.
72. *Tagebuch der K.B.W.*, 15.
73. Ibid., 17.
74. Ibid, 18.
75. Ibid.
76. See Phelps, "Theodor Fritsch."
77. *Presse und Funk im Dritten Reich*, 260 and 367.
78. *Hammer* 569, 25th year, March 1926, 104 f.
79. Cf. Fritsch, *Mein Streit mit dem Hause Warburg*. Fritsch was so sure of his cause and of his public that he also published statements from his accusers *in extenso*. This is confirmed by notes scribbled in the margin of the copy in the Hamburg Staatsbibliothek.
80. *Hammer* 502, 22nd year, May 1923, 186.
81. Lorenz, *Die Juden in Hamburg*, 1019 f.
82. *Hammer* 569, 25th year, March 1926, 100 f.
83. Ibid., 103.
84. Raulff, "Die Geburt eines Begriffs," 50–68; Le Goff, "Eine mehrdeutige Geschichte," 18–32.
85. Raulff, "Die Geburt eines Begriffs," 58.
86. WIA, *Zettelkasten* 36 (Jews), card no. 036/018453; *Der Türmer* 20, no.

3 (November 1917): 170.
87. Chernow, *The Warburgs,* 178–79.
88. Warnke, "Vier Stichworte," 54–83.
89. Ibid.; Gombrich, *Aby Warburg,* 206 f.; Heise, *Persönliche Erinnerungen an Aby Warburg.*
90. Warburg, *Renewal of Pagan Antiquity,* 599.
91. WIA, correspondence, copybook VI, letter to Professor Samter, 19 May 1918.
92. Gombrich, *Aby Warburg,* 207.
93. Warburg, *Renewal of Pagan Antiquity,* 621.
94. Ibid., 630.
95. Warnke, *Cranachs Luther,* esp. 61–68.
96. Warburg, *Renewal of Pagan Antiquity,* 650.
97. Liebeschütz, "Aby Warburg," 230.
98. WIA, correspondence, copybook VI, 304, 305; letter to Lore Strack, 1 July 1917.
99. For instance the Hamburg historian Max Lenz, see Lenz, "Luther und der deutsche Geist"; cf. also Jochmann, *Gesellschaftskrise und Judenfeindschaft,,* 268 f.
100. Cf. Erikson, *Young Man Luther,* a psychoanalytic study that did not go unchallenged but which very clearly shows Luther's ambiguities, among them the struggle between enlightened impulses and the fear of demons.
101. Schuster, *Melencolia I,* 32–34, 84–105.
102. Warburg, *Renewal of Pagan Antiquity,* 644.
103. Schuster, *Melencolia I,* 32.
104. Warburg states that he owed much to the decoding work done by Karl Giehlow, but that "Giehlow failed to carry his discovery through to its ultimate, and most enlightening, conclusion because he was unaware" of the *Picatrix,* a handbook of astrology and magic written by an Arab in the tenth century (Warburg, *Renewal of Pagan Antiquity,* 643).
105. Schuster, *Melencolia I,* 34 and note 135.
106. Böhme, *Albrecht Dürer,* 72 f.
107. Warburg, *Renewal of Pagan Antiquity,* 644.
108. Ibid., 691.
109. Ibid., 650.
110. *Hamburgischer Correspondent,* 17 November 1918, no. 582, morning edition, 2.
111. WIA, correspondence copybook VI, 336–37.
112. Meyer, "Aby Warburg in His Early Correspondence," 452.
113. Diers, *Warburg aus Briefen,* 4.
114. Iversen, "Retrieving Warburg's Tradition," 541–53.
115. Schuster, *Melencolia I,* 64.

116. Warburg's letter to his brothers Felix and Paul, printed in Stockhausen, *Die Kulturwissenschaftliche Bibliothek Warburg*, 174.
117. His "zest for organizing" thus need not be interpreted as a crisis in his creative work; see Warnke, "Aby Warburg," 118.
118. *Tagebuch der K.B.W.*, 144.
119. Grolle, *Bericht von einem schwierigen Leben*, 69: "Ein feste Warburg ist unser Institute." Solmitz was punning (untranslatably) upon a well-known hymn by Martin Luther, "Ein feste Burg ist unser Gott" ("A Mighty Fortress Is Our God"). This hymn also includes the line "Und wenn die Welt voll Teufel wär'" ("though the world were full of devils").

Chapter 6

1. WIA, GC, Fritz Saxl to Paul M. Warburg, 5 August 1926.
2. Huisstede, "De Mnemosyne Beeldatlas," 125–48.
3. The lecture notes are excerpted and partially translated by Gombrich, *Aby Warburg*, 313–14; there is also a transcription of the German in Huisstede, "De Mnemosyne Beeldatlas," 126–39. Further material used here is from WIA, III.101 "Italienische Antike im Zeitalter Rembrandts."
4. Huisstede, "De Mnemosyne Beeldatlas," 127.
5. Saxl's letter to Max M. Warburg, 5 August 1926 (referring to purchases of the year 1925).
6. "Italienische Antike im Zeitalter Rembrandts"; see Huisstede, "De Mnemosyne Beeldatlas," 125–48.
7. Fritz Saxl, speech at the memorial service for Professor Warburg, 5 December 1929 (typescript, Warburg Archive, Kunstgeschichtliches Seminar of the University of Hamburg): "Ever since I was a very young man, I have been trying to understand Rembrandt's work better. Then I grew interested in astrology. When after many years I told Warburg of my troubles and that I could not achieve a conspectus through working on Rembrandt and astrology at once, he answered that I must choose one or the other, and be with him (for at the time he was working on astrology) or against him, and for Rembrandt. Warburg's late work has taught us that Rembrandt and astrology must be seen together."
8. Saxl, "Rembrandt und Italien."
9. See Saxl's entry of 8 November 1926 in the Warburg library journal, *Tagebuch der K.B.W.*, 22.
10. Saxl, *Rembrandt's Sacrifice of Manoah* and *Lectures*, 298–310.
11. Panofsky, "Rembrandt und das Judentum."
12. Now in Berlin, Gemäldegalerie, Stiftung Preußischer Kulturbesitz.

13. Stockholm, National Museum; Carroll, "Civic Ideology and Its Subversion"; Alpers, *Rembrandt's Enterprise.*
14. On Rembrandt's treatment of the Medea theme see Saxl, *Lectures,* 304–8.
15. Gombrich, *Aby Warburg,* 230.
16. Ibid., 236.
17. Ibid., 238.
18. *Tagebuch der K.B.W.,* 6.
19. Gombrich, *Aby Warburg,* 230.
20. On the earlier reception of Rembrandt see Emmens, *Rembrandt en de regels van de kunst,* which does not however discuss the "Germanic" Rembrandt.
21. Bode, *Great Masters of Dutch and Flemish Painting,* 3.
22. Bode, "Rembrandt als Erzieher von einem Deutschen"; on this review see Behrendt, *Zwischen Paradox und Paralogismus,* 176 f. On Langbehn, see Stern, *Kulturpessimismus als politische Gefahr,* 190–220.
23. See *Catalog of The Warburg Institute Library,* 1:552 f.
24. Langbehn, *Rembrandt als Erzieher,* running to more than 70 editions and impressions.
25. *Tagebuch der K.B.W.,* 26.
26. Heise, *Persönliche Erinnerungen an Aby Warburg,* 18.
27. Behrendt, *Zwischen Paradox und Paralogismus,* 53.
28. Ibid.
29. Langbehn, *Rembrandt als Erzieher,* 67th–71st printing; this is the copy in the Warburg Institute. On the different editions and on Momme Nissen's alterations to the text, see Behrendt, *Zwischen Paradox und Paralogismus,* 44–52.
30. Behrendt, *Zwischen Paradox und Paralogismus,* 60–153; Stern, *Kulturpessimismus als politische Gefahr,* 190–220.
31. Behrendt, *Zwischen Paradox und Paralogismus,* 73.
32. Claussen, *Was heisst Rassismus?* 5.
33. Behrendt, *Zwischen Paradox und Paralogismus,* 154–210, gives a thorough account of the book's reception.
34. Cited in Behrendt, *Zwischen Paradox und Paralogismus,* 181, from an essay by Max Bewer, a figure in Langbehn's Dresden circle.
35. Behrendt, *Zwischen Paradox und Paralogismus,* 248–56.
36. See also Chernow, *The Warburgs,* 287 f. and his suggestion that this faith in the power of reason was misguided.
37. WIA; GC, Warburg to his friend Werner Weisbach, 3 April 1915; Warburg probably wrote this letter when Weisbach's work "The war aims and German idealism" was published in 1915, cf. Weisbach, *Geist und Gewalt,* 131.

38. Langbehn, *Rembrandt als Erzieher,* 77.
39. Gombrich, *Aby Warburg,* 231–32.
40. "Dürer and Italian Antiquity"; see 47 f.
41. Cf. Gombrich, *Aby Warburg,* plates 43b and 44a–c.
42. Rembrandt owned over two hundred copper plates by Tempesta; see ibid., 227 f.
43. We may also think here of "Dürer as Führer," also from the Langbehn-Nissen workshop, published in the *Kunstwart* in 1904 and later as Langbehn and Nissen, *Dürer als Führer.*
44. See 108–10.
45. The term became a successful slogan with a 1904 book of the same name by Adolf Bartels (1862–1945). The K.B.W. also contains further works by the anti-Semite Bartels.
46. Schmalenbach, "The Term 'Neue Sachlichkeit'"; Michels, "Ein Versuch über die K.B.W."
47. Langbehn, *Rembrandt als Erzieher,* 75.
48. On barbarism as a new ideal, cf. See, *Barbar, Germane, Arier.*
49. Gombrich, *Aby Warburg,* 234–35; see also Huisstede, "De Mnemosyne Beeldatlas," 137.
50. Margaret Deutsch Carroll (Carroll, "Civic Ideology and Its Subversion") concludes in much the same way as Warburg on the Amsterdam senate's reasons for rejecting Rembrandt's Claudius Civilis, although she does not know Warburg's work.
51. Warburg, *Renewal of Pagan Antiquity,* 711–17.
52. Gombrich, *Aby Warburg,* 236.
53. Ibid., 238.
54. Kedourie, *Nationalism,* 138.
55. *Tagebuch der K.B.W.,* 36–37; cf. also the report in Berger, "Erinnerungen an Aby Warburg (1979)," 52 f.
56. Motto for a print Warburg had designed and presented to Gustav Stresemann in the library on 20 July 1926; see Schoell-Glass, "Idea vincit?" and Michels and Schoell-Glass, "Aby Warburg."
57. *Tagebuch der K.B.W,* 39.
58. Neumann, *Rembrandt,* 27–30.
59. See the essay by Beat Wyss in Simmel, *Rembrandt* 1919, ix–xxxi.
60. Neumann, *Rembrandt,* 38.
61. WIA, GC, Warburg to Schwedeler-Meyer, 29 June 1917.
62. WIA, III.101.5.5; Ulrich Rauff identified Neumann as the recipient. Neumann's letter to Warburg is in GC, 3 January 1927.
63. Belting, *Das Ende der Kunstgeschichte,* 192.
64. Correspondence copybook VI, letter 215, 22 April 1916; "I, who was only made a 'politician' during the war."

65. Zafran, "Saturn and the Jews," 16: "Kilbansky, Panofsky and Saxl touch only indirectly upon one significant aspect or transformation of the ancient planetary deity—the interrelationship and even identification between Saturn and the Jews." Zafran's article draws on his dissertation, "The Iconography of Anti-Semitism, 1400–1600," Ph.D. diss., Institute of Fine Arts, 1973; on the publication history of Klibansky, Panofsky, and Saxl, *Saturn and Melancholy,* as far back as the 1920s, see its preface, v–vi).
66. Recently Borsi and Borsi, *Paolo Uccello,* 259–66, and catalog numbers 33, 336–38; Lavin, "The Altar of Corpus Domini."
67. Huisstede, "Der Mnemosyne-Atlas," 151.
68. The two most important reviews of the atlas's material and the circumstances of its growth are still those of Ernst Gombrich and, more recently, of Peter van Huisstede: Gombrich, *Aby Warburg,* 283–307, Huisstede, "De Mnemosyne Beeldatlas," and the German summary of this unpublished dissertation, Huisstede, "Der Mnemosyne-Atlas." Also on the picture-atlas see Hofmann, Syamken, and Warnke, *Die Menschenrechte des Auges*; Bauerle, *Gespenstergeschichten für ganz Erwachsene*; further Hofmann, "Der Mnemosyne-Atlas"; Forster, "Warburgs Versunkenheit."
69. Barta Fliedl and Geissmar, eds., *Die Beredsamkeit des Leibes,* 171–73.
70. Warburg, *Mnemosyne, Der Bilderatlas.*
71. Gombrich, *Aby Warburg,* 283.
72. Syamken "Warburgs Umwege als Hermeneutik 'More Majorum,'" 21.
73. Hofmann, "Der Mnemosyne-Atlas."
74. Gombrich, *Aby Warburg,* 261 and 284; Warnke, "Aby Warburg," 119.
75. First used by Heinrich Wölfflin in Berlin, 1901. Cf. Dilly, "Lichtbildprojektion."
76. See also Hofmann, "Der Mnemosyne-Atlas," 173 f.
77. Gombrich, *Aby Warburg,* 271.
78. Huisstede, "Der Mnemosyne-Atlas," 151.
79. Ibid., 191 f.
80. Ibid., 149–200; the titles for some plates are taken from exhibitions hung in the years 1926 and 1927; see also Warburg, *Mnemosyne, Der Bilderatlas,* for Gertrud Bing's captions for all plates.
81. Lavin, "The Altar of Corpus Domini," 3, with close attention to the sources; Lotter, "Aufkommen und Verbreitung," 68; Lotter, "Hostienfrevelvorwurf und Blutwunderfälschung," 536–60.
82. Rohrbacher and Schmidt, *Judenbilder,* 291 f.
83. Conciliorum Oecumenicorum Decreta, 227–71, here 266, Constitutio 68; *Jüdisches Lexikon,* vol. 3, "Judenabzeichen," columns 412–16.
84. Lavin, "The Altar of Corpus Domini," 4–6.

85. Ibid.
86. Backhaus, "Die Hostienschändungsprozesse."
87. See also Rohrbacher and Schmidt, *Judenbilder*, 298 f.
88. See also ibid., 299.
89. Schreiber, *Handbuch der Holz-und Metallschnitte*, 4:108–9, numbers 1965, 1966; WIA, Zetelkasten 36, "Jews." Under "Antisemitisches/ Antisemitics," card 036–018444, "Around 1491. Nuremberg. Host profanation by Jews. Profanation in Passau"; on the afterlife of this folio see Rohrbacher and Schmidt, *Judenbilder*, 295 and the illustrations on 296 f.
90. WIA, IV.31.1, "Religionswesen": *Frankfurter Zeitung*, 1912 (no date), "A medieval indictment."
91. *Jüdisches Lexikon*, vol. 2, "Hostienschändung" columns, 1679–1682; Warburg Institute: 27/2689; RR 102.
92. Schubring, *Cassoni.*
93. Gombrich, "Apollonio di Giovanni," reprinted in Gombrich, *Norm and Form.*
94. Schubring, *Cassoni*, appendix II, "Bottega-Buch des Marco del Buono und des Apollonio di Giovanni, 1446–1463" 443–50.
95. Oberhuber, "L'apparato decorativo di palazzo Tè," 353.
96. Warburg, *Renewal of Pagan Antiquity*, 171.
97. Gombrich, "Apollonio di Giovanni" and *Norm and Form.*
98. Pochat, *Theater und Bildende Kunst*, 156–67, here 159.
99. James, "Ritual, Drama and Social Body," 4.
100. Elias, *Was ist Soziologie?* 132–45.
101. Callmann, *Apollonio di Giovanni*, assembles Apollonio di Giovanni's oeuvre; on the iconographic aspects of the cassoni, see more recently Witthoft, "Marriage Rituals and Marriage Chests."
102. Lavin, "Altar of Corpus Domini," 17.
103. Lund, International Inter Arts Conference, May 1995.
104. Polleroß, "Interart Studies," 243.
105. Warburg, *Renewal of Pagan Antiquity*, 298n8.
106. Gombrich, *Aby Warburg*, 301 and plate 61.
107. Ibid., 279.
108. On the situation surrounding the Locarno negotiations see Jacobson, *Locarno Diplomacy*, and Turner, *Stresemann and the Politics of the Weimar Republic*, 154–219.
109. Gombrich, *Aby Warburg*, 280.
110. Schramm, *Herrschaftszeichen und Staatssymbolik*, illustration 105 on plate 84 and 697 f.
111. At the time art historians were not yet permitted to examine St Peter's chair; cf. ibid., 697.
112. Gombrich, *Aby Warburg*, 301.

113. Recently Nesselrath, "La Stanza d'Eliodoro," with a survey of earlier works.
114. Ibid., 226.
115. Cf. plates 46 and 47 of the picture-atlas.
116. Bauerle, *Gespenstergeschichten für ganz Erwachsene*, 141 f., though this interpretation perhaps overreaches.
117. Gombrich, *Aby Warburg*, 281.
118. Correspondence copybook, letter 264 of 13 November 1916 to the Hamburg Africanist Carl Meinhof, a member of Warburg's "circle."
119. *Tagebuch der K.B.W.*, 141. Warburg goes on to ask "Do we not have the French edition? If not, acquire it at once! Even in Kreuzlingen Ludwig Binswanger drew his strength from this work." Cf. Lévy-Bruhl, *Das Denken der Naturvölker*, important for Warburg above all because of the "law of participation," 51–82 and 199–267.
120. Ibid. For other remarks on abstraction and concretion in this context see Huisstede, "De Mnemosyne Beeldatlas," 159.
121. Wind, "Warburgs Begriff der Kulturwissenschaft," 401–17.
122. Vischer, *Kritische Gänge*, 4:420–56.
123. Wind, "Warburgs Begriff der Kulturwissenschaft," 409.
124. Ibid.
125. Buschendorf, "War ein sehr tüchtiges gegenseitiges Fördern," 183–88.
126. Wind, "Warburgs Begriff der Kulturwissenschaft," 410.
127. *Tagebuch der K.B.W.*, 327, emphasis in original.
128. Nietzsche, *Birth of Tragedy*, 42.
129. WIA, IV.31.1, "Religionswesen."
130. Ludwig Rieß (1861–1928), a student of Hans Delbruck, taught for 15 years at the Todai in Tokyo. He had been requested to come from Germany by the Japanese government to reform Japanese historiography along German lines; see Mehl, *Eine Vergangenheit für die japanische Nation*.
131. WIA, I.2, "Reise Ital. 28/29. Tagesereignisse."
132. Brafmann, *Das Buch vom Kahal*; the two-volume translation exists in manuscript, obviously corrected by Passarge, in the Staats-und Universitätsbibliothek in Hamburg, call number B/22574. Refutations by Stanjek, "Das Kahal-Märchen gründlich widerlegt!" and Carlebach, *Öffentliche Dank-und Huldigungsadresse*, are partly serious and partly satirical.
133. "Kahal" is Hebrew for "Jewish community"; see *Jüdisches Lexikon*, vol. 3, columns 525–30.
134. See Fischer and Sandner, "Die Geschichte des Geographischen Seminars," 1200–1217; Vogel, "Anpassung und Widerstand," 11 f. and 36; Ehlers, "Das Geologische Institut der Hamburger Universität,"

1229–34; Sandner and Rössler have also produced an unpublished bibliography for Passarge (held by the Hamburg University Library for university history).

135. Passarge, *Grundzüge der gesetzmäßigen Charakterentwicklung*; Warburg Institute DHD 25; 25/2970.
136. *Frankfurter Zeitung*, 7 May 1929, no. 336
137. *Frankfurter Zeitung*, 21 September 1928.
138. *B.T. (Berliner Tagblatt)*, 2 June 1929.
139. Huisstede, "De Mnemosyne Beeldatlas," 133.

Conclusion

1. Warburg, *Ausgewählte Schrifte und Würdigungen*, 464.

Bibliography

Works by Warburg and His Circle

Aby Warburg: Akten des internationalen Symposions Hamburg 1990, edited by Horst Bredekamp, Michael Diers, and Charlotte Schoell-Glass. Weinheim: VCH acta humaniora, 1991.

Aby M. Warburg: Bildersammlung zur Geschichte von Sternglaube und Sternkunde im Hamburger Planetarium, edited by Uwe Fleckner, Robert Galitz, Claudia Naber, and Herwart Nöldeke. Hamburg: Dölling und Galitz, 1993.

Catalog of the Warburg Institute Library, University of London, 12 vols. Boston: G. K. Hall, 1967.

Vorträge der Bibliothek Warburg, edited by Fritz Saxl. Vol. 1 (1921–22), pub. 1923; Vol. 2, part 1 (1922–23), pub. 1924; Vol. 2, part 2 (1922–23), pub. 1925; Vol. 3 (1923–24), pub. 1926; Vol. 4 (1924–25), pub. 1927; Vol. 5 (1925–26), pub. 1928; Vol. 6 (1927–28), pub. 1930; Vol. 7–9 pub. 1930 and 1931.

Warburg, Aby. "Artistic Exchanges between North and South in the Fifteenth Century" (1905). In Warburg, *Renewal of Pagan Antiquity,* 275–80, 468–69.

———. "The Art of Portraiture and the Florentine Bourgeoisie" (1902). In Warburg, *Renewal of Pagan Antiquity,* 185–221, 435–50.

———. *Ausgewählte Schriften und Würdigungen,* edited by Dieter Wuttke in association with Carl Georg Heise. 2nd ed. Baden-Baden: Valentin Körner, 1988.

———. "Dürer and Italian Antiqity" (1905). In Warburg, *Renewal of Pagan Antiquity,* 553–58, 729–30.

———. "*Ekstatische Nymphe . . . trauernder Flußgott*": *Portrait eines Gelehrten*, edited by Robert Galitz and Brita Reimers. Hamburg: Dölling und Galitz, 1995.

———. *Die Erneuerung der heidnischen Antike: Kulturwissenschaftliche Beiträge zur Geschichte der europäischen Renaissance.* Preface by Horst Bredekamp and Michael Diers. Vol. 1, bk. 2 of *Gesammelte Schriften: Studienausgabe.* Berlin: Akademie Verlag, 1998.

———. "Francesco Sassetti's Last Injunction to His Sons" (1907). In Warburg, *Renewal of Pagan Antiquity,* 223–62, 451–66.

———. *Gesammelte Schriften.* Vols. 1 and 2: *Die Erneuerung der heidnischen Antike: Kulturwissenschaftliche Beiträge zur Geschichte der europäischen Renaissance,* edited by Gertrud Bing. Leipzig: Teubner, 1932; reprint, Nendeln: Kraus, 1969.

———. "The Gods of Antiquity and the Early Renaissance in Southern and Northern Europe" (1908). In Warburg, *Renewal of Pagan Antiquity,* 559–60, 731.

———. *Images from the Region of the Pueblo Indians of North America.* Translated by Michael P. Steinberg. Ithaca: Cornell University Press, 1995.

———. *Mnemosyne, Der Bilderatlas,* edited by Martin Warnke and Claudia Brink. Vol. 2, bk. 1 of *Gesammelte Schriften: Studienausgabe.* Berlin: Akademie Verlag, 2000.

———. "The Mural Paintings in Hamburg City Hall" (1910). In Warburg, *Renewal of Pagan Antiquity,* 711–16, 776.

———. "On *Imprese Amorose* in the Earliest Florentine Engravings" (1905). In Warburg, *Renewal of Pagan Antiquity,* 169–83, 431–34.

———. "Pagan-Antique Prophecy in Words and Images in the Age of Luther" (1920). In Warburg, *Renewal of Pagan Antiquity,* 597–697, 760–75.

———. *The Renewal of Pagan Antiquity.* Translated by David Britt, introduction by Kurt W. Forster. Los Angeles: Getty Research Institute, 1999. English translation of Warburg's collected papers and articles, *Gesammelte Schriften.*

———. *Schlangenritual: Ein Reisebericht (Bilder aus dem Gebiet der Pueblo-Indianer in Nord Amerika).* Berlin: Wagenbach, 1988.

———. *Tagebuch der Kulturwissenschaftlichen Bibliothek Warburg, mit Einträgen von Gertrud Bing und Fritz Saxl,* edited by Karen Michels and Charlotte Schoell-Glass. Vol. 7 of *Gesammelte Schriften: Studienausgabe.* Berlin: Akademie Verlag, 2001.

General Literature

Adorno, Theodor W. "Antisemitismus und faschistische Propaganda." In

Antisemitismus, edited by Ernst Simmel, 148–61. Frankfurt am Main: Fischer Wissenschaft, 1993.

Alpers, Svetlana. *Rembrandt's Enterprise: The Studio and the Market.* Chicago: University of Chicago Press, 1988.

Alter, Peter, ed. *Nationalismus: Dokumente zur Geschichte und Gegenwart eines Phänomens.* Munich: Piper, 1994.

Angress, Werner T. "Prussia's Army and the Jewish Reserve Officer Controversy before World War I." *Publications of the Leo Baeck Institute: Year Book* 17 (1972): 19–42.

Anonymous. *Der jüdische Einjährig-Freiwillige im Deutschen Heere.* 2nd ed. Berlin: Walther und Apolant, 1888.

Anselm, Sigrun. "Angst und Angstprojektion in der Phantasie vom jüdischen Ritualmord." In *Die Legende vom Ritualmord: Zur Geschichte der Blutbeschuldigung gegen Juden*, edited by Rainer Erb, 253–65. Berlin: Metropol, 1993.

Armin, Otto. *Die Juden in den Kriegs-Gesellschaften und in der Kriegswirtschaft: Unter Benutzung amtlicher und anderer Quellen dargestellt.* Munich: Deutscher Volksverlag, 1921.

Aschheim, Steven E. *Brothers and Strangers: The East European Jew in German and German Jewish Consciousness, 1800–1923.* Madison: University of Wisconsin Press, 1982.

Backhaus, Fritz. "Die Hostienschändungsprozesse zu Sternberg (1492) und Berlin (1510) und die Ausweisung der Juden aus Mecklenburg und der Mark Brandenburg." *Jahrbuch für brandenburgische Landesgeschichte* 39 (1988): 7–26.

Barta Fliedl, Ilsebill, and Christoph Geissmar, eds. *Die Beredsamkeit des Leibes. Zur Körpersprache in der Kunst.* Salzburg: Residenz Verlag, 1992.

Bauerle, Dorothee. *Gespenstergeschichten für ganz Erwachsene. Ein Kommentar zu Aby Warburgs Bilderatlas Mnemosyne.* Münster: Lit-Verlag, 1988.

Behrendt, Bernd. "August Julius Langbehn, der 'Rembrandtdeutsche.'" In *Handbuch zur "Völkischen Bewegung" 1871–1918,* edited by Uwe Puschner, Walter Schmitz, and Justus H. Ulbricht, 94–113. Munich: Saur, 1996.

———. *Zwischen Paradox und Paralogismus: Weltanschauliche Grundzüge einer Kulturkritik in den neunziger Jahren des 19. Jahrhunderts am Beispiel August Julius Langbehn.* Frankfurt am Main: Lang, 1984.

Belke, Ingrid. *Moritz Lazarus und Heyman Steinthal: Die Begründer der Völkerpsychologie in ihren Briefen.* Tübingen: J. C. B. Mohr (Siebeck), 1971.

Belting, Hans. *Das Ende der Kunstgeschichte: Eine Revision nach zehn Jahren.* Munich: Beck, 1995.

Benoist, Jean-Marie, ed. *Identität: Ein interdisziplinäres Seminar unter Leitung von Claude Lévi-Strauss.* Stuttgart: Klett-Cotta, 1980.

Bendixen, Friedrich. *Briefe an Momme Nissen 1904–1916*. Hamburg: Gesellschaft der Bücherfreunde, 1969.

Berding, Helmut. *Moderner Antisemitismus in Deutschland*. Frankfurt am Main: Suhrkamp, 1988.

Berger, Klaus. "Erinnerungen an Aby Warburg (1979)." In *Mnemosyne: Zum 50. Todestag von Aby M. Warburg*, edited by Stephan Füssel, 49–57. Göttingen: Gratia-Verlag, 1979.

Bergmann, Martin S. "Moses and the Evolution of Freud's Jewish Identity." *Israel Annals of Psychiatry and Related Disciplines* 14 (1976): 3–26.

Bienert, Walther. *Martin Luther und die Juden: Ein Quellenbuch mit zeitgenössischen Illustrationen*. Frankfurt am Main: Evangelisches Verlagswerk, 1982.

Bing, Gertrud. "Aby M. Warburg." Lecture held on 31 October 1958 in the Hamburg Kunsthalle. In Warburg, *Ausgewählte Schriften und Würdigungen*, 455–64.

Bitterli, Urs. *Die 'Wilden' und die 'Zivilisierten': Grundzüge einer Geistes-und Kulturgeschichte der europäisch-überseeischen Begegnung*. 2nd rev. ed. Munich: Beck, 1991.

Blumenkranz, Bernhard. *Juden und Judentum in der mittelalterlichen Kunst*. Stuttgart: Kohlhammer, 1965.

Bock, Wolfgang. *Astrologie und Aufklärung: Über modernen Aberglauben*. Stuttgart: J. B. Metzlersche Verlagsbuchhandlung und Carl Ernst Poeschel Verlag, 1995.

Bode, Wilhelm. *Great Masters of Dutch and Flemish Painting*. Translated by Margaret L. Clarke. Freeport, N.Y.: Books for Libraries Press, 1967.

———. "Rembrandt als Erzieher von einem Deutschen." *Preußische Jahrbücher* 65 (January–June 1890): 301–14.

———. *Studien zur Geschichte der holländischen Malerei*. Braunschweig: Vieweg, 1883.

Boehlich, Walter, ed. *Der Berliner Antisemitismusstreit*. Frankfurt am Main: Insel, 1965.

Böhme, Hartmut. *Albrecht Dürer. Melencolia I. Im Labyrinth der Deutung*. Frankfurt am Main: Fischer, 1989.

Böhringer, Hannes, and Karlfried Gründer, eds. *Ästhetik und Soziologie um die Jahrhundertwende: Georg Simmel*. Frankfurt am Main: Vittorio Klostermann, 1976.

Bollenbeck, Georg. *Bildung und Kultur: Glanz und Elend eines deutschen Deutungsmusters*. 2nd ed. Frankfurt: Insel, 1994.

Bönisch, Michael. "Die 'Hammer'-Bewegung." In *Handbuch zur "Völkischen Bewegung" 1871–1918*, edited by Uwe Puschner, Walter Schmitz, and Justus H. Ulbricht, 341–65. Munich: Saur, 1996.

Borsi, Franco, and Stefano Borsi. *Paolo Uccello*. Milan: Leonardo Editore,

1992.

Borsook, Eve, and Johannes Offerhaus. *Francesco Sassetti and Ghirlandaio at Santa Trinita, Florence: History and Legend in a Renaissance Chapel.* Doornspijk: Davaco, 1981.

Brafmann, Jacob. "Das Buch vom Kahal," 2 vols. Typescript based on the editions of Vilnius 1869 and St. Petersburg 1875 (estate of Siegfried Passarge, now in the Staats-und Universitätsbibliothek Hamburg).

———. *Das Buch vom Kahal*, edited by Siegfried Passarge. 2 vols. Leipzig: Hammer Verlag, 1928.

Brandt, Susanne. "Kriegssammlungen im Ersten Weltkrieg: Denkmäler oder Laboratoires d'histoire?" In *Keiner fühlt sich hier mehr als Mensch . . . Erlebnis und Wirkung des Ersten Weltkriegs,* edited by Gerhard Hirschfeld and Gerd Krumeich, 241–58. Essen: Klartext Verlag, 1993.

Brauer, Ludolph, Albrecht Mendelssohn Bartholdy, and Adolf Meyer, eds. *Forschungsinstitute: Ihre Geschichte, Organisation und Ziele*, 2 vols. Hamburg: Hartung, 1930.

Brenner, Michael. *The Renaissance of Jewish Culture in Weimar Germany.* New Haven: Yale University Press, 1996.

Breuilly, John. *Nationalism and the State.* 2nd ed. Manchester: Manchester University Press, 1993.

Broich, Ulrich, and Manfred Pfister, eds. *Intertextualität: Formen, Funktionen, anglistische Fallstudien.* Tübingen: Niemeyer, 1985.

Brosseder, Johannes. *Luthers Stellung zu den Juden im Spiegel seiner Interpreten. Interpretation und Rezeption von Luthers Schriften und Äußerungen zum Judentum im 19. und 20. Jahrhundert vor allem im deutschsprachigen Raum.* Munich: Hueber, 1972.

Bruch, Rüdiger vom. "Weiterführung der Schmollerschen und Lamprechtschen Traditionen in der Weimarer Republik?" In *Karl Lamprecht weiterdenken: Universal-und Kulturgeschichte heute,* edited by Gerald Diesener, 225–41. Leipzig: Leipziger Universitätsverlag, 1993.

———. *Weltpolitik als Kulturmission. Auswärtige Kulturpolitik und Bildungsbürgertum in Deutschland am Vorabend des Ersten Weltkrieges.* Paderborn: Schöningh, 1982.

Bruch, Rüdiger vom, and Friedrich Wilhelm Graf, et al., eds. *Kultur und Kulturwissenschaften um 1900. Krise der Moderne und Glaube an die Wissenschaft.* Stuttgart: Steiner, 1989.

Buck, August. *Die Italienische Renaissance aus der Sicht des 20. Jahrhunderts.* Stuttgart: Steiner-Verlag Wiesbaden, 1988.

———. *Der Orpheus-Mythos in der italienischen Renaissance.* Krefeld: Scherpe, 1961.

———, ed. *Renaissance und Renaissancismus von Jacob Burckhardt bis Thomas Mann.* Tübingen: Max Niemeyer, 1990.

Burckhardt, Jacob. *Reflections on History.* Translated by M. D. Hottinger. Indianapolis: Liberty Classics, 1979.

Bureau für Statistik der Juden. *Statistik der Juden: Eine Sammelschrift.* Berlin: Jüdischer Verlag, 1918.

Buschendorf, Bernhard. "'War ein sehr tüchtiges gegenseitiges Fördern': Edgar Wind und Aby Warburg." *Idea: Jahrbuch der Hamburger Kunsthalle* 4 (1985): 164–209.

Callmann, Ellen. *Apollonio di Giovanni.* Oxford: Clarendon Press, 1974.

Carlebach, Joseph. *Öffentliche Dank-und Huldigungsadresse eines Odisten an den Sonnenmenschen Dr. Siegried Passarge o.ö. Professor der Geographie an der Universität Hamburg. Herausgeber des Buches vom Kahal.* Berlin: Philo Verlag, 1928.

Carroll, Margaret D. "Civic Ideology and Its Subversion: Rembrandt's *Oath of Claudius Civilis.*" *Art History* 9 (1986): 12–35.

Cecil, Lamar. "Wilhelm II. und die Juden." In *Juden im Wilhelminischen Deutschland 1890–1914,* edited by Werner E. Mosse, 313–47. Tübingen: J. C. B. Mohr (Siebeck), 1976.

Cestelli Guidi, Benedetta, and Nicholas Mann, eds. *Photographs at the Frontier: Aby Warburg in America 1895–1896.* London: Merrell Holberton in association with the Warburg Institute, 1998.

Chalcraft, David J., and Austin Harrington, eds. *Protestant Ethic Debate: Max Weber's Replies to His Critics, 1907–1910.* Liverpool: Liverpool University Press, 2001.

Chernow, Ron. *The Warburgs: A Family Saga.* London: Chatto & Windus, 1993.

Chevalier, Yves. *L'Antisémitisme. Le Juif comme bouc émissaire.* Paris: Les Éditions du Cerf, 1988.

Chickering, Roger. "Karl Lamprechts Konzeption einer Weltgeschichte." *Archiv für Kulturgeschichte* 73 (1991): 437–52.

———. "Ein schwieriges Heldenleben: Bekenntnisse eines Biographen." In *Karl Lamprecht weiterdenken: Universal-und Kulturgeschichte heute,* edited by Gerald Diesener, 207–22. Leipzig: Leipziger Universitätsverlag, 1993.

Claussen, Detlev. *Was heisst Rassismus?* Darmstadt: Wissenschaftliche Buchgesellschaft, 1994.

Conciliorum Oecumenicorum Decreta, edited by Centro di Documentazione and Giuseppe Alberigo, Giuseppe A. Dossetti, Perikle-P. Joannou, Claudio Leonardi, and Paolo Prodi, 227–71. Bologna: Istituto per le Scienze Religiose, 1973.

Corbey, Raymond. "Freud's Phylogenetic Narrative." In *Alterity, Identity, Image: Selves and Others in Society and Scholarship,* edited by Raymond Corbey and Joep Th. Leerssen, 37–56. Amsterdam: Rodopi, 1991.

Daxelmüller, Christoph. "Das 'Mauscheln.'" In *Antisemitismus: Vorurteile und Mythen,* edited by Julius H. Schoeps and Joachim Schlör. Munich: Piper, 1995.

Deppermann, Klaus. "Judenhaß und Judenfreundschaft im frühen Protestantismus." In *Die Juden als Minderheit in der Geschichte,* edited by Bernd Martin and Ernst Schulin, 110–30. Munich: Deutscher Taschenbuch Verlag, 1985.

Deppner, Martin Roman. "Bilder als Kommentare: R. B. Kitaj und Aby Warburg." In *Aby Warburg: Akten,* 235–60.

Das Deutsche Führerlexikon 1934/35. Berlin: Stollberg, 1934.

Deutsche jüdische Soldaten: Von der Epoche der Emanzipation bis zum Zeitalter der Weltkriege. Eine Ausstellung des Militärgeschichtlichen Forschungsamtes in Zusammenarbeit mit dem Moses Mendelssohn Zentrum, Potsdam und dem Centrum Judaicum, Berlin. Hamburg: E. S. Mittler, 1997. Exhibition catalog.

Didi-Huberman, Georges. *L'Image survivante: Histoire de l'art et temps des fantômes selon Aby Warburg.* Paris: Editions de Minuit, 2002.

Diers, Michael. "Kreuzlinger Passion." *Kritische Berichte* 7, no. 4 (1979): 5–14.

———. "Nagelmänner: Propaganda mit ephemeren Denkmälern im Ersten Weltkrieg." In *Mo(nu)mente: Formen und Funktionen ephemerer Denkmäler,* edited by Michael Diers, 113–35. Berlin: Akademie Verlag, 1993.

———. *Warburg aus Briefen: Kommentare zu den Kopierbüchern der Jahre 1905–1918.* Weinheim: VCH acta humaniora, 1991.

Diesener, Gerald, ed. *Karl Lamprecht weiterdenken: Universal-und Kulturgeschichte heute.* Leipzig: Leipziger Universitätsverlag, 1993.

Dilly, Heinrich. "Lichtbildprojektion—Prothese der Kunstbetrachtung." In *Kunstwissenschaft und Kunstvermittlung,* edited by Irene Below, 153–72. Gießen: Anabas Verlag, 1975.

Doren, Alfred. "Aby Warburg und sein Werk." *Archiv für Kulturgeschichte* 21 (1931): 1–25.

Dorowin, Hermann. *Retter des Abendlands: Kulturkritik im Vorfeld des europäischen Faschismus.* Stuttgart: Metzler, 1991.

Dudley, Edward, and M. Novak, eds. *The Wild Man Within: An Image in Western Thought from the Renaissance to Romanticism.* Pittsburgh: Pittsburgh University Press, 1972.

Duffy, Michael F., and Willard Mittelman. "Nietzsche's Attitudes toward the Jews." *Journal of the History of Ideas* 49 (1988): 301–17.

Dundes, Alan, ed. *The Blood Libel Legend: A Casebook in Anti-Semitic Folklore.* Madison: University of Wisconsin Press, 1991.

Eckardt, Julius von. *Lebenserinnerungen.* 2 Vols. Leipzig: S. Hirzel, 1910.

Ehlers, Jürgen. "Das Geologische Institut des Hamburger Universität in den dreißige Jahren." In *Hochschulalltag im "Dritten Reich": Die Hamburger Universität, 1933–1945,* edited by Eckart Krause, Ludwig Huber, and Holger Fischer, vol. 3, 1223–1244. Berlin: Dietrich Reimer, 1991.

Elias, Norbert. *Studien über die Deutschen: Machtkämpfe und Habitusentwicklung,* edited by Michael Schröter. 2nd ed. Frankfurt am Main: Suhrkamp, 1989.

———. *Was ist Soziologie?* 6th ed. Weinheim: Juventa Verlag, 1991.

Ellen, Roy, Ernest Gellner, et al., eds. *Malinowski between Two Worlds: The Polish Roots of an Anthropological Tradition.* Cambridge: Cambridge University Press, 1988.

Emmens, Jan A. *Rembrandt en de regels van de kunst.* Utrecht: Haentjens Dekker and Gumbert, 1968.

Erb, Rainer, ed. *Die Legende vom Ritualmord: Zur Geschichte der Blutbeschuldigung gegen Juden.* Berlin: Metropol, 1993.

Erikson, Erik H. *Identity and the Life Cycle: Selected Papers.* New York: International University Press, 1959.

———. *Young Man Luther: A Study in Psychoanalysis and History.* New York: Norton, 1958; 2nd ed. 1969.

Estel, Bernd. "Nationale Identität und Antisemitismus in Deutschland." In *Antisemitismus in der politischen Kultur nach 1945,* edited by Werner Bergmann and Rainer Erb, 57–78. Opladen: Westdeutscher Verlag, 1990.

Fischer, Holger, and Gerhard Sandner. "Die Geschichte des Geographischen Seminars der Hamburger Universität im 'Dritten Reich.'" In *Hochschulalltag im "Dritten Reich": Die Hamburger Universität 1933–1945,* edited by Eckart Krause, Ludwig Huber, and Holger Fischer, 1197–1222. Berlin: Reimer, 1991.

Foessel, Georges, Jean-Yves Marriotte, and Sylvain Morand. *Strasbourg: Passé et présent sous le même angle.* Paris: Èditions Champion, 1989.

Forster, Kurt W. "Warburgs Versunkenheit." In Warburg, *"Ekstatische Nymphe,"* 184–206.

Frank, Herfried. "Erik Homburger Erikson in Karlsruhe—Kindheit und Jugend." In *Trennungen: Kindliche Rettungsversuche bei Vernachlässigungen, Scheidungen und Tod,* edited by Christian Büttner and Aurel Ende, 164–73. Weinheim: Beltz, 1990.

Franke, Otto. "Der kosmische Gedanke in Philosophie und Staat der Chinesen." In *Vorträge der Bibliothek Warburg 1925–1926,* edited by Fritz Saxl, 1–44. Leipzig: Teubner, 1928.

Freimark, Peter, Alice Jankowski, and Ina S. Lorenz, eds. *Juden in Deutschland: Emanzipation, Integration, Verfolgung und Vernichtung. 25 Jahre Institut für die Geschichte der deutschen Juden Hamburg.* Hamburg:

Christians Verlag, 1991.

Frenkel-Brunswik, Else, and R. Nevitt Sanford. "Die Antisemitische Persönlichkeit: Ein Forschungsbericht." In *Antisemitismus,* edited by Ernst Simmel, 119–47. Frankfurt am Main: Fischer, 1993.

Freud, Sigmund. *Fragen der Gesellschaft: Ursprünge der Religion.* In *Studienausgabe.* Vol. 9. Frankfurt am Main: S. Fischer, 1972; reprint, 1994.

———. *The Interpretation of Dreams.* Translated by Joyce Crick. Oxford: Oxford University Press, 1999.

Fritsch, Theodor. *Mein Streit mit dem Hause Warburg: Eine Episode aus dem Kampfe gegen das Weltkapital.* Leipzig: Hammer-Verlag, 1925.

Gay, Peter. "Begegnung mit der Moderne-Deutsche Juden in der deutschen Kultur." In *Juden im Wilhelminischen Deutschland 1890–1914,* edited by Werner E. Mosse, 241–311. Tübingen: J. C. B. Mohr (Siebeck), 1976.

———. *Weimar Culture: The Outsider as Insider.* New York: Harper and Row, 1968.

Geffcken, Johannes. "Der Begriff des Tragischen in der Antike: Ein Beitrag zur Geschichte der antiken Ästhetik." In *Vorträge der Bibliothek Warburg 1927/28: Zur Geschichte des Dramas,* edited by Fritz Saxl, 89–166. Leipzig: Teubner, 1930.

———. "Neues und Neuestes vom Nachleben der Antike." *Süddeutsche Monatshefte* 23, no. 4 (1925/26): 324–28.

Gellner, Ernest. *Culture, Identity, and Politics.* Cambridge: Cambridge University Press, 1987.

Gellner, Ernest, and Anthony D. Smith. "The Nation: Real or Imagined? The Warwick Debates on Nationalism." *Nations and Nationalism* 2, no. 3 (1996): 357–70.

Gergen, Kenneth J. *The Saturated Self: Dilemmas of Identity in Contemporary Life.* New York: Basic Books and Harper Collins, 1991.

Gergen, Kenneth J., and Keith E. Davis, eds. *The Social Construction of the Person.* New York: Springer, 1985.

Giesen, Bernhard, ed. *Nationale und kulturelle Identität: Studien zur Entwicklung des kollektiven Bewußtseins in der Neuzeit.* 2nd ed. Frankfurt am Main: Suhrkamp, 1991.

Gilbert, Felix. "From Art History to the History of Civilization: Gombrich's Biography of Aby Warburg." *Journal of Modern History* 44, no. 3 (1972): 381–91.

Gilman, Sander L. *Freud, Identität und Geschlecht.* Frankfurt am Main: S. Fischer, 1994.

———. *Jewish Self-Hatred: Anti-Semitism and the Hidden Language of the Jews.* Baltimore: Johns Hopkins University Press, 1986.

———. *Rasse, Sexualität und Seuche: Stereotype aus der Innenwelt der westlichen Kultur.* Reinbek: Rowohlt, 1992.

Ginzburg, Carlo. "Kunst und soziales Gedächtnis: Die Warburg-Tradition." In *Spurensicherungen: Über verborgene Geschichte, Kunst und soziales Gedächtnis,* 149–233. Munich: Deutscher Taschenbuch Verlag, 1988.

Gleason, Philip. "Identifying Identity: A Semantic History." *Journal of American History* 69 (1983): 910–31.

Glum, Friedrich. "Die Kaiser-Wilhelm-Gesellschaft zur Förderung der Wissenschaften: Ihre Forschungsaufgaben, ihre Institute und ihre Organisation." In *Forschungsinstitute: Ihre Geschichte, Organisation und Ziele,* edited by Ludolph Brauer, Albrecht Mendelssohn Bartholdy, and Adolf Meyer, vol. 1, 359–73. Hamburg: Hartung, 1930.

Gobineau, Joseph. *Versuch über die Ungleichheit der Menschenracen.* 4 vols. Translated by Ludwig Schemann. 4th ed. Stuttgart: Frommann, 1922.

Goethe, Johann Wolfgang. "Maximen und Reflexionen." In *Goethes Werke, Hamburger Ausgabe.* Vol. 12. Munich: C. H. Beck, 1994.

———. *Wilhelm Meister's Years of Apprenticeship.* Translated by H. M. Waidson. London: Calder, 1978.

Goffman, Erving. *Stigma: Notes on the Management of Spoiled Identity.* Englewood Cliffs, N.J.: Prentice Hall, 1963.

Gombrich, Ernst H. *Aby Warburg: An Intellectual Biography.* London: Warburg Institute, 1970.

———. "Aby Warburg und der Evolutionismus des 19. Jahrhunderts." In Warburg, *"Ekstatische Nymphe,"* 52–73.

———. "The Ambivalence of the Classical Tradition: The Cultural Psychology of Aby Warburg (1866–1929)." In *Tributes: Interpreters of Our Cultural Tradition.* Ithaca: Cornell University Press, 1984.

———. "Apollonio di Giovanni: A Florentine Cassone Workshop Seen through the Eyes of a Humanist Poet." *Journal of the Warburg and Courtauld Institutes* 18 (1955): 16–34.

———. *Norm and Form: Studies in the Art of the Renaissance.* London: Phaidon, 1966.

Gossmann, Lionel. "Cultural History and Crisis: Burckhardt's *Civilisation of the Renaissance in Italy.*" In *Rediscovering History: Culture, Politics, and the Psyche,* edited by Michael S. Roth, 404–27. Stanford: Stanford University Press, 1994.

Grolle, Joist. *Bericht von einem schwierigen Leben: Walter Solmitz (1905 bis 1962) Schüler von Aby Warburg und Ernst Cassirer.* Berlin: Reimer, 1994.

———. "Die Büste Aby Warburgs in der Kunsthalle: Ein Hamburger 'Denkmalfall.'" *Im Blickfeld: Jahrbuch der Hamburger Kunsthalle* 1 (1994): 149–70.

Groß, Johannes T. *Ritualmordbeschuldigungen gegen Juden im deutschen Kaiserreich (1871–1914).* Berlin: Metropol, 2002.

Grubrich-Simitis, Ilse. *Freuds Moses-Studie als Tagtraum*. Weinheim: Verlag Internationale Psychoanalyse, 1991.

Hägler, Brigitte. *Die Christen und die "Judenfrage": Am Beispiel der Schriften Osianders und Ecks zum Ritualmordvorwurf*. Erlangen: Palm und Enke, 1992.

Halbwachs, Maurice. *Das Gedächtnis und seine sozialen Bedingungen*. Berlin: Luchterhand, 1966.

Hammerstein, Notker. *Antisemitismus und deutsche Universitäten 1871–1933*. Frankfurt am Main: Campus, 1995.

Haskins, Katherine. "Aby Warburg's Problembibliothek and German Art History in the 1920s." *Chicago Art Journal* 1 (1991): 21–31.

Heckscher, William S. "The Genesis of Iconology." In *Stil und Überlieferung in der Kunst des Abendlandes: Akten des XXI. Internationalen Kongresses für Kunstgeschichte in Bonn 1964*, 3:239–62. Berlin: Mann, 1967. Reprinted in *Art and Literature: Studies in Relationship*, edited by Egon Verkeysen, 253–80. 2nd ed. Baden-Baden: Verlag Valentin Koernes, 1994.

Heise, Carl Georg. *Persönliche Erinnerungen an Aby Warburg*. 2nd ed. Hamburg: Gesellschaft der Bücherfreunde, 1959.

Hermsen, Edmund. "Werk und Wirkung Erik H. Eriksons als Wegbereiter psychohistorischer Forschung." In *Psychohistorie-Ansätze und Perspektiven: Tagungsdokumentation d. 8. Jahrestagung der Dt. Ges. f. Psychohistorische Forschung in Heidelberg, 22.–24. April 1994*, edited by Ludwig Janus, 1–18. Heidelberg: Textstudio Groß, 1995.

Hertz, Friedrich Otto. *Rasse und Kultur: Eine kritische Untersuchung der Rassentheorien*. 2nd rev. exp. ed. Leipzig: A. Kroner, 1915.

Hertz, Hans W. "Wilhelm Ludwig Hertz, ein Sohn des Dichters Adelbert von Chamisso." *Archiv für Geschichte des Buchwesens* 10 (1969): 269–308.

Herzog, Max, ed. *Ludwig Binswanger und die Chronik der Klinik "Bellevue" in Kreuzlingen: Eine Psychiatrie in Lebensbildern*. Berlin: Quintessenz, 1995.

Hoecker, Rudolf. "Eine kunstwissenschaftliche Studienbibliothek: Die Bibliothek Prof. A. Warburgs in Hamburg." *Zentralblatt für die deutsche Kunst* (April 1917): 8–10.

Hoffmann, Christhard. "'Ostjuden' in Westeuropa: Großbritannien und Deutschland im Vergleich (1881–1914)." In *Mit Fremden leben: Eine Kulturgeschichte von der Antike bis zur Gegenwart*, edited by Alexander Demandt et al., 200–219, 281–85. Munich: Beck, 1995.

Hofmann, Werner. "Der Mnemosyne-Atlas: Zu Warburgs Konstellationen." In Warburg, *"Ekstatische Nymphe,"* 172–83.

Hofmann, Werner, Georg Syamken, and Martin Warnke. *Die Menschenrechte des Auges: Über Aby Warburg*. Frankfurt am Main: Europäische Verlagsanstalt, 1980.

Hsia, R. Po-Chia. *The Myth of Ritual Murder: Jews and Magic in Reformation Germany*. New Haven: Yale University Press, 1988.

Hubert, Henry, and Marcel Mauss. *Sacrifice: Its Nature and Function*. London: Cohen and West, 1964.

Huhn, Rosi, and Peter Rautmann. "'Gold gab ich für Eisen': Materialaspekte zur documenta 7." *Kritische Berichte* 10, no. 4 (1982): 21–36.

Huisstede, Peter van. "Der Mnemosyne-Atlas: Ein Laboratorium der Bildgeschichte." In Warburg, *"Ekstatische Nymphe,"* 130–71.

———. "De Mnemosyne Beeldatlas van Aby M. Warburg een laboratorium voor beeldgeschiedenis." Ph.D. diss., Leiden, 1992.

Iversen, Margaret. "Retrieving Warburg's Tradititon." *Art History* 16 (1993): 541–53.

Jacobson, Jon. *Locarno Diplomacy: Germany and the West, 1925–1929*. Princeton: Princeton University Press, 1972.

Jaeger, Friedrich. "Der Kulturbegriff im Werk Max Webers und seine Bedeutung für eine moderne Kulturgeschichte." *Geschichte und Gesellschaft* 18 (1992): 371–93.

James, Mervyn. "Ritual, Drama, and Social Body in the Late Medieval English Town." *Past and Present* 98 (1983): 3–29.

Jarausch, Konrad H. *Deutsche Studenten 1800–1970*. Frankfurt am Main: Suhrkamp, 1984.

———. *Students, Society, and Politics in Imperial Germany: The Rise of Academic Illiberalism*. Princeton: Princeton University Press, 1982.

———. "Die Vertreibung der jüdischen Studenten und Professoren von der Berliner Universität unter dem NS-Regime." Lecture, Humboldt Universität zu Berlin, June 15, 1993.

Jay, Martin. "Frankfurter Schule und Judentum: Die Antisemitismusanalyse der Kritischen Theorie." *Geschichte und Gesellschaft* 5 (1979): 439–54.

Jessen, Karl Detlev. *Heinses Stellung zur bildenden Kunst und ihrer Ästhetik: Zugleich ein Beitrag zur Quellenkunde des Ardinghello*. Berlin: Mayer und Müller, 1901.

Jochmann, Werner. "Antijüdische Traditionen im deutschen Protestantismus und nationalsozialistische Judenverfolgung." In *Gesellschaftskrise und Judenfeindschaft in Deutschland 1870–1945*, 265–81. 2nd ed. Hamburg: Christians, 1991.

———. "Die Ausbreitung des Antisemitismus." In *Deutsches Judentum in Krieg und Revolution 1916–1923*, edited by Werner E. Mosse and Arnold Paucker, 409–510. Tübingen: J. C. B. Mohr (Siebeck), 1971.

———. *Gesellschaftskrise und Judenfeindschaft in Deutschland 1870–1945*. 2nd ed. Hamburg: Christians, 1991.

———. "Struktur und Funktion des deutschen Antisemitismus." In *Juden im*

Wilhelminischen Deutschland 1890–1914, edited by Werner E. Mosse, 389–477. Tübingen: J. C. B. Mohr, 1976.

Jüdisches Lexikon: Ein enzyklopädisches Handbuch des jüdischen Wissens in vier Bänden. 2nd ed. Berlin: Jüdischer Verlag, 1927; reprint, Frankfurt am Main: Athenäum, 1987.

Kant, Immanuel. "Prolegomena zu einer jeden künftigen Metaphysik, die als Wissenschaft wird auftreten können." In *Schriften zur Metaphysik und Logik, Kant Werke,* vol. 5, 109–264. Darmstadt: Wissenschaftliche Buchgesellschaft, 1983.

Kany, Roland. "Aby M. Warburg." In *Handbuch religionswissenschaftlicher Grundbegriffe,* vol. 1, 298–300. Stuttgart: Kohlhammer, 1988.

———. *Mnemosyne als Programm: Geschichte, Erinnerung und die Andacht zum Unbedeutenden im Werk von Usener, Warburg und Benjamin.* Tübingen: Niemeyer, 1987.

———. *Die religionsgeschichtliche Forschung an der Kulturwissenschaftlichen Bibliothek Warburg.* Bamberg: Stefan Wendel Verlag, 1989.

Kedourie, Elie. *Nationalism.* 4th rev. ed. Oxford: Blackwell, 1993.

Kehr, Eckart. "Zur Genesis des königlich preußischen Reserveoffiziers." In *Der Primat der Innenpolitik: Gesammelte Aufsätze zur preußisch-deutschen Sozialgeschichte im 19. und 20. Jahrhundert,* edited by Hans-Ulrich Wehler, 53–63. Berlin: de Gruyter, 1965.

Klein, Dennis B. *Jewish Origins of the Psychoanalytic Movement.* Chicago: University of Chicago Press, 1985.

Kleinpaul, Rudolf. *Menschenopfer und Ritualmorde.* Leipzig: Schmidt and Günther, s.d. (after 1891).

Klibansky, Raymond, Erwin Panofsky, and Fritz Saxl. *Saturn and Melancholy: Studies in the History of Natural Philosophy, Religion and Art.* London: Nelson, 1964; reprint, Nendeln: Kraus Reprint, 1979.

Köhnke, Klaus Christian. "Soziologie als Kulturwissenschaft: Georg Simmel und die Völkerpsychologie." *Archiv für Kulturgeschichte* 72 (1990): 223–32.

Königseder, Karl. "Aby Warburg im 'Bellevue.'" In Warburg, "*Ekstatische Nymphe,*" 74–98.

Krause, Eckart, Ludwig Huber, and Holger Fischer, eds. *Hochschulalltag im "Dritten Reich": Die Hamburger Universität 1933–1945.* 3 vols. Berlin: Reimer, 1991.

Kremers, Heinz, ed. *Die Juden und Martin Luther-Martin Luther und die Juden: Geschichte, Wirkungsgeschichte, Herausforderung.* Neukirchen-Vluyn: Neukirchener Verlag, 1985.

Ein Krieg wird ausgestellt: Die Weltkriegssammlung des Historischen Museums (1914–1918). Themen einer Ausstellung, Inventarkatalog. Frankfurt am Main: Historisches Museum, 1976. Exhibition catalog.

Krohn, Helga. *Die Juden in Hamburg: Die politische, soziale und kulturelle Entwicklung einer jüdischen Großstadtgemeinde nach der Emanzipation 1848–1918.* Hamburg: Christians, 1974.

Krüger, Dieter. *Nationalökonomen im wilhelminischen Deutschland.* Göttingen: Vandenhoeck und Ruprecht, 1983.

Kultzen, Rolf. "Eine Anmerkung zur Vermittlung figürlicher Kompositionstypen durch die italienische Buchillustration des späten 15. Jahrhunderts." *Pantheon* 25 (1967): 407–17.

Lachmann, Renate. *Gedächtnis und Literatur: Intertextualität in der russischen Moderne.* Frankfurt am Main: Suhrkamp, 1990.

Landauer, Carl Hollis. "The Survival of Antiquity: The German Years of the Warburg Institute." Ph.D. diss., Yale University, 1984.

Langbehn, Julius. *Rembrandt als Erzieher.* Leipzig: C. L. Hirschfeld, 1890; reprint, 1922.

Langbehn, Julius, and Momme Nissen. *Dürer als Führer: Vom Rembrandtdeutschen und seinem Gehilfen.* Munich: Josef Müller, 1928.

Lavin, Marilyn Aronberg. "The Altar of Corpus Domini in Urbino: Paolo Uccello, Joos Van Ghent, Piero della Francesca." *Art Bulletin* 49 (1967): 1–24.

———. *The Place of Narrative: Mural Decoration in Italian Churches, 431–1600.* Chicago: University of Chicago Press, 1990.

Lazarus, Moritz. *Treu und Frei: Gesammelte Reden und Vorträge über Juden und Judenthum.* Leipzig: Winter'sche Verlagshandlung, 1887.

Le Goff, Jacques. "Eine mehrdeutige Geschichte." In *Mentalitäten-Geschichte: Zur historischen Rekonstruktion geistiger Prozesse,* edited by Ulrich Raulff, 18–32. Berlin: Wagenbach, 1987.

Lenz, Max. "Luther und der deutsche Geist: Zum 31. Oktober 1917." In *Kleine historische Schriften.* Vol. 2: *Von Luther zu Bismarck,* 9–24. Munich: Oldenbourg, 1920.

Lewin, Reinhold. *Luthers Stellung zu den Juden: Ein Beitrag zur Geschichte der Juden in Deutschland während des Reformationszeitalters.* Berlin: Trowitzsch, 1911; reprint, Aalen: Scientia, 1973.

Lichtblau, Albert. "Die Debatten über die Ritualmordbeschuldigungen im österreichischen Abgeordnetenhaus am Ende des 19. Jahrhunderts." In *Die Legende vom Ritualmord: Zur Geschichte der Blutbeschuldigung gegen Juden,* edited by Rainer Erb, 267–92. Berlin: Metropol, 1993.

Liebeschütz, Hans. "Aby Warburg (1866–1929) as Interpreter of Civilization." *Publications of the Leo Baeck Institute: Year Book* 16 (1971): 225–36.

———. "German Politics and Jewish Existence." *Publications of the Leo Baeck Institute: Year Book* 20 (1975): 27–33.

———. *Das Judentum im deutschen Geschichtsbild von Hegel bis Max Weber.*

Tübingen: J. C. B. Mohr (Siebeck), 1967.

———. "Das Judentum im Geschichtsbild Jacob Burckhardts." *Publications of the Leo Baeck Institute: Year Book* 4 (1959): 61–80.

———. "Max Weber's Historical Interpretation of Judaism." *Publications of the Leo Baeck Institute: Year Book* 9 (1964): 41–68.

———. "Treitschke and Mommsen on Jewry and Judaism." *Publications of the Leo Baeck Institute: Year Book* 7 (1962): 153–82.

Lightbown, Ronald. *Sandro Botticelli.* 2 vols. London: Paul Elek, 1978.

———. *Sandro Botticelli: Life and Work.* London: Thames and Hudson, 1989.

Lindner, Erik. "Houston Stewart Chamberlain: The Abwehrverein and the 'Praeceptor Germaniae' 1914–1918." *Publications of the Leo Baeck Institute: Year Book* 37 (1992): 213–36.

Lipp, Wolfgang. "Magie-Macht und Gefahr: Zur Soziologie des Irrationalen." *Archiv für Kulturgeschichte* 66 (1984): 389–423.

Lippincott, Kristen. "Aby Warburg, Fritz Saxl and the Astrological Ceiling of the Sala di Galatea." In *Aby Warburg: Akten,* 213–32.

Lipton, David R. *Ernst Cassirer: The Dilemma of a Liberal Intellectual in Germany 1914–1933.* Toronto: University of Toronto Press, 1978.

Loewenberg, Peter. "Antisemitismus und jüdischer Selbsthaß: Eine sich wechselseitig verstärkende sozialpsychologische Doppelbeziehung." *Geschichte und Gesellschaft* 5 (1979): 455–75.

Lonsbach, Richard Maximilian (i.e., Richard Maximilian Cahen). *Friedrich Nietzsche und die Juden: Ein Versuch,* edited by Heinz Robert Schlette. 2nd ed. Bonn: Bouvier, 1985.

Lorenz, Ina. *Die Juden in Hamburg zur Zeit der Weimarer Republik: Eine Dokumentation.* 2 vols. Hamburg: Christians, 1987.

Lotter, Friedrich. "Aufkommen und Verbreitung von Ritualmorden und Hostienfrevelanklagen gegen Juden." In *Die Macht der Bilder: Antisemitische Vorurteile und Mythen,* edited by Jüdisches Museum der Stadt Wien, 60–78. Vienna: Picus Verlag, 1995. Exhibition catalog.

———. "Hostienfrevelvorwurf und Blutwunderfälschung bei den Judenverfolgungen von 1298 ('Rintfleisch') und 1336–1338 ('Armleder')." In *Fälschungen im Mittelalter: Kongreß der Monumenta Germaniae Historica, München, 16.–19. September 1986.* Vol. 5: *Fingierte Briefe, Frömmigkeit und Fälschung, Realienfälschungen,* 533–83. Hannover: Hahnsche Buchhandlung, 1988.

Luhmann, Niklas. "Institutionalisierung-Funktion und Mechanismus im sozialen System der Gesellschaft." In *Zur Theorie der Institution,* edited by Helmut Schelsky, 27–41. Düsseldorf: Bertelsmann Universitätsverlag, 1970.

Die Macht der Bilder. Antisemitische Vorurteile und Mythen. Vienna: Picus Verlag, 1995. Exhibition catalog.

MacKinnon, Malcolm H. "Calvinism and the Infallible Assurance of Grace: The Weber Thesis Reconsidered (Part I)." *British Journal of Sociology* 39 (1988): 143–77.

———. "Weber's Exploration of Calvinism: The Undiscovered Provenance of Capitalism (Part II)." *British Journal of Sociology* 39 (1988): 178–210.

Mader, Andreas Evaristus. *Die Menschenopfer der alten Hebräer und der benachbarten Völker: Ein Beitrag zur alttestamentlichen Religionsgeschichte.* Freiburg: Herder, 1909.

Maikuma, Yoshihiko. *Der Begriff der Kultur bei Warburg, Nietzsche und Burckhardt.* Königstein im Taunus: Hain bei Athenäum, 1985.

Malkiel, David J. "Infanticide in Passover Iconography." *Journal of the Warburg and Courtauld Institutes* 56 (1993): 85–99.

Marquard, Odo, and Karlheinz Stierle, eds. *Identität.* Munich: Wilhelm Fink, 1979.

Megill, Alan, ed. *Rethinking Objectivity.* Durham: Duke University Press, 1994.

Mehl, Margaret. *Eine Vergangenheit für die japanische Nation: Die Entstehung des historischen Forschungsinstituts Tokyo daigaku Shiryo hensanjo (1869–1885).* Frankfurt am Main: Peter Lang, 1992.

Melamed, Samuel Max. *Die Psychologie des jüdischen Geistes: Zur Völker-und Kulturpsychologie.* 2nd ed. Berlin: Schwetschke und Sohn, 1921.

Mendelssohn Bartholdy, Albrecht. "Institut für Auswärtige Politik, Hamburg." In *Forschungsinstitute: Ihre Geschichte, Organisation und Ziele,* edited by Ludolph Brauer, Albrecht Mendelssohn Bartholdy, and Adolf Meyer, vol. 2, 332–46. Hamburg: Hartung, 1930.

———. "Rede zur Eröffnung des Instituts für Auswärtige Politik." In *Kolonialrechtswissenschaft, Kriegsursachenforschung, internationale Angelegenheiten: Materialien und Interpretationen zur Geschichte des Instituts für Internationale Angelegenheiten der Universität Hamburg 1923–1983,* edited by Klaus Jürgen Gantzel, 89–93. Baden-Baden: Nomos, 1983.

Meyer, Anne Marie. "Aby Warburg in His Early Correspondence." *American Scholar* 57, no. 3 (1988): 445–52.

Meyer, Michael A. *Jüdische Identität in der Moderne.* Frankfurt am Main: Jüdischer Verlag, 1992.

Michaud, Philippe-Alain. *Aby Warburg and the Image in Motion.* Translated by Sophie Hawkes. New York: Zone Books, 2004.

Michels, Karen. "Ein Versuch über die K.B.W. als Bau der Moderne." In *Porträt aus Büchern: Bibliothek Warburg und Warburg Institute,* edited by Michael Diers, 71–81. Hamburg: Dölling und Galitz, 1993.

Michels, Karen, and Charlotte Schoell-Glass. "Aby Warburg et les timbres en tant que document culturel." *Protée: Revue internationale de théories et pratiques sémiotiques* 30 (2002): 85–92.

Midgley, Mary. *Beast and Man: The Roots of Human Nature*. Hassocks: Harvester, 1978.

Mittenzwei, Werner. "Börries von Münchhausen." In *Neue deutsche Biographie*, 525–27. Berlin: Duncker und Humblot, 1997.

———. *Der Untergang einer Akademie oder die Mentalität des ewigen Deutschen: Der Einfluß der nationalkonservativen Dichter an der Preußischen Akademie der Künste 1918–1947*. Berlin: Aufbau Verlag, 1992.

Momigliano, Arnaldo. *Essays on Ancient and Modern Judaism*. Edited by Silvia Berti. Chicago: University of Chicago Press, 1987; reprint, 1994.

Moses, Julius. *Die Lösung der Judenfrage: Eine Rundfrage*. Berlin: Modernes Verlagsbureau Curt Wiegand, 1907.

Mosse, George L. *Confronting the Nation: Jewish and Western Nationalism*. Hanover: Brandeis University Press, 1993.

———. *Jüdische Intellektuelle in Deutschland: Zwischen Religion und Nationalismus*. Frankfurt am Main: Campus, 1992.

Mosse, Werner E. *Juden im Wilhelminischen Deutschland 1890–1914*. Tübingen: J.C.B. Mohr (Siebeck), 1976.

Mosse, Werner E., and Arnold Paucker, eds. *Deutsches Judentum in Krieg und Revolution, 1916–1923*. Tübingen: J. C. B. Mohr (Siebeck), 1971.

———. *Entscheidungsjahr 1932: Zur Judenfrage in der Endphase der Weimarer Republik*. 2nd ed. Tübingen: J. C. B. Mohr (Siebeck), 1965; reprint, 1966.

Münz, Ludwig. *Die Kunst Rembrandts und Goethes Sehen*. Leipzig: Heinrich Keller, 1934.

Naber, Claudia. ". . . die Fackel deutsch-jüdischer Geistigkeit weitertragen." In *Die Juden in Hamburg, 1590–1990: Wissenschaftliche Beiträge der Universität Hamburg zur Ausstellung Vierhundert Jahre Juden in Hamburg im Museum für Hamburgische Geschichte*, edited by Arno Herzig, 393–406. Hamburg: Dölling und Galitz, 1991.

Nesselrath, Arnold. "La Stanza d'Eliodoro." In *Raffaello nell'appartamento di Giulio II e Leone X*, 203–45. Milan: Electa, 1993.

Neumann, Carl. *Rembrandt*. 2 vols. 3rd rev. ed. Munich: Bruckmann, 1922.

———. *Rembrandt und Wir. (Rede bei der Rembrandtfeier der Königlichen Christian-Albrechts-Universität zu Kiel)*. Berlin: W. Spemann, 1906.

Nietzsche, Friedrich. *The Birth of Tragedy*. Translated by Shaun Whiteside. London: Penguin, 2003.

———. *Die Geburt der Tragödie, oder: Griechenthum und Pessimismus. Neue Ausgabe mit dem Versuch einer Selbstkritik*. Leipzig: E. W. Fritzsch, 1886.

———. *Unfashionable Observations*. Translated by Richard T. Gray. Stanford: Stanford University Press, 1995.

Nipperdey, Thomas. *Deutsche Geschichte 1866–1918*. Vol. 1: *Arbeitswelt und*

Bürgergeist. Munich: C. H. Beck, 1994.

———. *Deutsche Geschichte 1866–1918.* Vol. 2: *Machtstaat vor der Demokratie.* 2nd rev. ed. Munich: C. H. Beck, 1993.

Nipperdey, Thomas, and Reinhard Rürup. "Antisemitismus." In *Geschichtliche Grundbegriffe: Historisches Lexikon zur politisch-sozialen Sprache in Deutschland,* edited by O. Brunner, W. Conze, and R. Koselleck, vol. 1, 129–53. Stuttgart: Klett-Cotta, 1992.

Nirenberg, David. *Communities of Violence: Persecution of Minorities in the Middle Ages.* Princeton: Princeton University Press, 1996.

Nonn, Christoph. *Eine Stadt sucht einen Mörder: Gerücht, Gewalt und Antisemitismus im Kaiserreich.* Göttingen: Vandenhoeck und Ruprecht, 2002.

Oberhuber, Konrad. "L'apparato decorativo di palazzo Tè." In *Giulio Romano,* 336–79. Milan: Electa, 1989. Exhibition catalog.

Ohly, Friedrich. "Die Zerreißung als Strafe für Liebesverrat in der Antike und im Alten Testament." In *Sprache und Recht: Beiträge zur Kulturgeschichte des Mittelalters. Festschrift für Ruth Schmidt-Wiegand zum 60. Geburtstag,* edited by Karl Hauck et al., vol. 2, 554–624. Berlin: de Gruyter, 1986.

Olender, Maurice. *Die Sprachen des Paradieses: Religion, Philologie und Rassentheorie im 19. Jahrhundert.* Frankfurt am Main: Campus, 1995.

Oppenheimer, Franz. *Die Judenstatistik des preußischen Kriegsministeriums (Fragen der Zeit).* Munich: Verlag für Kulturpolitik, 1922.

Ortony, Andrew, ed. *Metaphor and Thought.* 2nd ed. Cambridge: Cambridge University Press, 1993.

Paetzold, Heinz. *Ernst Cassirer—Von Marburg nach New York: Eine philosophische Biographie.* Darmstadt: Wissenschaftliche Buchgesellschaft, 1995.

Panofsky, Erwin. "Rembrandt und das Judentum." *Jahrbuch der Hamburger Kunstsammlungen* 18 (1973): 75–108.

Passarge, Siegfried. *Grundzüge der gesetzmäßigen Charakterentwicklung der Völker auf religiöser und naturwissenschaftlicher Grundlage und in Abhängigkeit von der Landschaft.* Berlin: Gebrüder Borntraeger, 1925.

Paucker, Arnold. "Zur Problematik einer jüdischen Abwehrstrategie in der deutschen Gesellschaft." In *Juden im Wilhelminischen Deutschland 1890–1914,* edited by Werner E. Mosse, 479–548. Tübingen: J. C. B. Mohr (Siebeck), 1976.

Pfaff, William. *The Wrath of Nations: Civilization and the Furies of Nationalism.* New York: Simon and Schuster, 1993.

Pfotenhauer, Helmut. "Das Nachleben der Antike: Aby Warburgs Auseinandersetzung mit Nietzsche." In *Nietzsche-Studien: Internationales Jahrbuch für die Nietzsche-Forschung* 14 (1985): 298–313.

Phelps, Reginald H. "Theodor Fritsch und der Antisemitismus." *Deutsche Rundschau* 87 (1961): 442–49.

Plessner, Helmuth. *Die verspätete Nation: Über die politische Verführbarkeit bürgerlichen Geistes.* Frankfurt am Main: Suhrkamp, 1974.

Pochat, Götz. *Theater und Bildende Kunst im Mittelalter und in der Renaissance in Italien.* Graz: Akademische Druck-und Verlagsanstalt, 1990.

Poliakov, Léon. *Geschichte des Antisemitismus.* 8 vols. Worms: Heintz, 1977–88.

Polleroß, Friedrich. "Interart Studies—New Perspectives." *Frühneuzeit-Info* 6 (1995): 241–44.

Pollock, Friedrich. "Das Institut für Sozialforschung an der Universität Frankfurt am Main." In *Forschungsinstitute: Ihre Geschichte, Organisation und Ziele,* edited by Ludolph Brauer, Albrecht Mendelssohn Bartholdy, and Adolf Meyer, vol. 2, 347–54. Hamburg: Hartung, 1930.

Porter, Theodore M. *Trust in Numbers: The Pursuit of Objectivity in Science and Public Life.* Princeton: Princeton University Press, 1995.

Posèq, Avigdor W. G. "Left and Right Orientation of a *Pathosformel* in Dürer." *Source: Notes in the History of Art* 16 (1996): 7–17.

Presse und Funk im Dritten Reich: Eine Dokumentation von Joseph Wulf. Reinbek: Rowohlt, 1966.

Der Prozeß gegen Maßloff und Genossen (Konitz, 25. Oktober–10. November 1900) nach stenographischer Aufnahme. Berlin: H. G. Hermann, 1900.

Der Prozeß gegen Moritz Lewy (Konitz, 13.–16. Februar 1901) nach stenographischer Aufnahme. Berlin: H. G. Hermann, 1901.

Pulzer, Peter. "Die jüdische Beteiligung an der Politik." In *Juden im Wilhelminischen Deutschland 1890–1914,* edited by Werner E. Mosse, 143–239. Tübingen: J. C. B. Mohr (Siebeck), 1976.

Puschner, Uwe, Walter Schmitz, and Justus H. Ulbricht, eds. *Handbuch zur "Völkischen Bewegung" 1871–1918.* Munich: Saur, 1996.

Pyenson, Lewis. *The Young Einstein: The Advent of Relativity.* Bristol: Hilger, 1985.

Rathenau, Walther. "Staat und Judentum: Eine Polemik (1911)." In *Gesammelte Schriften in fünf Bänden,* vol. 1, 183–207. Berlin: S. Fischer, 1918.

Raulff, Ulrich. "Die Geburt eines Begriffs: Reden von 'Mentalität' zur Zeit der Affäre Dreyfus." In *Mentalitäten-Geschichte: Zur historischen Rekonstruktion geistiger Prozesse,* edited by Ulrich Raulff, 50–68. Berlin: Wagenbach, 1987.

Reck, Siegfried. *Identität, Rationalität und Verantwortung: Grundbegriffe und Grundzüge einer soziologischen Identitätstheorie.* Frankfurt am Main: Suhrkamp, 1981.

Reichmann, Eva G. "Der Bewußtseinswandel der deutschen Juden." In *Deutsches Judentum in Krieg und Revolution 1916–1923,* edited by

Werner E. Mosse and and Arnold Paucker, 511–612. Tübingen: J. C. B. Mohr (Siebeck), 1971.

Ringer, Fritz K. *The Decline of the German Mandarins: The German Academic Community 1890–1933.* Cambridge, Mass.: Harvard University Press, 1969.

Riquarts, Kurt-Gerhard. "Der Antisemitismus als politische Partei in Schleswig-Holstein und Hamburg 1871–1914." Ph.D. diss., Kiel, 1975.

Roeck, Bernd. "Burckhardt, Warburg und die italienische Renaissance." *Annali Istituto storico italiano-germanico in Trento* 17 (1991): 257–96.

———. *Der junge Aby Warburg.* Munich: Beck, 1996.

Roesler, Konrad. *Die Finanzpolitik des Deutschen Reiches im Ersten Weltkrieg.* Berlin: Duncker und Humblot, 1967.

Rohrbacher, Stefan, and Michael Schmidt. *Judenbilder: Kulturgeschichte antijüdischer Mythen und antisemitischer Vorurteile.* Hamburg: Rowohlt, 1991.

Rosenbaum, Eduard. "M. M. Warburg & Co. Merchant Bankers of Hamburg: A Survey of the First 140 Years." *Publications of the Leo Baeck Institute: Year Book* 7 (1962): 121–49.

Roth, Joseph. *Juden auf Wanderschaft.* Berlin: Verlag Die Schmiede, 1927.

Rubin, Miri. *Corpus Christi: The Eucharist in Late Medieval Culture.* Cambridge: Cambridge University Press, 1991.

———. "Der Körper der Eucharistie im Mittelalter." In *Gepeinigt, begehrt, vergessen: Symbolik und Sozialbezug des Körpers im späten Mittelalter und in der frühen Neuzeit,* edited by Klaus Schreiner and Norbert Schnitzler, 25–40. Munich: Wilhelm Fink, 1992.

Ruppin, Arthur. *Die Juden der Gegenwart: Eine sozialwissenschaftliche Studie.* Berlin: Calvary, 1904.

Rürup, Reinhard. "Emanzipation und Krise—Zur Geschichte der 'Judenfrage' in Deutschland vor 1890." In *Juden im Wilhelminischen Deutschland 1890–1914,* edited by Werner E. Mosse and Arnold Paucker, 1–56. Tübingen: J. C. B. Mohr (Siebeck), 1976.

Saxl, Fritz. "Die Kulturwissenschaftliche Bibliothek Warburg in Hamburg." In *Forschungsinstitute: Ihre Geschichte, Organisation und Ziele,* edited by Ludolph Brauer, Albrecht Mendelssohn Bartholdy, and Adolf Meyer, vol. 2, 355–58. Hamburg: Hartung, 1930.

———. *Lectures.* 2 vols. London: Warburg Institute, University of London, 1957.

———. "Rembrandt and Classical Antiquity" (1941). In *Lectures,* vol. 1, 298–310 and plates 208–17. London: Warburg Institute, 1957.

———. *Rembrandt's Sacrifice of Manoah.* In *Studies of the Warburg Institute.* London: Warburg Institute, 1939.

———. "Rembrandt und Italien." *Oud Holland* 41 (1923/24): 145–60.

Saxl, J. (Fritz). "Das Nachleben der Antike: Zur Einführung in die Bibliothek 'Warburg.'" *Hamburger Universitäts-Zeitung* 11, no. 4 (1920): 244–47.

Schelsky, Helmut. "Zur soziologischen Theorie der Institution." In *Zur Theorie der Institution,* edited by Helmut Schelsky, 9–26. Düsseldorf: Bertelsmann Universitätsverlag, 1970.

Schieder, Theodor. *Das Deutsche Kaiserreich als Nationalstaat,* edited by Hans-Ulrich Wehler. 2nd ed. Göttingen: Vandenhoeck und Ruprecht, 1992.

Schildt, Axel. "Radikale Antworten von rechts auf die Kulturkrise der Jahrhundertwende: Zur Herausbildung und Entwicklung der Ideologie einer 'Neuen Rechten' in der Wilhelminischen Gesellschaft des Kaiserreichs." In *Jahrbuch für Antisemitismusforschung,* vol. 4, 63–87. Frankfurt am Main: Campus, 1995.

Schluchter, Wolfgang. *Die Entwicklung des okzidentalen Rationalismus: Eine Analyse von Max Webers Gesellschaftsgeschichte.* Tübingen: J. C. B. Mohr (Siebeck), 1979.

———. *Rationalismus der Weltbeherrschung: Studien zu Max Weber.* Frankfurt am Main: Suhrkamp, 1980.

Schmalenbach, Fritz. "The Term 'Neue Sachlichkeit.'" *Art Bulletin* 22 (1940): 161–65.

Schmidt-Degener, Frederik. *Rembrandt und der holländische Barock.* Leipzig: Teubner, 1928.

Schnur, Roman, ed. *Die Theorie der Institution und zwei andere Aufsätze von Maurice Hauriou.* Berlin: Duncker und Humblot, 1965.

Schoeller, Felix M. "Darstellungen des Orpheus in der Antike." Ph.D. diss., Freiburg, 1969.

Schoell-Glass, Charlotte. "An Episode of Cultural Politics during the Weimar Republic: Aby Warburg and Thomas Mann Exchange a Letter Each." *Art History* 21 (1998): 107–28.

———. "Idea vincit? Das humanistische Projekt der Kulturwissenschaftlichen Bibliothek Warburg (1926–1929)." In *Humanismus in Geschichte und Gegenwart,* edited by V. R. Faber and E. Rudolph, 57–75. Tübingen: Mohr Siebeck, 2002.

Schoeps, Julius H., and Joachim Schlör, eds. *Antisemitismus: Vorurteile und Mythen.* Munich: Piper, 1995.

Schorn-Schütte, Luise. *Karl Lamprecht: Kulturgeschichtsschreibung zwischen Wissenschaft und Politik.* Göttingen: Vandenhoeck und Ruprecht, 1984.

———. "Karl Lamprecht und die internationale Geschichtswissenschaft an der Jahrhundertwende." *Archiv für Kulturgeschichte* 67 (1985): 417–64.

Schorske, Carl E. *Fin-de-Siècle Vienna: Politics and Culture.* New York: Knopf, 1980.

———. "Politics and Patricide in Freud's *Interpretation of Dreams.*" In *Fin-*

de-Siècle Vienna: Politics and Culture, 181–207. New York: Knopf, 1980.

Schramm, Percy Ernst. *Herrschaftszeichen und Staatssymbolik: Beiträge zu ihrer Geschichte vom dritten bis zum sechzehnten Jahrhundert.* Vol. 3. Stuttgart: Hiersemann, 1956.

Schreiber, Wilhelm Ludwig. *Handbuch der Holz-und Metallschnitte des 15. Jahrhunderts.* Vol. 4. Leipzig: Hiersemann, 1927.

Schroubek, Georg R. "Zur Tradierung und Diffusion einer europäischen Aberglaubensvorstellung." In *Die Legende vom Ritualmord: Zur Geschichte der Blutbeschuldigung gegen Juden,* edited by Rainer Erb, 17–24. Berlin: Metropol, 1993.

Schubring, Paul. *Cassoni: Truhen und Truhenbilder der italienischen Frührenaissance. Ein Beitrag zur Profanmalerei im Quattrocento.* 2nd exp. ed. Leipzig: Hiersemann, 1923.

Schulz, Andreas. "Liberalismus in Hamburg und Bremen zwischen Restauration und Reichsgründung (1830–1870)." In *Liberalismus und Region: Zur Geschichte des deutschen Liberalismus im 19. Jahrhundert,* edited by Lothar Gall and Dieter Langewiesche, 135–60. Munich: Oldenbourg, 1995.

———. "Weltbürger und Geldaristokraten: Hanseatisches Bürgertum im 19. Jahrhundert." *Historische Zeitschrift* 259 (1994): 637–70.

Schuster, Peter-Klaus. *Melencolia I: Dürers Denkbild,* 2 vols. Berlin: Gebr. Mann, 1991.

———. "Zu Dürers Zeichnung 'Der Tod des Orpheus' und verwandten Darstellungen." *Jahrbuch der Hamburger Kunstsammlungen* 23 (1978): 7–24.

See, Klaus von. *Barbar, Germane, Arier: Die Suche nach der Identität der Deutschen.* Heidelberg: C. Winter, 1994.

Settis, Salvatore. "Kunstgeschichte als vergleichende Kulturwissenschaft: Aby Warburg, die Pueblo-Indianer und das Nachleben der Antike." In *Künstlerischer Austausch-Artistic Exchange, Akten des XXVIII. Internationalen Kongresses für Kunstgeschichte, Berlin, 15.–20. Juli 1992,* edited by Thomas W. Gaethgens, vol. 1, 139–58. Berlin: Akademie Verlag, 1994.

———. "Pathos und Ethos, Morphologie und Funktion." In *Vorträge aus dem Warburg-Haus,* vol. 1, 33–73. Berlin: Akademie Verlag, 1997.

———. "Warburg 'continuatus': Description d'une bibliothèque." In *Le Pouvoir des bibliothèques: La mémoire des livres en Occident,* edited by Marc Baratin and Christian Jacob, 122–69. Paris: Albin Michel, 1996.

Simmel, Ernst, ed. *Antisemitismus.* Frankfurt am Main: Fischer Wissenschaft, 1993.

Simmel, Georg. *Rembrandt: Ein kunstphilosophischer Versuch.* 2nd ed. Leipzig:

Kurt Wolff, 1919.

———. *Rembrandt: Ein kunstphilosophischer Versuch.* Munich: Matthes und Seitz, 1985.

———. "Rembrandt als Erzieher (1890)." In *Vom Wesen der Moderne. Essays zur Philosophie und Ästhetik,* edited by Werner Jung, 145–61. Hamburg: Junius, 1990.

———. *Rembrandtstudien.* Darmstadt: Wissenschaftliche Buchgemeinschaft, 1953.

———. *Zur Philosophie der Kunst: Philosophische und kunstphilosophische Aufsätze.* Potsdam: Gustav Kiepenheuer Verlag, 1922.

Simon, Erika. "Dürer und Mantegna 1494." *Anzeiger des Germanischen Nationalmuseums* (1971/72): 21–40.

Smith, Helmut Walser. *The Butcher's Tale: Murder and Anti-Semitism in a German Town.* New York: W. W. Norton, 2002.

Stanjek, J. "Das Kahal-Märchen gründlich widerlegt!" *Abwehr-Blätter: Mitteilungen aus dem Verein zur Abwehr des Antisemitismus* 37, nos. 23/24 (1927).

Starobinski, Jean. *Blessings in Disguise; or, the Morality of Evil.* Cambridge, Mass.: Harvard University Press, 1993.

———. "Sur quelques formes de critique de la notion d'identité." In *Identität,* edited by Odo Marquard and Karlheinz Stierle, 644–50. Munich: Wilhelm Fink, 1979.

Steinberg, Michael P. "Aby Warburg's Kreuzlingen Lecture: A Reading." In Warburg, *Images from the Region of the Pueblo,* 59–114.

Steinhausen, Georg, ed. *Monographien zur deutschen Kulturgeschichte.* Vols. 1–12. Leipzig: Diederichs, 1899–1905.

Stern, Fritz. *Kulturpessimismus als politische Gefahr: Eine Analyse nationaler Ideologie in Deutschland.* Bern: Scherz, 1963.

Stern, Heinrich. *Angriff und Abwehr: Ein Handbuch über die Judenfrage.* Berlin: Philo-Verlag, 1924.

Stimilli, Davide, ed. *Ludwig Binswanger–Aby Warburg: La guarigione infinita. Storia clinica di Aby Warburg.* Translated by Chantal Marazia and Davide Stimilli. Vicenza: Neri Pozza Editore, 2005.

Stockhausen, Tilmann von. *Die Kulturwissenschaftliche Bibliothek Warburg: Architektur, Einrichtung und Organisation.* Hamburg: Dölling und Galitz, 1992.

Stockhorst, Erich. *Fünftausend Köpfe: Wer war was im Dritten Reich.* Velbert: blick + bild Verlag, 1967.

Stocking, George W., Jr. *Race, Culture, and Evolution: Essays in the History of Anthropology.* 2nd ed. Chicago: University of Chicago Press, 1982.

———. *Victorian Anthropology.* New York: Macmillan, Free Press, 1987.

Strack, Hermann Leberecht. *Das Blut im Glauben und Aberglauben der Men-*

schheit: Mit besonderer Berücksichtigung der "Volksmedizin" und des "jüdischen Blutritus." Munich: Beck, 1900.

Strieder, Peter. *Dürer: Mit Beiträgen von Gisela Goldberg, Joseph Harnest und Matthias Mende.* Königstein im Taunus: Köster (Langewiesche Nachf.), 1981.

Syamken, Georg. "Aby Warburg—Ideen und Initiativen." In *Die Menschenrechte des Auges: Über Aby Warburg* edited by Werner Hofmann, Georg Syamken, and Martin Warnke, 13–51. Frankfurt am Main: Europäische Verlagsanstalt, 1980.

———. "Warburgs Umwege als Hermeneutik 'More Majorum.'" *Jahrbuch der Hamburger Kunstsammlungen* 25 (1980): 15–26.

Theweleit, Klaus. *Männerphantasien.* 2 vols. Frankfurt am Main: Stroemfeld/Roter Stern, 1977; reprint, Reinbek: Rowohlt, 1993.

Toury, Jakob. "Die bangen Jahre (1887–1891): Juden in Deutschland zwischen Integrationshoffnung und Isolationsfurcht." In *Juden in Deutschland: Emanzipation, Integration, Verfolgung und Vernichtung. 25 Jahre Institut für die Geschichte der deutschen Juden Hamburg,* edited by Peter Freimark, Alice Jankowski, and Ina S. Lorenz, 164–85. Hamburg: Christians, 1991.

———. "Der Eintritt der Juden ins deutsche Bürgertum." In *Das Judentum in der deutschen Umwelt: Studien zur Frühgeschichte der Emanzipation,* edited by Hans Liebeschütz and Arnold Paucker, 139–242. Tübingen: J. C. B. Mohr (Siebeck), 1977.

———. *Die politischen Orientierungen der Juden in Deutschland: Von Jena bis Weimar.* Tübingen: J. C. B. Mohr (Siebeck), 1966.

Traeger, Jörg. "Raffaels Stanza d'Eliodoro und ihr Bildprogramm." *Römisches Jahrbuch für Kunstgeschichte* 13 (1971): 29–99.

Tramer, Hans. "Die Hamburger Kaiserjuden." *Bulletin: Publikationen des Leo Baeck Instituts* 3 (1960): 177–89.

Trützschler von Falkenstein, Kurt. *Die Lösung der Judenfrage im Deutschen Reiche.* Darmstadt: Falken, 1917.

Turner, Henry Ashby, Jr. *Stresemann and the Politics of the Weimar Republic.* Princeton: Princeton University Press, 1963.

Tyrell, Hartmann. "Worum geht es in der 'Protestantischen Ethik'? Ein Versuch zum besseren Verständnis Max Webers." *Saeculum: Jahrbuch für Universalgeschichte* 41 (1990): 130–77.

Vagts, Alfred. "Albrecht Mendelssohn Bartholdy: Ein Lebensbild." In *Mendelssohn Studien: Beiträge zur neueren deutschen Kultur-und Wirtschaftsgeschichte,* vol. 3, 201–25. Berlin: Duncker und Humblot, 1979.

———. "Erinnerungen an Hamburg 1923–1932." In *Kolonialrechtswissenschaft, Kriegsursachenforschung, internationale Angelegenheiten:*

Materialien und Interpretationen zur Geschichte des Instituts für Internationale Angelegenheiten der Universität Hamburg 1923–1983, edited by Klaus Jürgen Gantzel, 97–111. Baden-Baden: Nomos, 1983.

Vischer, Friedrich Theodor. *Kritische Gänge*, edited by Robert Vischer. Vol. 4. 2nd exp. ed. Munich: Meyer und Jessen, 1922.

Vogel, Barbara. "Anpassung und Widerstand: Das Verhältnis Hamburger Hochschullehrer zum Staat 1919 bis 1945." In *Hochschulalltag im "Dritten Reich": Die Hamburger Universität 1933–1945*, edited by Eckart Krause, Ludwig Huber and Holger Fischer, 3–83. Berlin: Reimer, 1991.

Volkov, Shulamit. "Die Erfindung einer Tradition: Zur Entstehung des modernen Judentums in Deutschland." *Historische Zeitschrift* 253 (1991): 603–28.

———. *The Rise of Popular Antimodernism in Germany: The Urban Master Artisans, 1873–1896*. Princeton: Princeton University Press, 1978.

———. "Selbstgefälligkeit und Selbsthaß: Die deutschen Juden zu Beginn des 20. Jahrhunderts." *Geschichte in Wissenschaft und Unterricht* 37 (1986): 1–13.

———. "Soziale Ursachen des Erfolgs in der Wissenschaft: Juden im Kaiserreich." *Historische Zeitschrift* 245 (1987): 315–42.

Warburg, Max. *Die Judenfrage im Rahmen der deutschen Gesamtpolitik*. N.p.: privately printed, 1916.

Warburg Spinelli, Ingrid. *Die Dringlichkeit des Mitleids und die Einsamkeit, nein zu sagen: Lebenserinnerungen*. Hamburg: Dölling und Galitz, 1990.

Warnke, Martin. "Aby Warburg (1866–1929)." In *Altmeister moderner Kunstgeschichte*, edited by Heinrich Dilly, 116–30. Berlin: Reimer, 1990.

———. *Cranachs Luther: Entwürfe für ein Image*. Frankfurt am Main: Fischer, 1984.

———. "Der Leidschatz der Menschheit wird humaner Besitz." In *Die Menschenrechte des Auges: Über Aby Warburg*, edited by Werner Hofmann, Georg Syamken, and Martin Warnke, 113–86. Frankfurt am Main: Europäische Verlagsanstalt, 1980.

———. "On Heinrich Wölfflin." *Representations* 27 (1989): 172–87.

———. "Vier Stichworte: Ikonologie-Pathosformel-Polarität und Ausgleich-Schlagbilder und Bilderfahrzeuge." In *Die Menschenrechte des Auges: Über Aby Warburg*, edited by Werner Hofmann, Georg Syamken, and Martin Warnke, 54–83. Frankfurt am Main: Europäische Verlagsanstalt, 1980.

Weber, Max. "Bismarcks Außenpolitik und die Gegenwart." In *Politische Schriften*, 31–59. Munich: Drei Maskenverlag, 1921.

———. *Gesammelte Aufsätze zur Religionssoziologie*, edited by Marianne Weber. vol. 1. Tübingen: J .C. B. Mohr, 1920.

———. *Gesammelte Aufsätze zur Religionssoziologie.* Vol. 2. 2nd ed. Tübingen: J .C. B. Mohr, 1923.

———. *Gesammelte Aufsätze zur Religionssoziologie.* Vol. 3. 2nd ed. Tübingen: J. C. B. Mohr, 1923.

———. *Gesammelte politische Schriften.* 3rd ed. Edited by J. Winckelmann. Tübingen: J. C. B. Mohr, 1971.

———. *The Protestant Ethic and the Spirit of Capitalism.* London: Routledge, 2001.

———. *Science as a Vocation.* Translated by Michael John. Edited by Peter Lassman and Irving Velody. London: Unwin Hyman, 1989.

Wehler, Hans-Ulrich. *Das Deutsche Kaiserreich 1871–1918.* 7th ed. Göttingen: Vandenhoeck und Ruprecht, 1994.

Weltsch, Robert. "Die schleichende Krise der jüdischen Identität—Ein Nachwort." In *Juden im Wilhelminischen Deutschland 1890–1914,* edited by Werner E. Mosse, 689–702. Tübingen: J. C. B. Mohr (Siebeck), 1976.

Weisbach, Werner. *Geist und Gewalt.* Vienna: Schroll, 1956.

Wenzel, Edith. "Martin Luther und der mittelalterliche Antisemitismus." In *Die Juden in ihrer mittelalterlichen Umwelt,* edited by Alfred Ebenbauer and Klaus Zatloukal, 301–19. Vienna: Böhlau, 1991.

White, Hayden. *Metahistory: The Historical Imagination in Nineteenth-Century Europe.* Baltimore: Johns Hopkins University Press, 1973.

Winckelmann, Johannes, ed. *Max Weber, Die protestantische Ethik und Die protestantische Ethik II: Kritiken und Antikritiken.* Munich: Siebenstern Taschenbuchverlag, 1968.

Wind, Edgar. "Warburgs Begriff der Kulturwissenschaft und seine Bedeutung für die Ästhetik." *Vierter Kongreß für Ästhetik und Allgemeine Kulturwissenschaft, Beilageheft der Zeitschrift für Ästhetik und Allgemeine Kulturwissenschaft* 25 (1931): 163–79.

———. "'Hercules' and 'Orpheus': Two Mock-Heroic Designs by Dürer." *Journal of the Warburg Institute* 2 (1938/39): 206–18.

———. "Appendix: On a Recent Biography of Warburg." In *The Eloquence of Symbols: Studies in Humanist Art,* edited by Jaynie Anderson, 106–13. Oxford: Clarendon Press, 1983.

Wistrich, Robert S. *Between Redemption and Perdition: Modern Antisemitism and Jewish Identity.* London: Routledge, 1990.

Witthoft, Brucia. "Marriage Rituals and Marriage Chests in Quattrocento Florence." *Artibus et Historiae* 5 (1982): 43–59.

Wölfflin, Heinrich. *Kunstgeschichtliche Grundbegriffe: Das Problem der Stilentwicklung in der neueren Kunst.* 5th ed. Munich: Bruckmann, 1921.

Woodfield, Richard, ed. *Art History as Cultural History: Warburg's Projects.* Amsterdam: Overseas Publishers, 2001.

Worte zur Beisetzung von Professor Dr. Aby M. Warburg (Aby M. Warburg zum

Gedächtnis). Hamburg: Privately printed, 1929.

Wuttke, Dieter. *Aby M. Warburg–Bibliographie 1866 bis 1995: Werk und Wirkung. Mit Annotationen*. Baden-Baden: Valentin Koerner, 1998.

———, ed. *Kosmopolis der Wissenschaft: E. R. Curtius und das Warburg Institute. Briefe 1928 bis 1953 und andere Dokumente*. Baden-Baden: Koerner, 1989.

Yerushalmi, Yosef Hayim. *Freud's Moses: Judaism Terminable and Interminable*. New Haven: Yale University Press, 1991.

Zafran, Eric. "Saturn and the Jews." *Journal of the Warburg and Courtauld Institutes* 42 (1979): 16–27.

Zimmermann, Mosche. "Antisemitismus im Kaiserreich zwischen Modernität und Antimodernismus im Urteil der Renegaten." In *Juden in Deutschland: Emanzipation, Integration, Verfolgung und Vernichtung. 25 Jahre Institut für die Geschichte der deutschen Juden Hamburg*, edited by Peter Freimark, Alice Jankowski, and Ina S. Lorenz, 196–206. Hamburg: Christians Verlag, 1991.

Zollschan, Ignaz. *Das Rassenproblem unter besonderer Berücksichtigung der theoretischen Grundlagen der jüdischen Rassenfrage*. 5th ed. Vienna: Braumüller, 1925.

Index

www.ingramcontent.com/pod-product-compliance
Lightning Source LLC
LaVergne TN
LVHW010353080826
844660LV00004B/263
9780814332559